Endless Love and Second Chances

To Paul,

Live a Life that matters!

Endless Love and Second Chances

THE WIFE OF MEDAL OF HONOR RECIPIENT SAMMY DAVIS SHARES THEIR LOVE STORY THROUGH GRIEF, FAITH, AND JOYFUL NEW BEGINNINGS

Dixie Davis

with Sherry Maves

ISBN: 0692589759
ISBN 13: 9780692589755
Library of Congress Control Number: 2015920015
Dixie Davis: Freedom, IN

To my husband, Sammy.
My best friend, my hero, and my endless love.

Acknowledgments

As Sammy and I crisscross the country for speaking engagements, I've often been asked if I had a book. People want to know more about our personal lives.

After thinking about it for a long time, I finally persuaded my best forever friend and freelance writer, Sherry Maves, to be my cowriter. We've been sisters-of-the-heart for close to fifty years, and she's lived many of these experiences with me. We both prayed a lot about it and finally decided to give it a go. A six-month plan turned into a two-year project; we collaborated by phone and e-mail as Sam and I toured many states, Germany, and even went on a cruise in the Bahamas. As chapters came to life, it was hard to relive the tough times but wonderful to remember the good experiences. Sherry, Sam, and I laughed, cried, and experienced every emotion in between. By the final chapter, I realized that every event in my life led me to the next step toward my second chance at love with Sammy, and that we are surrounded by endless love at every turn.

Our readers were lifesavers as we navigated uncharted waters. With heartfelt appreciation, I say thank you to: retired General Perry Smith and his wife, Connor, for tearing the first chapter apart, helping me find my voice, for setting us on the right track, and for their editing skills and endless encouragement; my sister, Roxanne Gordon, for helping me keep our childhood memories straight; Lee Garner for his sensitive insight and unique perspective; Elizabeth Schellenger for attention to detail and for being a lifesaver when the clock was ticking; Janet Deetz for diligently catching grammatical errors we all seemed to miss; Bob Jerome for his enthusiasm, great support, and always being available; and Marie and Scott Harabuda for edits, tech savvy, and for being great cheerleaders.

Caroline Lambert, who coauthored Sam's memoir, which will be published in spring 2016, showed us how to step outside the frame so we could see the picture inside. I am grateful for her exceptional editing skills and fresh perspective that helped us polish this project.

Thanks to Detective Ron Gray, Captain Jerry Martin, and Lieutenant Michael Scott for sharing their dramatic stories surrounding the investigation of Sam's stolen Medal of Honor.

Gary Sinise is an amazing friend. I appreciate his writing the foreword for my book and for supporting Sam and me in our mission to serve veterans.

To my husband, Sammy, for his unfaltering support, for contributing his personal narrative, and for helping me remember Tim stories and details about the Last Patrol, I love you.

In memory of my parents, grandparents, family members, teachers, and others who helped shape my life, I am deeply grateful. To our friends and all of our children and grandchildren, thank you for your love and support. I am also thankful to our Heavenly Father for his guidance and direction in this endeavor.

Contents

Foreword

When September 11, 2001, came along and our country was attacked, I just thought the best way I could serve was by helping the military. It was that involvement that led me to meet Sammy and Dixie Davis. In August 2005, my Lieutenant Dan Band was playing a veterans event at Cantigny Park in Wheaton, Illinois. We were setting up that afternoon and a blond-haired man in a military uniform wearing the Medal of Honor around his neck came up to me and introduced himself as Sammy Davis.

"I'm the real Forrest Gump," he said.

When I played the role of Lieutenant Dan, an injured Vietnam veteran in the movie *Forrest Gump*, I had known there was a Medal of Honor recipient named Sammy Davis; it was the footage of him receiving the Medal of Honor from President Johnson that was used in the movie. They had superimposed Tom Hanks's head on Sammy's body, but that was actual footage from Sammy's Medal of Honor ceremony at the White House in 1968. However, Sammy and I had never met during filming.

That afternoon at Cantigny Park I was honored to meet Sammy, and I have a picture from that day sitting in my living room. I also remember Sammy playing harmonica on stage at that event. After meeting Sammy, we just kept bumping into each other at USO and other events.

In 2006, I had my first interaction with the Medal of Honor Society when they gave me their Bob Hope Excellence and Entertainment Award at an event in Seattle, Washington. I was very honored to receive it. I met so many recipients at that time, shaking hands with a lot of different folks, but not really getting a chance to have any conversations. Sammy and Dixie were probably there, but we didn't get to talk then.

In 2007, I was a cohost of an annual event called Celebration of Freedom at the Reagan Library in California. It was a very, very special event with usually upward of fifty of the living Medal of Honor recipients in attendance. Each year of the five years the event was held, I would see Sammy and Dixie there.

Later, I became one of the members on the executive council for the Medal of Honor Foundation, supporting them in different ways. Interacting with the society continually brought Sammy, Dixie, and me together, and we just started becoming pals. Now they are very good friends and have just been totally inspiring to me. The story of both of them losing their loved ones and then coming together is truly beautiful. They are just wonderful human beings and a wonderful couple.

An interesting side note, in conversation we found out that my Uncle Jack, who was a navigator on a B17 and flew thirty combat missions in World War II, lived next door to Dixie's brother, Roger, in northern Illinois. How crazy is that? I hardly ever got up there, but one time I took Uncle Jack home from one of our trips because I wanted to see where he and my cousin lived. When they were taking me back to the airport, Uncle Jack pointed out a farmhouse and said that's where Dixie grew up. I told them to stop the car, and I jumped out and took a picture. I e-mailed it to her right away from my phone. There was her house looking very pretty, the house she grew up in, and she said when she got the picture, it brought tears to her eyes.

Later when I saw Sammy and Dixie, they mentioned they were going back home to Illinois and would run by and see Uncle Jack. They did and sent me some pictures. It's just wonderful that they knew him and took the time to go visit him. Sadly we lost Uncle Jack in 2015, but it meant a lot to him and to me that they went to see him.

I saw Sammy tell his Shenandoah story at an event for the Joe Foss Institute. We had known each other, but I'd never seen him get up and tell the story; it was fantastic and very moving. The experience of playing the character of Lieutenant Dan in the *Forrest Gump* movie really opened my eyes to what our severely wounded veterans were going through, and it was pivotal for me. So later I asked Sammy if he would come help me with my foundation that raises money for wounded service members and all kinds of things that support our veterans. I invited him to tell the Shenandoah story and talk a little bit at one of our fund-raisers. He agreed.

It was clear to me that both Sammy and Dixie have such big hearts, and they use their time on the road throughout the year to spread a message of sacrifice, service, honor, and selflessness. All of these are very important messages to send to people. Sammy is so eloquent the way he tells his story, and I thought that folks attending our fund-raiser would respond to that. Of course, they did.

Now Sammy has become one of the ambassadors for the Gary Sinise Foundation. We were starting to build this ambassadors council of supporters, people who would help me in my mission to change lives and help other people. We carefully select those who have exceptional character and patriotism for the council. Sammy's heart is so big, and he knows the needs of the veterans out there. Both he and Dixie understand that, and they want to give back and do things to help. Sammy didn't hesitate when I asked him to be on the ambassador's council. I am honored to have his support and to call Dixie and Sammy my friends.

Certainly a big part of their story is that you may lose somebody that is very, very close to you, and you feel devastated and lost. You're not sure where to turn, or how life can go on. You wonder if you can ever be happy again. Their story shows there can be life after grieving. They've found that.

God brought them together, and they make a great team, people who want to do good things in this life. Sammy has certainly seen his share of terrible things that he's survived. They have both survived their tragedies and their difficulties, and they know that by sharing their story they can help other people, and that's a beautiful thing.

Gary Sinise

Actor, Film director, Musician, Founder of Gary Sinise Foundation

Prologue

Frigid winds whip through the frosty forest of trees behind our house, and I feel like we are gazing out from the inside of a snow globe in our cozy living room. It is a night for pondering. A cheery fire crackles and hisses in the hearth, edged with rugged boards from a long ago barn. Like those boards, we humans often have to be rugged and enduring as we travel the road that life has laid out for us. Sometimes I wonder how we manage to survive the tribulations on this journey, and I marvel at just how resilient we can be. I am also grateful for the joy that can come after the darkest voids in our lives.

Above the thick, oak mantle, a framed portrait of my husband, Sammy Davis, Congressional Medal of Honor recipient, and me reflects the happiness we share. I am grateful for the warmth, for the love of this man sitting next to me, and for the extraordinary story that chronicles our life journey. Looking back at my darkest days and most painful heartaches from losing a spouse to cancer, I could never have imagined this beautiful life I have today with Sammy Lee Davis. He, too, experienced his own pain when he lost his wife to cancer. We have been blessed beyond measure with a love that neither of us thought we would ever find again. It makes both of us want to reassure others that there really can be something wonderful after the deepest tragedies of our lives.

Reflecting on the winding path that brought me to Sammy, I lay aside some beaded needlework and sit mesmerized by the colorful flames; then my mind wanders back to the mid-1990s, the little town of Hawkins, Texas, and my late husband, Tim "Doc Holiday" Taylor.

As strange as it sounds, my marriage with Tim ultimately paved the way, following the death of our spouses, for Sammy and me to find each other.

CHAPTER 1

Feelings

I first saw Tim at a veterans reunion campout at Lake LaDonna near Oregon, Illinois, in the mid-1980s. Several of us from VietNow, a veterans organization in northwest Illinois, were attending for the weekend. While there were some solemn ceremonies, much of the reunion was a social affair with a lot of laughs and camaraderie. The highlight of the weekend was a performance by a couple of crazy Texas singers called Martin and Holiday, both Vietnam veterans. Accompanied only by their guitars, playing off of each other, they created a special kind of magic. It was the kind of thing that only happens when people really connect and have worked together for a long time.

Michael J. Martin was brash, earthy, and soulful, and he sounded like he gleaned every note straight from the cotton fields. Tim "Doc Holiday" Taylor, sporting a long, wheat-colored ponytail, had a softer manner. He added smooth harmonies and was a master of improvising and witty quips. He possessed a different kind of soulfulness that pulled me right into the core of emotion, and his solo portion of their performance spoke to me. Both Michael and Tim possessed charisma, each in his own special way, which drew people in.

Their original veteran music was powerful and poignant; some of it made me laugh, and some of it cut straight to the heart. I found myself wiping away a lot of tears that day. In between songs they spoke of issues that veterans often face.

Michael told the crowd that Tim spoke Latin. "Yeah, I speak Latin," Tim grinned with a slow Southern drawl. "E pluribus thinkum. That's Latin.

What it means is that it's our job to pick and sing and make y'all think about some things. If we do that, then we've done what we set out to do."

For all their soulful and thoughtful music, Michael and Tim were eccentric with a capital E. They drove a big old boat of a car, a faded green Buick LeSabre, dubbed the "High Plains Drifter." How it ever made it across town, let alone across country with three hundred thousand miles on it, I don't know. That day, after the concert, they parked the Drifter next to the stage with the trunk open to load up their equipment. A bunch of us were gathered around to say hello, and somebody offered Tim an alcoholic drink. He declined.

"What? Holiday turning down a drink!" Michael exclaimed.

With that Michael literally flopped backward into the open trunk. That was my first introduction to Martin and Holiday. Oh, boy, who were these characters? Tim was so quiet, and Michael was the one holding court with everyone. I'm not even certain I actually go to say hello to either of them that day. At that moment, I didn't know if I would ever see them again, but I hoped I would. I sure liked their music and their spirit.

I was also intrigued with their story. I found out that Tim and Michael had been performing together since the early 1980s. The duo of Martin and Holiday had written and recorded a number of poignant songs that became anthems in the veteran movement at that time. Tim referred to their veteran songs, the ones that made a difference to others, as "righteous music." Their lyrics raised awareness about American prisoners of war still being held in Southeast Asia and the plight of veterans seeking better government care for their war-induced health problems.

Tim and Michael's songs also inspired hope for veterans at home who had never been able to step out into the light and deal with their experiences in Vietnam. Post-traumatic stress (PTS) was a huge but largely unaddressed issue, and Tim and Michael's music assured the vets that they were not alone. That weekend at Lake LaDonna, I also got a lump in my throat when I heard Tim sing "Suitcase Full of Secrets," a song that paid homage to the nurses and medics, the unsung heroes of war, who carried heart-wrenching memories of the dying and wounded that they attended.

Music is the gift of a universal language that can bridge the widest gap, touch the deepest emotions, and can heal the wounds of the soul. I think Michael and Tim were each given a special dose of that musical medicine to share with others, and I loved that they were making a difference for the veterans. The powerful lyrics of their self-penned songs stung with truth and passion that could only have been written by those who had been there. It helped galvanize the veterans' movement of the day.

By then veteran communities all over the country were inviting Martin and Holiday to play big welcome home parades and veteran reunions. They played bars, prisons, churches, colleges, big cities, and Podunk Holler towns; it didn't matter. It had become evident to Tim and Michael that something bigger than the two of them had come out of their music, so their professional aspirations took a back seat, and they embraced a new mission.

To further serve veterans, Tim and Michael formed a group called the Last Patrol that evolved into a support network for veterans and their families. They began walking all over the country carrying the United States and POW flags; the walks became a vehicle to bring veterans groups together, to create awareness, and to encourage veterans to take a stand on issues that affected them, including: health problems from Agent Orange, PTS, and the prisoners of war and soldiers listed as missing in action issues. Veterans were also encouraged to register to vote to make their voices heard with elected officials.

The first walk was a three-hundred-mile trek from Dallas, Texas, to the Alamo in San Antonio, Texas, in 1985. The message of that journey was "Remember the Alamo, and quit telling us to forget about Vietnam." Thousands of miles and several states later, Michael and Tim led a group on a sixteen-hundred-mile, sixty-six-day walk from the Alamo to the Vietnam Wall in Washington, DC, in 1987. An army of supporters, veterans, and their families and friends continued walking additional thousands of miles across the country as momentum built for the Last Patrol.

At their concerts following a walk, Michael and Tim often asked veterans to draw an imaginary line. The suicide rate for Vietnam veterans was alarming, and they implored the veterans as they stepped over that line to promise they would never take their own lives.

I could not have imagined that day at the reunion in Lake LaDonna that I, too, would become part of the Last Patrol. I had grown up honoring our country and its veterans, but in those days, that kind of activism wasn't part of it. We were proud to be Americans, and that meant reciting the Pledge of Allegiance and praying at school. George Washington and Lincoln's birthdays weren't just days off. We studied about these presidents, and for their birthday celebration, we sometimes made silhouettes of their profiles during art time; we knew they were very important leaders in our country's history and that many people had sacrificed for our freedom. This was also the early days of TV, when the two or three stations available signed off at midnight with "The Star-Spangled Banner."

As kids, living next to the Blackhawk Monument Park in the rolling hills of northwest Illinois, we learned lessons in patriotism at an early age by raising and lowering the American flag at the park on Sundays and holidays. The Kent, Illinois, Fire Department paid us twenty-five cents each day for the task. In those days, there were no lights to illuminate the flag at night, so protocol said it had to be taken down at dusk.

On Memorial Day, everyone in our small town of Pearl City, Illinois, always turned out for the little parade. My sister, Roxie, played sax in the school band, and I twirled the baton. Kids with decorated bikes in red, white, and blue fell in behind us. Riders on horses brought up the rear. We marched to Highland Cemetery, where the American Legion had placed flags on the graves of veterans, and stood at attention throughout a solemn program. We understood that it was important to honor those who had given their lives for our country.

The homecoming parade was also a very big deal. Everyone wanted to ride the lead horse that carried the flag. It was a huge honor, and the person selected to ride practiced at home with the flag so the horse wouldn't be spooked. The veterans came next behind that horse, and the thing I remember most is that the minute people saw the flag they would stand with their hands over their hearts as a sign of respect. They would stay standing until the flags and veterans had passed. Nobody questioned patriotism: it was part of our moral fiber, and we knew we were blessed to live in a country like America.

By the time I encountered Tim and Michael, patriotism and honoring veterans was part of the fabric of my life. I had long been part of veterans groups and events, but I had never really thought of myself as an activist. However, I believed in what the Last Patrol stood for, so before long, I put on my walking shoes to join them. In September 1988, a group of Last Patrollers led by Michael and Tim departed from the Vietnam Veterans' Memorial in Springfield, Illinois, for a two-hundred-mile trek culminating in a large rally at Chicago's Daily Plaza on October 1. They were walking to raise awareness about the Prisoner of War/Missing in Action (POW/MIA) issues, post-traumatic stress, and the impact of Agent Orange, the defoliant widely used in Vietnam that has since been linked to serious health problems. The theme for the walk was "United We Stand—Divided We Fall."

Several of us from the local VietNow chapter joined the group at Miller Park in Bloomington, Illinois, for Michael and Tim's concert. We stayed the night with the walkers, crashing in sleeping bags on the rock-hard floor of the local armory. A number of the walkers had already put in twenty-five miles that day, so they were just glad for a place to lay their heads.

I never expected to meet such a diverse and inspiring group of people: homeless folks, veterans, blue-collar workers, professionals, wives, and families. We met Floyd Kitchen, a man from New Mexico who had walked across the desert carrying a POW flag, while Richard Campos from Colorado had walked a thousand miles by himself for his brothers unaccounted for in Vietnam. That kind of dedication was amazing to me. There were people of all ages, and I was most humbled to meet the disabled veterans in wheelchairs who were rolling down the highway with us to do their part. They were an inspiration to me and a real lesson in courage. They all made me feel proud to be part of the movement. Some of these people I will never forget. To this day, I still stay in touch with some of them.

In Vietnam, the guys all had nicknames, and it was the same on the walks. Among them were names like Hot Wheels, Fast Eddie, and Indiana Jim. Some like Sugar Bear and Mama Mia and Whippoorwill made it into the lyrics of Michael and Tim's songs.

Mama Mia and Whippoorwill (their CB handles) were an older couple from Texas who had lost their son, Roy Jr. in Vietnam. Mama had seen TV reports about the Last Patrol heading their direction, found out how close they were, and asked her daughter to take her to Walmart so she could watch them pass by. The Last Patrol never got to the store, so Mama Mia and her daughter rode around until they found them. Mama Mia jumped out of the car and fell in with the veterans. Her stunned daughter took off for home to tell Pop that Mama had run off with those wild-looking vets, and he needed to go get her back. By the time Pop got there, the walkers were in a field getting ready to pitch camp for the night. Pop talked to Michael and some of the others, then relayed that he had walked many a mile delivering mail. He asked if he could walk a mile in Roy's place the next day. Mama Mia joined them as well, and the next morning they all walked into Milford, Texas, under a magnificent double rainbow. That image in my mind gives me goose bumps; it was like God was smiling down on them. The song about them always makes me cry, and much later Tim introduced me to them. They were a precious couple that I will never forget.

As we hoofed up I-55 the next morning, with colorful state flags waving in the wind, there was an indescribable excitement as truckers blew their horns and drivers gave us the thumb-up sign. The twenty-plus miles to our destination in Chenoa, Illinois, were a long way to walk.

It was on that walk that I first talked to Tim. I've always had a weak ankle from cheerleading in high school, and he wrapped it so I could continue walking. I just remember that he was a gentle person and a sweet spirit. I don't know what we talked about, nothing much, but he was funny. I could tell he cared about the people on the march. Tim always followed at the rear, watching the way people walked, always on the lookout for somebody who was having trouble. I really liked him and felt we would become good friends.

Cheering townspeople from Chenoa on the off ramp greeted us as we left the freeway, and I'll always remember the hospitality of the folks at the Lutheran Church who fed us as well as the camaraderie of the group. Everybody was worn out, including Michael and Tim, but they had a way of energizing and pulling everyone together when they sang that night. Lyrics of the music reminded us why we were there. Circling together, hand in hand at the end of the concert, we all joined Tim and Michael singing "Will the Circle Be Unbroken."

It was that night I really got it and understood on a much more profound level the importance of what we were doing. I had heard these issues discussed at the VietNow meetings and among veterans, but meeting people on that march, hearing their stories, and feeling their commitment and conviction somehow switched on the proverbial light bulb in my mind. It was no longer a head thing for me; it became a commitment that grew roots deep in my heart. I didn't know yet that this heartfelt commitment would turn into a lifelong endeavor, but I knew it would not be my last walk.

Subsequent walks would further open my eyes and heart to the plight of veterans and their families. I embraced Gold Star moms, women who had lost a son or daughter to war, and my heart was broken. I hugged Colonel Earl Hopper and his wife, whose son was unaccounted for in Vietnam; I could not imagine the anguish they experienced every day of their lives, never knowing what happened to their boy. As a mom, I thought it would probably be easier to know that my child had died than to wonder every day if he was being held prisoner and brutally tortured by the enemy. How could I live with myself if I thought that my son wondered why nobody cared enough to come bring him home, and I was helpless to do anything about it? I couldn't conceive how they could deal with it. I'd seen the POW statistics and heard about it on the news, but it really hit home when I came to know grieving parents firsthand.

During these walks, I also met spouses of veterans who tearfully relayed the effects of post-traumatic stress on them and their families. I especially remember a woman who woke up to find her husband on the floor beside the bed, spreading the fibers of the carpet with his fingers, flashing back to Vietnam as he would have spread the grass while inching his way on his stomach on the ground. I was touched by the love of total strangers for one another as they shared a common bond, and most of all, I realized how important it was for people to know they were not facing traumatic issues alone. Sometimes just knowing somebody else cared is all they needed to help lighten a heavy burden.

After Chenoa, we went home and then returned on the weekend for the last leg of the walk to Daily Plaza in Chicago. Approximately two hundred of us walked the eight miles of the Chicago leg, which ended in a sea of cheering supporters waving flags to greet us at the Plaza. Michael and Tim performed, and they introduced the speaker, a blond-haired man in dress blues. I really didn't know much about him except that he was a Congressional Medal of Honor recipient, and all the vets talked about him with such reverence. The Medal of Honor is America's highest military honor awarded for personal acts of valor above and beyond the call of duty. I was briefly introduced to him and his wife, Peggy. His name was Sammy Davis. I knew Tim and Michael had the greatest respect for him; they had even written a song, "Who's Gonna Fight the Fight When the Last Warrior is Gone," to honor him. But there were too many people and too much going on for any conversation, and I really didn't think too much about it at the time.

A year or so later, I became involved with coordinating a Last Patrol walk in Stephenson County where I lived. Until then, I really hadn't had the occasion to talk much with Tim except for the few minutes when he bandaged my ankle. During that walk, however, we discovered we had a mutual interest in Native American culture.

Some years before, Tim had been invited to the Pine Ridge Reservation in South Dakota by a Native American veteran to study the culture of the Lakota Sioux. He had learned about the sacred spiritual practices of the sweat lodge and sun dance. The sweat lodge relates to personal purification plus prayers for one's family and friends, and the sun dance is offered as a sacrifice and prayer for the benefit of one's family and community. Out of great respect for the protection of the traditional ways, the details of these ceremonies are not discussed in public. It was Tim's interest in the spirituality of the Native American culture that saved him; he gave up drugs and drinking because he wanted to sun dance, and one has to live a clean life in order to do that. He also cared enough to learn their tongue, spoke the Lakota language quite well, and he would sing in Lakota during the ceremonies. Tim told me about Grandfather Pete Catches, an old Lakota medicine man he loved dearly. Pete Catches had given Tim the Lakota name "Cetan

Tan Inchia," which alluded to "hawks around him." There truly were always hawks around Tim.

I had been fascinated by Native American culture since I was a little girl. My family's dairy farm was on historical land near Kellogg's Grove, close to the little towns of Kent and Pearl City, Illinois. That area was very significant in the Black Hawk War of June 1832. Centering on the disputed 1804 Treaty of Saint Louis between the United States and Native Americans, the conflict left several on both sides dead during the two battles that occurred near the grove. After the second battle, Abraham Lincoln arrived as a soldier to help bury the dead. At a spring between our house and the barn, a little drummer boy named Benjamin Scott was killed in the skirmish; my son, Tony, named his youngest son after that little boy. There were a couple of cabins on our property left from the time of the Black Hawk War, but back then they were no big deal. Nobody realized the historical value, so my grandpa tore them down. I still have a pair of spats made of wool and canvas with original hooks from one of those cabins. As kids, we would follow Dad behind the tractor and plow, picking up scads of arrow heads. Contemplating these relics as a little girl, I wondered who they'd belonged to and how their owners had lived. Native American stories always held me spellbound.

Like Tim, I had also visited the Pine Ridge Reservation, where I had learned to do Native American beadwork. Tim saw some beadwork bands I had designed with the words "Last Patrol" on them, and he asked if I could make something for him. I was so thrilled there was someone who was as interested as I was in beadwork. I had always loved crafts and needlework, and I found that I could express myself in custom designs. We talked back and forth on the phone and sent design ideas by mail so he could tell me what he wanted for a Native American medicine bag. We also talked about Lakota ceremonies and the things that had special meaning in his life, and we would find a suitable design to express that area of his life.

Through these discussions I began to know the real Tim Taylor, the man behind the righteous music and the veteran movement. He was funny as all get out, laid back, polite, mannerly, and kind. I loved that he used his

God-given talents for a higher purpose than just himself; I couldn't help but be attracted to him.

Still, we remained friends for several years before discovering that our feelings had started to grow into something more. Then I began to feel that something bigger than both of us was drawing me to Tim and to Texas.

CHAPTER 2

Waltz across Texas

On a brisk December day in 1993, I pulled out of Freeport, Illinois, heading south for a new life in the Piney Wood Hills of East Texas. Nine hundred seventy-five miles and the unknown stretched between me and my destination. Ahead of my van, my son, Tony, drove a U-Haul containing everything I owned. There was no turning back.

At forty-seven years of age, I had made a decision that was turning my world upside down. The promise of a new life and a new love with Tim Taylor was irresistible. To find out whether this was the real thing, I needed to get to know him better on his turf, which was just outside the little town of Hawkins, Texas. This would be a courtship period to discover if he was truly the man I believed him to be. I knew the pain of divorce, and I didn't want to make another mistake. But I still believed in for better or worse until death do us part. If I was ever to marry again, I wanted it to be the real thing.

As I drove, I considered what love and marriage meant to me. Growing up in a small farming community, I don't think there were any kids in our class who came from divorced homes. Both sets of my grandparents had life-long marriages. I remember them working together, caring for each other if one was sick, and there was never a feeling of contention in their homes. Grandma and Grandpa Fehr even shared the same room when they moved on to a nursing home. That's the kind of marriage I wanted.

I was devastated when, after thirty-eight years of marriage, my own parents divorced. I was an adult with a grown son when that happened, but age doesn't matter when you watch your family fall apart. At the time I married, I was sure I knew what I was doing, but sometimes people marry for the wrong reasons. In the rural culture where I grew up, it was just expected that I would marry a person I had dated for a long time. I certainly never intended to be divorced, but when I knew it wasn't working, and we weren't suited for each other, it didn't help either of us to stay married.

Despite the difficult experiences of divorce, I still believed that marriage was sacred. There is an old song called "Sunday Kind of Love," and that is the kind of love I longed for. I wanted someone who believed in God, somebody with family values, manners, and a friendly, outgoing personality. I wanted somebody loyal who would treat me with respect, who would make me laugh, and someone I enjoyed being with no matter what we were doing. In my heart of hearts, I felt that Tim Taylor was that kind of man. I knew I wanted and needed something drastically different from where I was in my life, and I was drawn to Tim like a magnet.

As a young married mom, I had stayed at home until my son, Tony, went to school. Then I worked as a bookkeeper and receptionist for both a dentist and an employment service. For more than a decade, I was a mail carrier in nearby Freeport, Illinois, and I also attended Highland Community College there.

After studying to become an interior decorator, I had worked my way up to national design director in a successful interior design company. Managing my shop and employees, consulting with clients, and occasionally flying to large cities for conferences constituted my career. I enjoyed it, yet life was a whirlwind, and sometimes I felt like a spider caught in the intricate threads of her own web. I still wanted to be a decorator, but on a much simpler scale.

On both sides of the highway, as I drove toward a new life, light from the early morning sun glinted on scattered farms dotting the gently rolling land-scape. I could almost smell the aroma of perking coffee and sizzling bacon as wives in aprons prepared hearty breakfasts in country kitchens. Their hus-bands donned feed store caps and pulled on heavy coats and boots for frosty barn chores. I was the daughter of a dairy farmer, and I knew that life well.

While I had made the transition from the farm to town, northwest Illinois was the only home I had ever known, and saying good-bye to everything and everyone I knew pierced my heart. In my mind, I saw my five-year-old self clad in snow pants, a head scarf, a little button-up coat and red boots, standing under the indigo sky on a frigid northern Illinois evening. Stars twinkled overhead, and I could see my breath in the frozen air as I trudged back to the house with Dad after the milking was done and the animals were fed and bedded down. The sweet fragrance of hay in the barn and the crunch of our boots in the snow echoed gently in my memory. I loved being with my dad on the farm where my little girl world felt safe and secure. I wanted to feel safe and secure again. Alone at the wheel, tears rolled down my cheeks. I was grateful that no one was in the car with me. I needed the space and the freedom to let go completely.

My stomach did flip-flops, and with every mile, I waffled between excitement and trepidation about whether or not I was making the right decision. How would I take to all the changes in my life? Would I fit into a place that was so different from where I had lived? Could Tim and I mesh our lives and different worlds together?

The thing that always sticks in my mind about that trip was the unusual number of hawks along the way. At one point I started to count them, and within a hundred-mile stretch, I counted one hundred hawks. As I was making my way toward the man known to the Lakota as "Cetan Tan Inchia," it felt like they were an omen that I was going where I was supposed to be.

Perhaps there was some truth in that omen, because a year and a half later Tim and I were married. It is strange how hawks have made their presence known to me in uncanny ways ever since.

Once in Texas, I quickly realized there were so many facets to Tim that I loved. He was fiercely loyal and deeply vulnerable. He was quirky and unconventional and kept me laughing like nobody I had ever known. Tim was a collector of old cans because he might need them someday, and he was a dancing fool. When he was a teenager he would hear a song on the car radio and just had to pull over and get out and dance; it didn't matter where it was, the music was in him. As a kid he'd tag along on dates with his sisters when they went to the drive-in. During intermission, with 50s music blaring, somebody would put a piece of cardboard on the gravel, and Tim would dance and put on a show, always drawing a crowd. Even during our marriage, he'd break out in the Watusi or whatever dance struck him, no matter who was around. There was no pretense about him; he just did his own thing.

For all his easygoing, laid-back, and carefree attitude, there was an intensely spiritual side to Tim as well, and I loved that about him. Our mutual interest in Native American culture became a very strong bond between us. I have no idea why, but even as a child, Tim always wanted to be the Indian, not the cowboy. Once as a little boy playing cowboys and Indians, he and the son of his mom's housekeeper decided they were going to burn out the settler's cabin. They got matches from somewhere and proceeded to set fire all around the perimeter of the house. It was the housekeeper's home, and she was inside! Fortunately for all concerned, neighbors put the fire out before the fire trucks arrived.

Later, Tim and I would visit the Pine Ridge Reservation together. I made him a Native American shirt with beadwork of custom designs, horsehair, and other symbols that meant a lot to each of us. He was very proud of that shirt and wore it for an album cover. Tim was my biggest beadwork fan, and after he passed away, for nearly fourteen years, I just couldn't pick up a needle and beads.

Tim was truly a gifted musician, a talented songwriter, and his singing voice was smooth and mellow. How I loved to hear him sing. He once told me that he never chose to live the life of a musician—it chose him. I remember seeing photos of him as a child holding a guitar.

At two years of age, Tim had been adopted by a surgeon and his wife in Abilene, Texas. Dr. Floyd Taylor had been a military doctor before going into private practice. After Tim and I were married, I did some digging to help Tim discover who his birth parents were. They were not married, and Tim's mother had left him with his grandmother in Abilene, Texas, so she could join the circus. According to Tim's original birth certificate, his dad was a musician.

Music was in Tim's blood, but his adoptive father didn't understand and didn't approve. Dr. Taylor's aspirations for Tim included medicine, not clubs and honky-tonks. Although Tim desperately wanted his dad's approval, the music in his soul was leading him on a different journey.

Not wanting to embarrass his dad, Tim started performing under the stage name of Doc Holiday. Before my time with him, he had a recording contract with United Artists in Nashville, and his song "Bottle of Wine," written by Tom Paxton, as well as a song called "Champagne Lady," received radio play.

When we married, I think most of Tim's friends were just happy for him to have a respectable woman in his life that was not from the club scene. The first thing he always told the other musicians was, "She is not from the clubs." That meant I was to be treated with respect.

I was always so proud of Tim. He gave up the rough and rowdy musician life years before he met me. If he had not, I would not have given him the time of day. No drinking, no drugging, and no club girls. I hadn't known him during those days, but I sure had heard the stories, and I was thankful that was behind him. I never worried about groupies because he always took me with him, and he would proudly introduce me from the stage as his lady.

He once told me he could no longer write blues songs because when you are happy, you can't write the blues. That was always a good joke between us, but it made me happy, too.

Before a concert, Tim would have me braid his hair. It was middle-of-his-back long, and he liked how it looked. Unless it was on a Last Patrol walk where he wore jeans and T-shirts stating something about veterans, he was a very neat dresser; his jeans had sharp creases, his boots were polished, and his shirts went to the laundry for heavy starch. A true Texan, he wore a Stetson hat. His singing partner, Michael J. Martin, would have a fit because he was carting equipment and tuning up while Tim was still primping. In some ways, Tim and Michael were like an old married couple, and they tickled me.

I learned what it meant to be married to a celebrity and a public figure, which I hadn't thought of before. It didn't matter if we were tired and weary, if people had been kind enough to come hear Tim sing and wanted an autograph or to say hello, we stayed to talk with them. I learned quickly that going to grab a meal in a restaurant where people recognized Tim meant that we would have no privacy. On the Last Patrol walks, people wanted to talk to Michael and Tim at all hours, so our time was not our own.

It's a strange phenomenon, but people hung on to every word Tim said. As his wife, I became an extension of that. They would ask me if Tim had any lasting effects from the war or about other veteran issues. I realized that I had the responsibility to make sure I knew what I was talking about because people thought if Tim's wife said it, then it must be absolutely true. Sometimes I felt kind of like a teacher who has to be "on" all the time. Even though there were times we were tired and would have just liked to relax, I wouldn't have missed that experience for the world. Little did I know back then that this was a rehearsal for what was to come later in my life.

Growing up in an affluent, country-club family in Abilene, Tim had impeccable manners and Southern charm. He was very polite and said, "Yes, ma'am," or "Yes, sir." It had nothing to do with a person's age; he addressed adults that way out of respect. He always wore a shirt to the table or removed his hat at mealtime, and he knew how to use all the correct pieces of silverware and glasses at a formal setting. If he had to sneeze or cough while eating, he'd excuse himself away from the table to do it. Of course, he opened doors for ladies. Ever the gentleman, he would never pass gas in the house. It became a big joke with friends when he would discreetly get up, go outside, and then return without a word to anyone.

Tim was full of stories and quick-witted retorts that he delivered in a Texas drawl as long as the braid that hung down his back. I just loved that accent. When he heard this Yankee girl talk, he said I talked way too fast, and I needed to slow down. I asked why he talked so slow, and he drawled, "Well, honey, it's just too hot in Texas to talk any faster."

I still smile when I remember the first time he took me fishing on beautiful Lake Fork, known for its "lunker bass." Every time we pulled one in, we always said, "Nice fish," even if it was only a minnow. That day I actually caught a three-pounder. I know guys always lie about the size of the fish they catch, so by the time we got back to the boat ramp, I told Tim I was so thrilled about the nine-pound bass I caught. With a deadpan expression, he came back

with, "Baby, one thing y'all need to remember 'bout catchin' and braggin'—
y'all jumped too big too soon."

Fishing and monthly neighborhood get-togethers were a regular part of
our lives. We spent a lot of time with friends, and both of us were card players.
Texans were partial to the games of spades, poker, and euchre. I felt right at
home. As I was growing up, my folks would get together with friends many
evenings after the farm chores were finished and take us kids along with
them. The visits rotated from home to home. Our parents played the card
game euchre, drinking beer from bottles that had to be opened with a church
key, and we kids became pretty good at cards hanging around the card table
trying to snitch candy and nuts from the party bowl. I remember trying to be
just like my dad, slamming my hand down on the table as I yelled, "Euchre!"
It was fun doing the same with Tim and our friends in Texas.

Tim and I both loved to garden. How we laughed about growing the okra
that ate Mineola, a little town up the road. It was twelve feet tall, and we had
to use a stepladder to pick it.

We also shared a love of critters. Animals had always been part of my life
on the farm, so having a brood of five dogs with Tim just seemed normal
to me. I guess they were kind of like the kids he and I never had together.
Wishbone and Sister were two big, old, red dogs. Mooney was white with
brown spots, and Dancer was white with black spots. They were all of ques-
tionable heritage. Then there was little Cheesi, who was left in the men's room
of the Beckham Hotel in Mineola. She was the sweetest dog with a pleasant
face and never had a bad word to say about anybody. She looked like a Welsh
Corgi, but we thought her father was a drummer in a rock and roll band (the
kind that blows into town and hightails it out in a hurry.)

Tim got the cats, Annie and Hobbie, from the humane society in Tyler;
they were Siamese "kinda." Both of them traveled across the country with
us in a motor home while we sought treatment and a cure for Tim's cancer.
Animals seem to have a sixth sense when their owners are ill or distressed, and
our animals were our companions and such a source of comfort for me when
Tim became so sick. They gave me a reason to get up every morning after he
died.

However, Tim's experiences spanned much deeper than music and the gentle life in the Piney Wood Hills. After high school, he wanted his dad to be proud of him, and he wanted to serve his country, so he enlisted in the navy. His enlistment turned into three grueling tours of duty as a Fleet Marine Force line corpsman (a combat medical corpsman attached to the Marines) in Vietnam. A combat medical corpsman is an enlisted medical specialist with extensive medical training who is often assigned to Marine units on extended deployment. In addition to advanced training in battlefield medicine, Tim had to have the same combat knowledge and skills as his Marine unit. The docs in a combat situation see the worst of the worst, the hellish carnage of battle, trying to save those who can be saved and comforting those who are losing their battles. "Doc" is a highly revered title in the military, and Tim wore it proudly. He earned the rank of E-6 petty officer, first class and returned home as a decorated Vietnam veteran. Altogether, he spent nearly fourteen years in the navy.

Although Tim had seen the worst in Vietnam, he hadn't lost his gentle and caring side. As I think of him being a "doc," I can't help but smile when I remember the time I had a sliver in my arm. He asked if I wanted him to take it out. I thought he would grab a pair of tweezers and whisk that little thing right out. Well, a doc is always a doc. He got a pan out and filled it with water and put it on the stove to boil. Then he laid a clean, white towel on the table. He grabbed my magnifying craft light and set that up by the table. When his instruments were boiled, he put on surgical gloves. I got a little worried when I saw a scalpel, but he proceeded to take out the sliver, which took all of two seconds.

"Wow, this thing is gigantic!" he exclaimed.

I laughed and told him to take it away from the magnifying glass. Then he disappeared, and I found him sitting outside on the back step with his head between his knees. When I asked him what was wrong, I was so touched when he mumbled, "I can sew a man's ear back on in Vietnam, but I can't take a sliver out of my baby without getting faint."

The Vietnam War took its toll on Tim, and like many others veterans from many wars, he suffered from post-traumatic stress. He couldn't go to sleep until the early morning hours because he dreaded the nightmares about the war; it was medication that allowed him to sleep. Tim used to sleep with a gun under his pillow, but that was so unnerving to me that he moved it to the nightstand drawer. Performing on a stage in front of a thousand people was fine, but he didn't want to be mingling in a crowd. On stage, there was nobody behind him, and he felt in control. In a crowd he was ever vigilant and very uneasy. He said it helped when I held his hand if we had to walk through a crowd, and even carrying his guitar seemed to help because it gave him something to focus on. In a restaurant he would never sit with his back to the door; he had to see who was coming and going. I knew never to startle a veteran with PTS, and Tim was no different. If he was asleep, I would speak softly to wake him, but never shake him. A combat veteran's first impulse may be to immediately react in a physical manner as he was trained to do in combat. Tim never lashed out at me that way, but I have known others veterans who have.

Being too close to fireworks unhinged Tim. The reverberating percussion, the acrid sulfur smell, and brilliant exploding lights of fireworks were much too close to the enemy tracers he'd experienced in battle.

However, Tim knew I loved fireworks, so one night we parked a long distance from where they were being set off so they weren't so loud. Knowing how fireworks unnerved him, it meant a lot that he would make that concession for me to see them.

I never experienced unreasonable anger, disrespect, or rage from Tim, but I knew many wives of Vietnam vets who had. Yet like other combat veterans, Tim fought his share of demons. I had previously been married to a Vietnam veteran and had been around enough Vietnam vets that none of it was really new to me. I accepted it as part of our lives and relationship; it's just what you do when you love someone.

I loved Tim with all his quirks, his big heart, and his funny bone; I loved him for better or for worse, more than I ever imagined possible.

As much as it hurt me to leave Illinois, I also fell in love with Texas. I felt I was where I belonged. Tim always described our place as eleven acres of heaven on earth, and I felt that way, too. The land was pretty and so peaceful and quiet with the pines, the sassafras, maples, oaks, and sweet gum trees. It didn't take me long to become accustomed to the laid-back Texas culture as I traded my tailored suits and makeup for ponytails and blue jeans. Soon the pressures of business rolled off my shoulders down the slopes of the Piney Wood Hills; I relished the tranquil setting there with Tim.

East Texas in the spring is magical and green with bluebonnets and Indian paintbrushes popping up everywhere. The faint smell of pine and fragrance of honeysuckle and Carolina jessamine would waft through the soft breeze; in summer there was the scent of fresh mown hay. It all smelled like home to me. The red and gold leaves in the fall looked like a postcard. We lived in a clearing in the woods, down a lane so there was no traffic…just quiet. It was our respite from the outside world.

I loved the Texans, too. They were so friendly. Tim's dad and mom and Tim's kids from a previous marriage lived out of town, but when we saw them, they were all very sweet to me and made me feel accepted. Neighbors stopped in just to say, "Welcome to Texas," and locals from town told me, "We were so anxious to meet you. Welcome to your new hometown."

Besides the beauty of the land and the warmth of its people, I fit right into the quirky, small towns with their East Texas charm. It's not every town that has a restaurant in the hardware store, but Mineola, up the road from Hawkins does. With antiques and picnic tables outside the front of the vintage brick building, the window at Kitchen's Hardware said it was established in 1899. I loved the creaky, wood floors, exposed brick walls, and mismatched chairs and tables. You could find everything from canning supplies to watering cans, rakes, shovels, and bins full of loose nails and screws that you bagged and weighed at the counter. The owner knew the locals by name, and the food was great. Tim and I spent a lot of time at Kitchen's Hardware. He had his own stool there, and I got mine by default.

With Tim being a musician, it was only natural that our other favorite place in Mineola was the Piney Woods Pickin' Parlor in the Beckham Hotel, owned by Tim's close friend, John DeFoore. During Tim's Dallas days playing clubs, before his musical partnership with Michael J. Martin, John had been the lead guitar player in their band, Stump Broke. John once came to visit Tim on his eleven acres of heaven and fell in love with the area. He bought the old Beckham Hotel, and that's how the Piney Woods Pickin' Parlor came to be. Concerts were held in what had been the old ballroom upstairs.

More than a hundred years old, the hotel is a red brick building across the street from the railroad with a colorful history of travelers, gamblers, and even a ghost or two. John hired me to decorate the Victorian parlor with its rich wood, tin ceiling, French doors, and open staircase. There was a kitchen and a restaurant off one side of the large parlor, and on the other side was John's personal quarters.

With John's ownership of the hotel came the DeFoore Music Institute, where he taught guitar and songwriting in one of the side rooms. His illustrious stable of students included Kacey Musgraves, Michelle Shocked, Jon Wolfe, Jeff Allen, and Ryan Beaver. I remember walking in one day and hearing the most glorious music coming from the side room. I glanced in and saw a stunning blond girl singing her heart out. When John stepped out of the room, I asked him, "Who is *that*?"

"Miranda Lambert," he replied. "She's a high school student from Lindale." Miranda would go on to become a megastar in country music.

A lot of locals, including Tim, would often get together to jam at the Pickin' Parlor, the downstairs parlor of the hotel. Many colorful performers of note including the Dixie Chicks, Ray Wylie Hubbard, Billy Joe Shaver, Tony Lane, Druha Trava, Kacey Musgraves, and Shake Russell also performed there. We had such great times at the Pickin' Parlor.

My life with Tim was steeped in love, music, good times, and good friends. Ours was a simple life, Americana at its best, and it fit me like a glove. We looked forward to growing old together. Until that unthinkable day Tim was diagnosed with cancer.

CHAPTER 3

First and Final Chapter

In the summer of 1995, Tim had a sore throat. He hadn't told me about it, but he later said it had bothered him off and on for a couple of months. Tim wasn't a complainer, but if he'd suspected it was anything serious, he would have seen about it sooner. He left for an appointment for his regular checkup at the Veterans Administration (VA) in Dallas, and I didn't think anything of it. When he got back, he sat in his recliner, and I was on the love seat; I just thought we were going to have a normal conversation.

"They told me it could be cancer," he announced. There was no emotion; he just told me like he might say it was raining outside. For a moment the silence was deafening.

My blood turned cold, and I trembled inside. I couldn't wrap my mind around that possibility. It just couldn't be. Our life together was only eighteen months old, and we had just married. I went over and kneeled by his chair, and we held each other. I couldn't let him see how panicked I was, so I kept trying to reassure him that what they told him was probably a mistake and everything would be fine. With denial, I was trying to reassure myself as well.

That afternoon we decided to go to the riverboat in nearby Shreveport, Louisiana, to try to have a good time and not think about it. While we were putting our coins in the slots, Tim told me, "I'm giving myself the gift of life. I'm throwing my cigarettes away today."

I wished he'd done it earlier, but at that moment he seemed resolved to quit, and I was glad he made that decision on his own.

Tim had smoked a pack or more a day since he joined the service as a young man. He gave up drugs years before, but he said that was a piece of cake compared to the cigarettes that were so addicting. From time to time Tim would say he was going to the barn to check on the boat or some crazy thing; usually it was after a meal, and he finally admitted that he was backsliding on the cigarettes. He was only taking a couple of puffs each time and then he would put the cigarette out, but still they controlled him. I didn't want to nag him, but I was terrified because his life hung in the balance. I was on my knees a lot about the smoking and praying that the doctors were wrong.

Between that time and when we got the final diagnosis, Tim and I tried to live as normally as possible, and we talked about everything but cancer. I think we were trying to protect each other. We had to take control of little things in our lives because so much was not in our control.

Within a month, however, Tim got a call from the VA to tell him that the diagnosis was cancer. Once again he was very calm and matter of fact when he told me. I felt sick to my stomach and that frightening feeling of panic settled over me once more. This was certainly not the life we had planned together. Our entire future changed in one split second with one ugly word.

What were we to do next? What could I do to help Tim, and how could I make things better? My immediate reaction was that of wanting to fix everything for this man that I loved so dearly.

I first contacted the American Cancer Society and told them all the details about his cancer. I guess I hoped they would give me some definite answer of exactly what we needed to do to cure him. I asked if there was any new treatment where he could be part of a trial or something. It just doesn't work that way, but at that point I was desperate and grasping at straws. Their information was general, and they told me that everything would have to go through his doctor.

The VA doctor gave Tim two options: radiation or a laryngectomy (the removal of his voice box). What a heartbreaking choice for someone whose life was singing. The specialist was so deadpan without an ounce of compassion; it was just, "Here are your choices; what do you want to do?" To me, it felt like the word empathy didn't exist in his vocabulary.

I guess I needed a doctor with the compassion that Tim showed to people he had cared for. Both Tim and I needed to feel that somebody in charge cared about us, we needed some kind of reassurance; instead at that moment we both felt apprehensive and very much alone. I bombarded the doctor with questions, and Tim asked what his chances were if he chose radiation. Finally, when the doctor said, "I can get this," meaning with radiation, I started to feel more hopeful.

We drove the two hours from Hawkins to Dallas each way, five days a week, for thirty-five treatments, and I went with him to all but a couple of appointments. Then a church friend whose wife had survived throat cancer took him. The Shellys were so supportive of Tim because they understood what he was going through. During that time I tried to make hope my daily companion, and I still believed Tim was going to get well, but nothing about it was easy.

Prior to Tim's initial treatments, we had gone out to Pine Ridge for Native American prayers and healing ceremonies. We prayed for a miracle of healing. I contacted Native American friends who were into holistic medicine, and we learned about herbs. I did later confer with the doctors before Tim took any of those, and I read every book I could get my hands on about vitamins and minerals as well as cancer treatments. I needed to be educated, and it helped me know what questions to ask the doctors. We also discussed treatments with Dr. Taylor, Tim's dad, who only advocated conventional medicine.

Through my reading, I learned that nutrition was key to helping Tim's body fight the cancer, so we started a juicing program right away. He drank one quart of fresh vegetable juice in the morning that I processed in a juicer, and then he had a pint of fruit in a yogurt smoothie in the evening. He ate no processed meat, no fried foods, and we kept sugary foods to a minimum. We used everything as fresh as possible from the garden, and we bought large quantities of organic carrots from a co-op in Dallas. I felt confident because Tim was getting the nutrients he needed to fight the cancer, and I really thought he was going to win the battle.

When a serious illness strikes, people often fight emotional battles within themselves as they watch a loved one deal with illness. I loved Tim with all my heart, but at first I was angry with him. Why did he smoke, why did he volunteer for Vietnam, and why in the world did he go back for two additional tours? Then I would feel guilty for having those thoughts.

I was angry with our government for not telling the truth about Agent Orange and how it affected our veterans. Everything revolved around cancer—what we ate, how much exercise Tim needed each day to maintain muscle mass, what drugs and supplements would help, and when the next doctor appointment or treatment was. Everything that had been normal in our lives was now secondary to cancer. I resented the illness, but I never let Tim see my feelings. As I prayed, I learned to accept what I couldn't change and tried to work on the things I could change. I realized that those initial feelings were all a reaction to fear and not having control over much of anything in our lives.

Tim didn't get sick from radiation on his throat, but his glands stopped making saliva, so he had to take medication for that. Dry mouth bothered him a lot, and a metallic taste lingered, but mostly he did pretty well. His voice didn't sound the same, but the doctor told him it would slowly come back, and he clung to that hope.

Tim wanted to record another album, "The Life and Times of Tim Holiday," to chronicle his life in music, so he worked hard on it after the radiation treatments. It was his legacy. When I had discovered who Tim's birth parents were, I also found out that Tim's birth name was Henry Kaiser. A character named Henry Kaiser narrates the album. In the studio, just by chance, Tim had come across some lyrics lying on the table; perhaps it really wasn't by chance. The song was called "First and Final Chapter," written by his producer, Randy Brown. After reading the words, Tim knew it had to be the final song of his project. He didn't know it at the time, but it was also to be the last song he would ever record.

Following the final radiation, Tim's doctor believed he was cured, and for the next two years we tried to live life as normally as possible, cautiously planning for the future. We didn't even want to mention the word cancer. We fished and drove our motor home back to Freeport to visit my family and to Abilene to visit his family. We took trips to visit other friends. While we were optimistic, we also realized more than ever how important it was to make every day count.

In the spring of 1997, Tim and I and the two cats were planning a trip to join Michael for a Last Patrol walk from Florida to Washington, DC. Before we left, I came outside to find Tim leaning up against the back of the motor home. He said he didn't feel well. I had my reservations about starting out, but he wanted to go and said he was sure he'd feel better. He started driving, but I later took over because he was feeling worse. By the time we got near Nashville, Tennessee, Tim told me to take him to the emergency room at the VA hospital. I was scared and drove like a maniac to get there.

Tim was very congested, and as I looked at x-rays in ER with the doctor, a cloudy film almost covered both of his lungs. The doctor said it was fluid, and then in a very blunt manner, he said to me, "We'll take him upstairs, but just so you know, not many people survive this." I started shaking and nearly collapsed on a nearby stool. I put my head in my hands and didn't think I could move. I felt so alone and frightened for both of us. Almost as an afterthought, the doctor said he was sorry. My husband was gravely ill, and I needed a compassionate nurse or somebody to come alongside me and give me some reassurance, but there was nobody. Tim needed the same compassion. In that ER room, it just appeared to be business as usual.

At the hospital Tim was diagnosed with pneumonia, and during a very painful procedure to drain fluid from around his lungs, one lung was accidently punctured. Tim was on his side, and he gripped the bedrail with pain. He peppered the doctors with a litany of questions; had they done this, had they done that? With his medical knowledge, he knew very well what was going on. While he never got combative, PTS was kicking in, and he was agitated. I kept trying to reassure him to calm him down. I don't know what I was doing that irritated the nurse, but in a very curt manner she told me that if I couldn't cooperate with them, I needed to step out of the room. Throughout the procedure, they were so brisk with Tim, and I flatly refused to step out of the room. There was no way I was going to leave him.

Later, I asked to speak to the chief of staff of the VA hospital, and I told him how I felt Tim had not been treated with the respect that a veteran, or anyone for that matter, should receive, not to mention his punctured lung. I had also called Michael to tell him what happened, and he and someone else from the walk had called the chief of staff to make sure the hospital knew who Tim was. Michael was not one to mince words, and since "VA Runaround" was one of his pet issues, I can only imagine what he said. It was amazing, though, to see the courtesy Tim and I received after that. Tim had to stay for two months, and we couldn't have asked for better care.

I lived in the motor home in the hospital parking lot during that time, and I continued juicing for Tim. Our good friends Roger and Sandy Walker, whom we'd met on the walks, drove some distance to see me. They were so kind and took me out to eat just to get me away from the hospital because I rarely left Tim's room. Michael and several Last Patrollers drove a number of miles from the walk to see Tim. Included in that group was Ron "Doc" Smith. Tim had known Doc for a long time, and they shared a common bond as navy corpsmen. Since Tim wasn't going to be able to care for blistered feet on the walk, Doc would take over, and he conferred with Tim about those duties.

During Tim's stay in Nashville, he started getting major headaches, so they did a number of scans, but nothing showed up. They continued draining his lungs throughout that time, a procedure that only the doctor could do. I watched them do it each day, and finally at the end of two months, the doctor told me he was sending us home. Tim had a drain inserted in his side, and the doctor said I could do the procedure at home. Tim was so tired, and I worried about the drive home, but he was able to lie down and made it OK. After massive doses of antibiotics, the fluid finally subsided from Tim's lungs, but within the month his sore throat returned. He thought it was connected to his bout with pneumonia, or maybe he just needed to think that. He didn't want to consider that the cancer had returned.

However, a private ear, nose, and throat doctor in Tyler, Texas, confirmed the worst. This time, in order to try to keep cancer from spreading, he gave us no choice but the complete laryngectomy. He said Tim's type of cancer didn't respond well to chemotherapy.

Tim was devastated. As usual, he hid his feelings with a stoic face, but I could see in his eyes that he knew he would never sing again and would never speak in his normal voice. A suffocating sadness engulfed both of us.

My heart was broken for him. His singing was the way he had related to the world, the way he shared what was in his heart. Knowing he would no longer have his voice seemed cruel beyond comprehension.

My mind slipped back to the Dallas VA. Before radiation was started, Tim was measured for a facial mask that would hold his head in the exact same position when the treatment was administered. At a checkup after the final radiation treatments, when we thought he was cured, the doctor picked up Tim's long braid, and he started to laugh. He said, "Oops, I forgot to take this into consideration when we measured."

That meant that Tim's braid could have altered his position on the treatment table. It was my understanding that if he was even out of position ever so slightly, the radiation could have missed part of the cancer cells. Now that Tim's cancer had returned, I was appalled at the doctor's cavalier attitude, and I wondered how much difference that initial error could have made. I'll never know; that doctor was long gone from the VA by then, but I've always wondered if that slip could have contributed to Tim's cancer returning. The thought pierced my heart.

Around the time Tim was diagnosed, we also learned that numerous veterans who had been in contact with Agent Orange were being diagnosed with throat cancer. Since Tim had been a heavy smoker for years, there was no way to know for sure what caused his cancer. However, it seemed cruelly ironic that he had been educating others about the Agent Orange issue through his music and the marches, and now it was all hitting home for us.

Before Tim went in for surgery to remove his voice box, I wanted to hold on to his bed and scream to the nurses not to take him. I wanted to tell them we hadn't had enough time together that was normal. We needed more years, Tim needed his voice to sing, and I needed to be able to hear that gentle voice I loved so much. Those words pounded in my heart and my head.

Instead, I leaned over and whispered to him, "I love you, and I will be here waiting for you when you wake up. It won't be easy, but we will go on, and we can do it together."

Because Tim had been abandoned as a child and because of failed marriages, he always felt deep insecurities. Michael once told me that Tim needed to hear every day that I loved him. He needed to know that I wasn't with him just because of the music and that I would stay for the long haul. More than anything at that moment, it was important for him to know that he was loved and wouldn't go through his trial alone.

With pain in his eyes, Tim looked up at me and answered, "I love you, baby. I want those words to be the last you hear from me." They were the last words I would ever hear in his natural voice.

In the recovery room after surgery, the nurse said he was waking up and seemed very upset. I wrapped my arms around him and just held him and rocked him, murmuring softly that everything would be OK. When he was fully awake, I grabbed a pen and paper and asked him to let me know about pain levels and anything else that would help him be comfortable. The first thing he wrote was, "It seems I can no longer talk." Always the comedian, even in his distressed condition, he was trying to make a wisecrack.

Within a week Tim had a Servox, a voice prosthesis that utilized vibrations to produce a mechanical voice sound. A speech pathologist instructed him to press the button on a metal cylinder as he held it to his cheek or neck and attempted to speak. There was no tonal inflection, and Tim couldn't yell. That was a concern in case he needed to let someone know he was in distress.

Some people couldn't understand him, and they were put off by the device. They stopped coming around. Michael called Tim to sing the latest songs he'd written, and then he would ask to talk to me. He couldn't seem to understand Tim, and Tim was hurt. There were those who were patient and made the effort to understand, and Tim wanted his dear friend to try a little harder. He missed conversations with Michael and needed his support. I tried to tell Michael that Tim needed him, but I guess he did the best he could.

An inscription on Tim's memorial bench comes from the title of one of Tim and Michael's compositions, "How Far Can You Go for a Friend." When people find out someone is facing cancer, one of two things usually happens. Either they jump in and lend their support with every ounce of their beings, or they back away. Maybe it's because they don't know how to handle it, but that's the time when your friend or loved one needs you the most. The chorus of this song seems to say it all:

How far can you for a friend? Will you walk through the rain and the wind?

How many miles is too much to depend? How far can you go till you call it the end?

How far can you go for a friend?

Tim worked at the Servox and got to where he could use it pretty well. As long as he was able, he still fed the dogs, and he'd call them with the buzz of the device. They came to understand his signal. I knew Tim's distress signal, or when he was making a joke by the number of buzzes the Servox made. We kind of created our own code to help us communicate better.

Neighbors and church friends often brought food and stopped to offer a word of encouragement. If we traveled, another neighbor cared for our dogs. That was a godsend knowing I could rely on her.

The most difficult part for me was watching Tim not be able to speak and to have to act as his voice. When ordering in a restaurant, waitresses often could not understand the Servox. I felt so bad for him having to repeat everything, with me filling in what wasn't understood. Tim couldn't go any-place alone because he couldn't talk. He no longer cared to listen to any of his recorded music or even play the guitar.

Our lives as we knew it no longer existed, and in some ways it was hard to never have a moment to myself. In other ways, I was just thankful I could be there for him. Once in a while I'd go to the store, and my daughter-in-law would stay with Tim, but I could never relax when I left him.

About four months after the laryngectomy, Tim underwent another surgery. A device was inserted in his throat that allowed air to be drawn in, and as he expelled, he could speak in a monotone. His voice sounded more human instead of mechanical. He still used the Servox, but at least he could communicate a little better.

During the next two years we survived day by day, but we tried to live our days together to the fullest, finding enjoyable moments when Tim felt good. We sat outside in the morning sunshine, Tim with a coffee cup in his hand and me with hot chocolate. The dogs lazed on the grass nearby, the birds sang and the flowers bloomed. We prayed, and people prayed for us.

I remember earlier in Tim's illness when somebody had asked me if we were trying to pack as much in as possible in case the worst happened. I had been so taken aback with that statement because I couldn't fathom that Tim would not get well. I tried so hard to cling to hope, but on those peaceful mornings that we spent together, there was always that dreaded thought in the recesses of my mind that things might not be as tranquil as they seemed. As time progressed, I could see Tim growing weaker. Our future consisted of the time between each checkup. I feared each checkup for both of us.

It became increasingly important for me to take over our daily chores; lawn care, gardening, housekeeping, driving, the bills, taking care of the animals, and keeping track of all of Tim's appointments and medical care. I missed Tim's input on decisions I had to make, and sometimes I felt totally overwhelmed with the responsibilities that we used to split fifty-fifty. There were days when the stress made me feel physically sick, but I couldn't let on to Tim, or it would have upset him. The feelings of anger over the cancer had long since subsided, and Tim finally rested in the confidence that he was the center of my world and that I had married him for better or worse. I needed to try my best to stay strong for him.

In 1998, the threat of what the doctor might find hung thick in the air as we went to Tim's appointment in Tyler. Tim never said much; it was just what we had to do. All of the fears I'd tried to shove to the back of my mind came tumbling out that day when the doctor told us there was a spot on Tim's lung. Perhaps a type of numbness sets in after so much bad news. I wanted to breakdown in sobs, but I asked the doctor what the next step would be.

We were told that a hospital in Staten Island, New York, was doing very specialized pinpoint radiation treatment. We didn't know a soul there, so Tim asked me to call his friend Sammy Davis to see if he knew anyone in Staten

Island that could help us. I made the call and then let Tim relay the situation as well as he could with his limited verbal ability. He returned the phone to me to discuss details. Sam directed us to someone he knew as a contact, and then we stayed in hospital quarters when Tim underwent the radiation. That was the only time I talked with Sammy about Tim's condition.

We ended up making two more trips to Staten Island for treatments, and twice we stayed with Doc Smith and his wife, Carolyn, who lived two hours away in Delaware. Both had served in the military, and she was a nurse. They knew just what we needed, and we had such fun with them and laughed so hard. It was such a respite that we sorely needed. We even went to a rodeo in New Jersey.

They took us to an orchard, and I remember the peaceful walk and buying cider donuts at a market. For years after Tim died, Doc and Carolyn continued to send me cider donuts in the fall.

I was so grateful to neighbors and people from our church who stepped up to take care of our property and animals while we had to be away in New York. Their love and compassion was overwhelming, and I will never forget it.

We talked all the way to Staten Island that last trip, discussing financial matters, special Native American items Tim wanted people to have, and what I needed to give his kids. He wanted me to stay in our home as long as I wanted to; he knew how much I loved the Piney Wood Hills. Tim never mentioned anything about the possibility of my remarrying, but he said I had to make up my own mind about a future without him. That was the only real conversation we ever had about the possibility of him not pulling through. It was a lot easier to talk about our adventures together, the fun times we had shared, and the crazy things our friends had done. We both wanted to laugh, not to cry.

The pinpoint radiation did shrink some of Tim's tumors for a time, but they never completely disappeared. When I thought things couldn't get any worse, in 1999, Tim's cancer exploded with a vengeance with more spots on his lungs, and the cancer spread to his brain. He underwent more radiation, and finally they gave him chemo treatments.

Tim knew his hair would fall out, so before that happened we went to the barber to have it cut. Before we left, I braided it one last time, and with tears in my eyes, I watched as the scissors severed it from his head. I thought of all the times I had braided it for him to perform and how proud he was of his hair. I knew I had to keep it. I told him he looked younger with short hair, and he didn't seem to mind losing the braid as much as I thought he would. I still tried to cling to hope that Tim would somehow beat the cancer, but deep down I knew there was more to be concerned with than his hair.

After the radiation and chemo, Tim and the cancer fought a standoff. I watched him grow weaker, and there were days I didn't know if I could survive as a caregiver. I cried alone, and I pretended to be OK, but I wasn't. I forced myself to remain as positive as I could for Tim. For some reason, I also felt like I had to be positive for everyone else around Tim and help them hold up. I had watched the women in my family react to difficulties with great strength, and I felt that's what I had to do as well. It was all about Tim, and no matter what, I couldn't give up or let on how rough things were. I know it was only the strength from my Heavenly Father that kept me from completely falling apart.

It was so difficult to watch Tim losing ground. One evening, after another round of radiation on his brain, it was time for bed. Tim tried to get up, but he couldn't walk. I was so scared and called my son, Tony, to help. We soon got a wheelchair, and Tony would help me get Tim in the car to go for his treatments. I always tried to lift him from his recliner to the wheelchair, but sometimes he slipped, and I had to call a neighbor to help. Once Tim couldn't walk, the doctor suspended his treatments. It was just too hard on him, and the bad things started to move ahead way too fast.

We got a hospital bed for the family room so Tim could see what I was doing during the day. He quit using the Servox, and his movements became very limited, but sometimes he would thrash around in bed. After checking tubes and clearing his throat, I'd turn him or reposition him and rub his back and or his legs. I knew that my touching him calmed him, and sometimes I just held him in my arms. I needed to touch him, too.

The sound of my voice seemed to calm him as well, so I often read to him; sometimes it was the Bible or the Book of Mormon, and I read mail and vet magazines. Sometimes I even read recipes to him. I brought the dogs in to visit and told him about everyone who called and what they said. I talked about our lives and adventures together and told him how much he meant to me. I tried in every way to comfort him as best I could, and still I wondered if there was something else I should be doing.

That last year there was no longer any good news. I wanted Tim's suffering to end, but I didn't want to lose him. Only someone who has watched a loved one slowly slip away from cancer can really understand. I did what I could to make Tim comfortable and reassured him how much I loved him. Doctors had shown me how to feed him through a feeding tube in his stomach and to take care of his physical needs at that point, so that was just part of what I did every day. I still did the juicing through the tube.

During the last two months of Tim's life, I had to finally come to grips with the fact that he was going to die. I felt numb, I felt hollow, and the sadness threatened to pull me into a dark place where I could never get out. I was afraid of a future without Tim, and the emotional pain hurt more than any physical pain I had ever endured.

There is an ebb and flow to life, just as there is in nature. The tide comes in and goes out, the moon emerges from darkness into a brilliant sphere each month, and there are cycles in our lives. At that time I could not have imagined that I would ever see a cycle of joy or light again.

As the summer of 2000 gave way to fall, and Tim deteriorated, we knew the end was near. He couldn't smile much anymore, but for a few days he kept staring up at the corner of the ceiling with a faint smile on his lips. He could no longer use the mechanical devices to talk, but I asked him if he could see someone. Again that slight smile. I asked if Grandfather Pete Catches, the old Lakota medicine man who had given him his Lakota name and who was like a real grandfather to him, was waiting to take him home. A weak smile spread across his face, and he nodded ever so slightly.

On the evening of October 24, I moved the oxygen tubes and climbed in bed with Tim and told him it was OK for him to leave. I was honest that I wouldn't be fine, but I'd survive with family and friends for support. I told him to look for my dad when he got to Heaven. Tim had never met him, but I knew he would recognize him and love him. I also told him that his friends who had gone before him would be waiting for him so he wouldn't be alone.

Tim passed away the next morning. It was a beautiful fall morning with the trees just starting to turn gold. The tiny leaves on the Chinese elm floated on the breeze, and the birds sang so cheerfully. Our dear friends Doc and Carolyn Smith had arrived about midnight the night before. I had told Tim that Doc and Carolyn were coming, and I believe he waited for them so I wouldn't be alone.

About six hours after their arrival, Doc pronounced him dead. He shaved Tim, and Carolyn and I washed and dressed him. We wrapped him in his orange and white Lakota sunburst star quilt that he'd received as a gift on the reservation. I placed a little stuffed dog in his hand, one he often held toward the end. We put his beloved navy corpsman cap on his head, and I kissed him good-bye. I remember opening the windows because I wanted the sounds of his piney woods to be the last thing he heard; he loved the woods so much. I was numb with grief, torn with wanting him to be free of his suffering, yet devastated by the loss I felt. I wasn't sure how I could ever go on without him.

The day after Tim's celebration of life, some of our closest friends stood in a prayer circle in our driveway, holding hands, praying, and reflecting on Tim's life. In the Lakota tradition, I burned some sage, which is to cleanse, purify, and send the bad spirits away. It is also used for blessing, and the smoke is believed to carry prayers to the Creator. Suddenly Rich Campos, from the Last Patrol, looked up and yelled, "Here comes the hawk!" From out of nowhere, a hawk soared in, circled twice above our heads, and then flew off toward the south. Cetan Tan Inchia. Hawks were still around Tim! It was one of those sacred moments that I can't explain, but it deeply touched each person there.

As I saw the hawk circle, lyrics from the final song Tim recorded tumbled out of my heart as tears ran down my face. In my mind, so clearly I could hear him singing:

When we meet again someday either here or miles away

Will you recall that our hearts once flew together before you heard another call?

Then your heart will finally understand what it is now your mind can only doubt.

Your spirit rises like a red tail hawk

Circles twice
And heads off to the south

Right then, standing in our driveway celebrating Tim's life, I remembered all the hawks that had kept me company on my drive from Illinois to Texas. It had only been a few years, but it felt like a lifetime. Seeing the hawk was deeply moving, but it was also comforting: I felt Tim was watching over me, and I believe he still does.

Part of Tim's ashes are buried in Abilene, Texas. His parents were too old to make the trip to visit Tim at the end of his life, so I thought perhaps they would have closure if we buried part of his ashes there. The rest are buried in the backyard of our home, under the sassafras trees, next to his memorial bench that says, "How Far Can You Go for a Friend." His final wish was to be buried in his beautiful Piney Wood Hills that he loved so much.

From time to time it seemed like Tim still made his presence known. Michael wrote a song about him called "The Ghost of Old Doc Holiday." As soon as he finished performing the song in Melbourne, Florida, at a veterans reunion where Tim often played, a hawk circled over the stage area. Michael threw up his hands and said, "Well, Holiday has upstaged me again."

When I was having a rough time after Tim died, a hawk would always appear. Now that Sam and I are married, they seem to come in pairs. They always make us think of Tim and Sam's late wife, Peggy.

After Tim died, I received over three hundred e-mails in one day. I once said I should write a book entitled *You Don't Know Me But* because that's how many of the e-mails started. They would tell me how Tim and Michael had saved their lives, and they would often ask to reorder tapes of their albums. The originals had been worn out from playing them so often.

More than one veteran stepped forward at Tim's memorial service to share that Tim was the reason he was still alive. During Tim's lifetime, he also heard from veterans with similar messages. It always made me so proud of him, and it validated Tim and helped him emotionally as well. Knowing that their original music helped mend broken lives meant a great deal to both of us. Tim lived his life making a difference to others.

Some things, indeed, seem more than coincidence. I consider the connection between Tim and Sammy and marvel at how very strange life is. Some years earlier, before the Last Patrol was in full swing, Sammy was at a small veterans gathering near Kankakee, Illinois. Michael and Tim had played at a Veterans of Foreign War (VFW) or Moose Lodge. The next day twenty or so vets met at a little park where they sat on picnic tables and talked; it was the start of several large veterans events that would happen in the coming years. That was where Sammy and Tim met for the first time.

This was the beginning of a friendship that would span years. Sammy enjoyed Tim's wit, sense of humor, and outlook on life. Whenever they had the opportunity to spend time together, they made it happen. On several occasions, Tim and Michael stopped at Sammy and Peggy's house for a meal and a bed and a great evening's conversation. They considered each other brothers.

As a Medal of Honor recipient, Sammy would on many occasions speak at events where Tim and Michael performed. Peggy often accompanied him and would sing a few songs as well.

Sammy also recalls a particular veterans reunion, back in the 80s, at Lake LaDonna in Illinois. At that time, those events were full of great festivities and family camaraderie. Music was playing over the loudspeaker, and he watched in amusement as two young women exuberantly led a group of friends in the hand jive. We didn't know each other, and I sure don't remember Sammy being there. However, I cannot tell a lie—I was one of those two.

Like the faintest of shadows, we waltzed on the periphery of each other's lives, none of us realizing how we would become connected. Yet it gives me the shivers when I recall that Peggy used to be called up to the stage to sing the final song with Tim and Michael at many of their concerts. That song was "Will the Circle Be Unbroken." Sammy and I have often wondered if somehow Tim and Peggy weren't up there pulling strings to help bless our relationship.

CHAPTER 4

How Can You Mend a Broken Heart

Those first days and weeks after Tim died were surreal. People went about their business, but for me, life stood still, and I couldn't move forward. Nothing had any meaning, and nothing really made sense. I found myself wondering how others could shop in the stores, deliver the mail, and do a thousand ordinary things that make up a day. Didn't they know Tim had died? Shouldn't the whole world stop and grieve as I was grieving? My mind knew Tim was gone, but my heart wouldn't let me grasp it. It didn't feel real; any minute now I was going to wake up and realize it had all been a bad dream. Perhaps it was God's way of letting in only what I could emotionally handle at the time.

I have read that grief comes in five stages: denial; anger; bargaining; depression; and acceptance. I think I went through each stage and some more than once.

With Tim sick for years, I grieved before he passed away. I grieved because he was suffering from the treatments he was receiving. I grieved for the life we had together, and I grieved for many things we could no longer do together as a couple. I grieved because I knew he was going to die. I had to come to grips with that certainty, and things that were once important lost their meaning. I feared the uncertainty of life alone without him. The sadness was almost unbearable, and I kept wondering if I had done absolutely everything I could to help Tim.

Autumn with its flaming colors was beautiful when Tim died in October 2000. The days were the kind that he and I would have loved walking side by side in the Piney Wood Hills. So after his death, I walked, and I walked, and I walked. My thinking went all over the place. I tried to relive the fun times with Tim; I just missed him so much. With each step, his songs would run through my head, and I would think of special things he said to me.

He once told me that if he could still sing, he would sing me a song by Leon Russell called "A Song for You." The lyrics were so beautiful; they spoke of remembering when we were together and about a lifelong love in a place where there is no space and time. I especially loved the line that alluded to Tim knowing that my image of him was what he hoped to be. I'd never had a song that was just for me, and it touched me to the core that he would want to sing it for me.

I dug out all of Tim's old practice tapes and put them in the tape player in the truck just to hear his voice. Suddenly he was back with me, and I could almost feel his presence and touch him. It made me realize how important it is to have the voices of our loved ones recorded.

Every time I saw a hawk, it would feel comforting in one way yet almost bring me to my knees at the same time. Everything reminded me of Tim. Every room in the house, every golden leaf that fluttered to the ground, his guitars, his fishing poles, even the old cans he collected in the barn. Our dogs and cats helped to fend off the crippling sense of loneliness that engulfed me, and sometimes having them around was like a warm blanket when I needed comfort the most. Yet they were also a reminder of what I had lost; years that I had thought Tim and I would spend together loomed ahead of me, empty and desolate. The dream we'd had for our lives together had been laid to rest with him, and there was no road map for what lay ahead. I stopped going anywhere at night. If I did go out, I made sure I was home before dark because I couldn't face coming home to a dark, empty house.

Drowning in sorrow, I wondered how I could go on, and I prayed a lot. Tim used to say I could pray the phone book because I always prayed for others. I still did that, but I needed strength and direction for my life as well. I now know that my Heavenly Father was aware of my grief and pain, and he never left me alone. Yet in spite of my strong faith, there were moments when, in my pain, I sometimes wondered where He was. My heart was broken, and I felt a bottomless sense of loss. Still, I learned to lean heavily on my Heavenly Father. My walks became time to pour my heart out to Him.

The most ordinary thing like a smell, a song, or perusing the greeting card aisle at the store could trigger a reaction when I least expected it. I just couldn't consider getting rid of Tim's clothes that first year, and one day I opened his side of the closet. I saw his cowboy boots and sank to the floor. I just fell apart, cradling them to me as I sobbed. Small things like that took me by surprise. I came to realize that crying was part of healing; holding everything in made it worse. Later, when Sammy and I got together, he said he also went to pieces at the sight of Peggy Jo's shoes in the closet.

Sometimes people say the most insensitive things when someone dies; I'm sure they don't mean to, but sometimes they do. About a week after Tim passed away, his stepmother, of all people, told me I was young yet, I would get over it, and I would find somebody else. I was shocked. Get over it? Why would anyone say something like that to a person who had just lost her husband? It would have been better if she had just hugged me and said nothing.

I went a bit crazy, too. When Tim was sick, nutrition and juicing had been a big part of our lives. It was all about vegetables. During that time I, too, ate healthier than I ever had before. After Tim passed away, our oncologist wrote me a note and said our juicing and nutrition program likely added three additional years to Tim's life.

However, when I went to the grocery store for the first time after Tim passed away, I just stopped in the middle of an aisle and realized I didn't know what to buy. At that moment, I didn't want to see another carrot as long as I lived. So I went on a binge and grabbed breads, yogurts, bananas, lunch meat, and cheeses. Then I hit the Blue Bell ice cream, and the next aisle was the bakery. Then I guess I felt a slight twinge of guilt because I went back for a head of cauliflower. After eating like that for two weeks, I started to crave "healthy" again, but I thoroughly enjoyed my fall off the nutrition wagon. Perhaps in some way that was a small taste of acceptance because it was moving forward with something that didn't involve sickness and death.

To make things worse, there were huge medical bills to pay. Despite my grief, I had to return to work right away. When Tim died, Social Security took back about $1,200 from our joint account because he died before the end of the month. It was a shock. There was no warning letter; they just took it back. I needed money to live on, and the checking account was empty. Thankfully there was always garden produce in the freezer, and I had frozen some of the leftover food from Tim's memorial celebration. However, the financial burden was heavy.

Tim and I owned a shaved ice concession trailer that we bought in 1994. We would set up at First Monday in Canton, Texas, a huge flea market that covered a couple hundred acres. In addition, we would set up one weekend a month at Trade Days in Longview and Tyler, Texas. Besides the shaved ice, coffee, and hot chocolate, we sold sandwiches and Frito pies. Also, my neighbor Loretta Moon sometimes made wonderful buttermilk pies for us to sell. On weekdays I would set the trailer up at the local Super Walmart parking lot. During the last year when Tim was sick, my daughter-in-law, Christie, and other friends would take my hours so we could keep the business going.

I was back selling sandwiches within a week or so after Tim died. I don't know how I did it, but I had no choice. The bills had to be paid, and I just operated on automatic pilot. Somehow it seemed when some bill was due, and I didn't know how I would pay it, the amount needed was just what I would make that weekend. I believe strongly in tithing ten percent of my income to my church, and I found out those are the kinds of little miracles that happen on a regular basis when one tithes.

Also, I wouldn't have made it without the neighboring concessionaires who had their trailers near me at Canton, people like Jerry and Margie Welch, who made kettle corn in their little log cabin on wheels. When Tim was sick, they would help me set up, and after he died, they watched out for me like they were family. Those folks were all like special angels who held me up so I wouldn't fall apart.

An established Avon route also landed in my lap when a lady at church got sick and could no longer take care of her business. Between that and the concession stand, I managed and was able to whittle away at the medical bills.

I had given up the interior decorating when Tim was sick because I couldn't be there for clients, so I worked long hours selling concessions and delivering Avon. It wasn't easy, but somehow I made it. I think having my lonely hours filled with work was a godsend in disguise. It gave me a sense of purpose and kept me busy. I couldn't afford to crumble.

The first year, as I learned to live as a widow, was the hardest. Each holiday was so difficult. There were no more sweetheart cards on Valentine's Day and no birthday or anniversary celebrations with Tim. There were no more fishing trips, no more music gigs, and no more walks with him in the Piney Wood Hills. Eventually I had to face the task of what to do with Tim's clothes and personal things. I also learned that it was probably wise to avoid making any major decisions, if possible, that first year.

As heart-wrenching as it is, somehow we have to find a way to get through grief. We can't go around it or cross over it. We have to go through it. Like walking through shadowed woods, there is finally that glimmer in a clearing ahead that leads you out to the other side. Finally, one day you arrive at a place where you can see the light again, a place where the heart can start to mend.

As I crossed my own shadowed woods, I was very blessed to have many caring people help me through it. My church family, my family back in Illinois, and my dear neighbors, the Moons, the Attaways, and the Hubbards were a great support to me as well. I was so fortunate that my son, Tony, his wife, Christie, and their babies lived next door. They were a godsend. Later on, Tony was transferred to Wimberley, Texas, so I would take the Amtrak to visit. I'd bring the kids back with me, and they loved those train trips. Sometimes I drove, so even in my darkest hours I found something to look forward to, which was a great help.

My sister and hometown friends from Illinois called often to check on me. Many from the veteran community, the Last Patrol, and the Few made sure I knew they were thinking of me. The Few is group of Marines and hospital corpsmen to which Tim belonged, and they made me an honorary member, staying in touch through e-mail. Tim's singing partner, Michael J. Martin, called often; I think he missed Tim almost as much as I did, and we comforted each other by talking about Tim. I really needed to talk to someone who was close to Tim, and I think Michael did as well. A great spinner of tales, Michael had a truckload of Tim stories that would make both of us laugh, and I learned that laughter helps so much with healing.

Tim's singing buddy John DeFoore also saw to it that I was included in the music world. He invited me to concerts at the Pickin' Parlor and to some of the gigs with his band. Sometimes he'd just invite me to go with him to Tyler for something to eat. He also needed to talk about Tim, and our conversations brought me comfort. One time I dragged John to the worst animal movie in the world, and we laughed so much. He was kind enough to stay through the whole thing.

I can't say enough about girlfriends. My dearest forever friend, Sherry, from northern Illinois, with whom I exchanged daily e-mails and phone calls, saved my sanity on several occasions. She always seemed to call or write when I needed a friend the most. We've known each other for more years than either of us wants to admit, and for some reason, whether by phone or in person, we seem to set each other laughing like hyenas over the dumbest things. So we sobbed and blubbered and cackled through the tears. Sherry knew Tim and never minded that I needed to talk about him all the time. She traveled to Texas for Tim's memorial, and after everyone went home, we stayed up half the night sitting on the bed talking, crying, and laughing. While it may sound strange to laugh after your husband's memorial, it was all part of the healing process. We laughed about the good times; the last few months with Tim's illness had been so difficult, and I needed to remember the fun times with him and let a few rays of sunshine into a heart that was shattered. She helped me do that.

I found out that girlfriends were there for me when I cried and to laugh with me when I was ready. As young women, when we marry, our friends tend to be mostly couple friends. But when things went awry, my girlfriends came through for me. We could pick up a conversation started seven years before. It didn't matter; they understood. I realized it's so important never to let those girlfriends go; I needed to cultivate these friendships like my favorite flowering plants. I didn't know how much of a treasure they were until I was in the depths of grief.

Cultivating plants gave me comfort as well. If you want to heal a heart, plant a garden or even a flower in a small pot. I found that something so simple, so organic, can have lasting consequences for health and healing. I needed to watch something grow. Maybe it was the new life just springing from the ground and turning into something edible or into a beautiful flower. I wanted to watch plants thrive, not wither and die. It was very symbolic, I guess, and it was all beautiful and therapeutic for me.

I loved the vegetable garden and walking barefoot in the freshly turned earth. I suppose that is the farm girl in me. I would plop down in the grass to eat vegetables right off the vine or brush dirt off a freshly dug carrot to taste its goodness. Usually a dog or two would flop down next to me, and I could find a lot of peace in the moment.

My grandma, Flory Busch, was an avid gardener, and the shelves in her fruit cellar were always loaded with canned food. As a kid I would just stand and gaze at the colorful jars that looked like bright-colored gemstones. I know she was with me in spirit as I canned some of the produce, a satisfying task that gave me an additional purpose.

When I had canned, frozen, and eaten all of the fresh food that I could, then it was time to give it away. In nourishing another's life, I found out that mine was being nourished in return. Sharing my garden bounty and doing something for others was one of the great healers of grief.

Gardening also made me look at dying with new eyes. In 1 Corinthians 15:36, Scripture talks about new bodies for those who have died in Christ. It says the answer is found in the garden. When we drop a brown, shriveled seed in the earth, the green shoot that comes up looks nothing like the dead-looking thing you put in the ground. It becomes a beautiful flower, stalk of wheat, or whatever you planted. In the same way, our old bodies shrivel and die like the seed, but the Heavenly bodies we will be given will be beautiful and lasting. Tim would no longer be trapped in a cancer-ravaged body, and he would be able to talk and sing again. How comforting it was to think of him in that light.

Involvement in my church was a great help, too. Every Wednesday night I began to serve as an advisor to a young women's program, and there were church carry-in dinners and Ladies Relief Society meetings. My neighbor Linda Davis (no relation) came every Monday night for Bible study. She brought her little Schnauzer, and my little Cheesi would come in the house; they would lay in the den with us and pretend to listen while the cats would make fun of the dogs. Of course, we always had some kind of comfort food. It all helped to fill the void, and I so appreciated everyone who shared their time with me.

One Monday, my granddaughter, August, was with me for our Bible study. She was about four, and I asked her if she'd like to tell a Bible story. In her story, Mary and Joseph went to a different town to get a baby. Joseph rode a donkey, and Mary rode a little lamb. Instead of baby Jesus being born in a stable in Bethlehem, it was a stadium in Buffalo. She continued very earnestly telling us that when He was born, they put Him in a cow bowl (her version of a manger).

Then she turned to me, wide-eyed, and said, "Grandma, how would you feel if the second you got born somebody put you in cow spit?"

Children have such a way of filling a broken heart with love and laughter.

Comfort is important during grief, and that comes in different forms. Thinking about my Grandma Busch baking bread and buns was one of those special comforts for me. Closing my eyes, I could almost smell the scrumptious fragrance wafting through the kitchen door as we kids came in from school. It made everything seem right in our world. I needed that kind of comfort, so I began making my own bread. My friend Mitch Mitchell showed me how to make a wonderful wheat bread from scratch. The recipe called for nuts and all kinds of seeds, so I even ground my own wheat and flaxseeds. Since it made three loaves, I made one for myself, one for the freezer, and one to give away.

Every loaf of bread I made, every seed I planted, the hours I worked, and most of all the people who loved and supported me became a stitch in mending my broken heart. The pain of losing a loved one never goes away, but it finds a place in your heart to softly settle so the jagged edges are no longer your constant companion. Little by little, the acceptance of Tim's death allowed me to move forward. I missed him terribly, but I knew my Heavenly Father had given me the strength to go on without him.

Through the dreadful ordeal of cancer, I had also learned from Tim how to be strong, and I knew that I wasn't a quitter. I understood that there are no guarantees for tomorrow, so I needed to use my time wisely. I learned compassion for those who are dealing with illness or disabilities, and I knew that I needed to use the lessons I had learned to help others. I just didn't know exactly how yet.

By 2004, men were asking me out, but I had no interest in seeking a new relationship. I had reached a stage of relative contentment, and I saw myself living out my life as a grandma, enjoying the kids, the dogs, my cats, and taking care of my little home in the Piney Wood Hills of East Texas. I would find joy in simple things and do whatever I could to reach out to others in my own little space.

But God had other plans for me.

CHAPTER 5

Getting to Know You

In March 2004, an e-mail from Sammy Davis, addressed to a number of people, flashed across my computer screen. I just hung my head and took a deep breath as I read that after a five-year battle, cancer had taken his Peggy Jo, too. I stared off into space, trying to blink back the tears. Some seven hundred miles from Hawkins, in Flat Rock, Illinois, a man I barely knew was walking the same devastating journey I had traveled with Tim. All the memories from the morning I lost Tim came tumbling out, and hearing of Peggy's death showered me with that deep sadness all over again. My heart ached for Sammy and his family; I knew the layers of grief that lay ahead of them.

Peggy was actually going through cancer treatment when Tim consulted Sam about his treatment in Staten, Island, New York. Tim put me on the phone with Sammy, and we discussed juicing and nutrition for Peggy during that phone call, but I had not talked to him since. Occasionally I would hear updates about Peggy from mutual friends, and I was very sad to receive the news that day. Even though Sam and Tim were friends, and I had spoken to Sam by phone that one time, I somehow didn't feel like I knew him well enough to call. Still, I wanted him to know that I cared about him and his family, so I sent a sympathy card instead.

In the summer of 2004, I was still working many hours with both my Avon route and shaved ice business. My usual routine was to get up early, put on my walking shoes, and hit the road. This was my alone time. I tried to walk four miles each morning. During that time, I talked to God and then made my plans for the day. As I remembered others in my prayers, I often prayed for Sammy and his family and hoped they were holding up OK. When I returned home, I normally collapsed for a bit, tidied the house, and made breakfast. After breakfast I sat down in front of my computer to see what was happening in the world and to check my e-mail.

One morning I was totally taken back to see Sammy Davis's name on my list of incoming e-mails. His message was short and to the point. *"Dixie, thought I'd better check in and make sure you are doing OK."*

I sat and stared at the screen and wondered what to write back. I remembered the hollowness, the sense of not knowing what to do next when Tim died, the pain, and the feeling that I just couldn't move forward. I wanted to say something that would let him know he was not alone. So I assured him that I often kept his family in my prayers, kept him in my thoughts, and wondered how he was getting along. I tried to find words that would encourage him. Memories are bittersweet at first, I wrote, but a time would come when his thoughts of Peggy would simply be sweet, and it wouldn't hurt so much to remember.

"Some days are diamonds, and some days are stone," Sammy wrote back. His words were wise and elegant; how well I understood the journey he was on. Sam knew I was getting ready for a trip back to Freeport, and he wished me a safe trip up north.

That was the start of a regular e-mail correspondence between us. I never expected that Sammy's first message would turn into what quickly became a comfortable and comforting exchange; after all, we barely knew each other. Yet, there we were, traveling down the same road, fumbling to find a way to recover from the immense loss we'd both suffered. That gave us a lot to write about, and our shared sense of grief provided the first foundation of the connection that developed between us.

I shared how I believed that he and I had been blessed to have the time we had with Tim and Peggy. We got to say things that needed to be said, and we let them know how deeply we loved them. I couldn't imagine the pain of couples who had left the house one morning, and one of them had not returned because of an accident or tragedy. No time to even say good-bye.

I wrote him about the feelings I had after Tim died, wondering if I could have done something more for him to change the outcome of his illness. I knew when Tim passed away that I needed to talk to somebody who had really been through the same thing, and I wanted to know if my splintered feelings were normal. I suspected Sam might be having those feelings as well and might want to talk about it. I mentioned that there was no timetable for the acceptance part of grief, but once I got there, I found an inner peace. I believed that if Peggy or Tim had the chance to come back, they wouldn't because life in Heaven with God was too wonderful for the earth mind to comprehend. If they had found each other in Heaven, I was sure she was singing backup for Tim at concerts for vets. They were just missing one heck of a good harmonica player.

We quickly discovered that we were both thinking the same way about loss and grief and decided that if we ever needed to talk, we should feel free to call each other. While that invitation was open on both ends, we didn't speak by phone for quite some time. I was still feeling that I just didn't know him that well, and I wasn't sure I was ready for a phone call. As we talked about Tim and Peggy and the pain of losing them, I could think things out before I wrote them. For me, and I think for Sammy as well, e-mails felt like a more comfortable way to communicate at that time.

During the next several weeks Sam traveled a lot. Back then, neither of us had iPads and smart phones, so there were only sporadic e-mails when he was home near a computer. It was nice to hear from him when he did write. While I was in a slightly different place emotionally than Sam because I'd had four years to deal with my grief, it meant a lot to be in touch with someone who could relate.

I wrote a lot about my faith in God and the comfort it gave me; I knew Sammy understood. One day I found a Bible verse in Psalm 30:5 that I thought maybe he would identify with. I had read it after Tim died, but at that time my profound grief wouldn't let me grasp its meaning. Then when I found it again, it made sense. In this verse, the psalmist has been persecuted, and he is giving thanks that the Lord has saved him through his ordeal. The

Psalm goes on to say that we may shed tears of despair through a night of sorrow, but joy will come in the morning.

As I thought of time with my grandkids and my peaceful days in the Piney Wood Hills, I was learning to find joy in life again, and I knew that someday Sammy would find it, too. I wanted him to know that I believed the sorrow he was feeling would eventually give way to peace and, in time, there would be something to look forward to.

At times we comforted each other in our grief. Other times we joked a lot. We both needed to find humor in our lives and to laugh again because everything had been so serious when we had taken care of our sick spouses. I was delighted to discover that Sammy had a wicked sense of humor, and I wanted to make him laugh, so I told him about me and my neighbor Linda Davis taking a "Thelma and Louise" trip to West Texas. To clear up any misunderstanding, it wasn't *exactly* a Thelma and Louise trip like in the movies. No trucks were blown up, and we did not pick up Brad Pitt or anyone else along the way. We just wanted to hit the open road. I joked in an e-mail to Sammy that after we'd returned, the Texas panhandle was still in shock, and the Dallas Cowboys had moved their summer training camp from Wichita Falls because of the whirlwind we created. Most of the town was destroyed!

As our e-mail correspondence continued, we laughed about so many things, some of it really dumb stuff, and that was important to me. I've always had a sense of humor that was a little left of center—probably inherited that from my dad—and Sam got it.

I told Sam about Dad's big, white, pet goose named Charlie that followed him around like a dog. However, Charlie didn't care for the rest of the family and chased us whenever we invaded his territory, which was pretty much the entire farmyard. He also liked to team up with the dog to chase cars. Always the jokester, Dad would put a cigarette in Charlie's beak. Ol' Charlie just left it dangling there as if he was James Dean reincarnated. It was a sight to see this smug, cigarette-smoking goose chasing cars, and I could only imagine what passersby thought.

By then an easy friendship with Sammy was taking root, and I looked forward to seeing his name on my e-mail list. We began to reveal stories about our lives. It was fun to share our backgrounds and life experiences, and I enjoyed getting to know him. We found out we had a lot in common.

We'd both grown up in America's rural heartland, and Sammy had spent the first few years of his life in Illinois like I had. When Sam was in elementary school, his dad worked for a construction company associated with oil refineries, and every six months or so his family moved, often living on farms. My grandpa, John Busch, was an industrious farmer who owned our family farm in Illinois before my dad bought it from him. Sam and I were the products of a rural upbringing and lifestyle; it was in our blood, and we understood where each other came from. We'd both been raised in hardworking families in which everyone had a job to do. We'd been brought up helping our parents and neighbors and taking care of animals around the farm. Sammy was full of family stories about fishing and playing cards, bingo, and dominos. His folks sounded so like my own parents, with their card club, playing the game of euchre every chance they got. Both our families did almost everything together and had a lot fun.

I loved the respect he had for his mom, and the loving way he spoke of her. The fact that she canned and gardened felt so familiar. She would have gotten along famously with the women in my family who gardened, canned, and prepared all of our food from scratch. His mom's life wasn't easy moving all the time, but she was a strong woman who was willing to pick up and follow his dad. That said a lot to me about the love she had for her husband and for her family, and the more we talked, the more I realized that we shared the same family values. Sammy and I also held similar spiritual beliefs, and we both believed in hanging in there when the going gets tough.

In addition, we were both raised with a strong sense of patriotism. Sammy came from a long line of men who served in the military, and like Tim, he had volunteered to become a soldier. Ironically my son, Tony, and Sammy were both in the 9th Infantry Division in the army. In my family, farmers didn't serve in the military because they were doing their duty to provide food for the country. But they honored veterans and were proud to be Americans.

Then there was the music. Of course, Sam knew Tim's music; in fact, before I knew Tim, Sam had played harmonica on one of Tim's albums, so that was an immediate connection between us.

When Sam was a kid, his dad played the harmonica. In fact his uncles Mel, Boo, and Jessie also played, and they all gathered for jam sessions, playing Irish jigs and old-time tunes. Sam's family didn't have much money, so Sam wasn't allowed to touch his dad's harmonica; that was a treasured possession. Later he would learn to play harmonica on his own.

I told Sam about Grandpa Busch with his beautiful bass voice. Each year people looked forward to his rendition of "Old Man River" as one of the highlights of the annual Lions Club show in Pearl City. That show was a really big deal in our little town, and everyone attended. My dad also sang in a barbershop quartet, and Mom played the piano. She'd accompany the men if they came over to the house to practice, and the quartet always performed at the Lions Club show as well. Many times there were sing-a-longs around the piano with Mom and Dad's friends after a euchre game, and the kids could join in too. It was always a family Christmas Eve tradition at our house to sing carols either before or after the oyster stew.

We talked about our families and grandkids. I learned that he liked to take his little ones fishing, riding on a four-wheeler, and in the winter he'd pull them in round sleds behind the four-wheeler. The picture in my mind of him as a doting grandpa made me smile. I discovered Sammy loved to cook, and I love to bake. He seemed gung ho to try new things, and I loved that about him.

Through our e-mail conversations, I learned that he cared deeply about people and reaching out to those who struggle with life, especially veterans.

I had known of Sammy Davis, Congressional Medal of Honor recipient, for years. While I didn't know details, I knew Sammy had saved three men in Vietnam while being badly wounded himself. He was a living legend among the veterans I knew, and they revered him with the utmost respect. However, Sammy didn't say much about his Vietnam experience during our early e-mails. There was humbleness about him, and sometimes I sensed a vulnerability that reminded me of Tim's.

I've been asked if I was intimidated by who he was. Sammy has an uncanny ability to put anyone at ease, so I really wasn't, but I was curious about him. I was finding out about the genuine person behind the medal and the unique position he held in American history. I was getting acquainted with the private Sammy Davis, and the more I got to know him, the more I liked what was in his heart.

One evening about midway through the summer my phone rang. I didn't have caller ID, so I picked up without knowing who it was. "Hello, Dixie, this is Sammy," said the voice on the other end. I was taken by surprise, and my heart started to pound. Luckily I was sitting down when I first heard his voice. After all of those e-mails I didn't know what to say. I don't think he did either. Once we both got over our initial awkwardness, the words started to flow like water. It seemed like we had a lifetime of experiences to share with each other, and we laughed so hard that first conversation. Sammy has a laugh like one of the old cartoon dogs, and that alone cracked me up.

He roared when I told him how I seem to always get myself in messes and do really dumb things, like unwittingly picking up a glass pitcher of soapy water and dumping it into the Thanksgiving dressing. My friend gasped when she saw me do it, but our lips were sealed at the dinner table. We bit our tongues and dared not even look at each other because we knew we would burst out laughing.

We talked for two hours that night, our conversation easily moving from one topic to the next. It was like chatting with an old friend. We talked about our kids, and I let the cat out of the bag that Tony had checked Sam out on the Internet and said he might be OK, but I should be careful. I laughed that my mom had said those things when I was a teenager, and now my kid was worrying about me.

It was an election year, so our conversation turned to politics. However, I was most fascinated when Sam told me about the first inauguration he attended in January 1969, which was also his first official Medal of Honor function. Peggy Jo was eighteen, it was about two weeks after they were married, and they were also on their honeymoon. I was interested in the women's fashions for the balls, so he described the dazzling gowns the women wore, and he said Peggy, in her high school prom gown, looked as beautiful as anyone there. She never met a stranger and was the one who led him around at those first events when neither of them knew what they were doing. Sammy was so impressed by the sea of people from all over the world who cared enough to attend a presidential inauguration in the United States. They also met the newly elected President Nixon, who treated them both like they were family.

Sammy regaled me with tales of playing harmonica on stage with Willie Nelson and John Mellencamp at one of the early Farm Aid concerts. Years before, Sam had met Willie's longtime stage manager Poodie Locke, who was a veteran. When Poodie saw Sam at the Farm Aid concert, he invited him to the stage with Willie and John. Sam also told me how he'd spoken at a high school in Indiana where Lee Greenwood was performing. Sam was in uniform, and Lee called him up on stage to play harmonica on Lee's signature song, "God Bless the USA." I loved his stories, but Tim had played with some big name performers, too, so that wasn't completely out of my realm of experiences.

Sam also talked about his life on the road for speaking engagements, the interesting places he visited, and the fascinating people he met. His experiences were anything but ordinary, and I think he wanted me to know that he was constantly on the go and in the public eye. He later told me that he initially let me know about those things because if we did ever get together, his lifestyle would mean that I would forfeit a lot of my privacy.

But what amazed me the most about the first conversation was when he told me what prompted him to call. While cleaning out his desk, he picked up a phone ledger, and a yellow Post-it fell out and floated to his desktop. The note was in Peggy Jo's handwriting and read, "Call Dixie." My number was also written in her hand. It must have been written during the time we talked back and forth about the New York trip for Tim's radiation treatment and nutrition for Peggy. Still, it felt immensely surreal to both of us for him to find it at that time.

After I finally hung up, I sat in stunned silence. I could not believe that I enjoyed that call so much. Sam's personality was so alive, his experiences so extraordinary, and I loved the sound of his laughter. I wanted more! After that, we continued our e-mails but also talked on the phone often. I wasn't sure where this ride was taking me, but I wanted to be on it with the seatbelt fastened tight.

I'd read a story about a woman named Rose who went to college at eighty-seven years old because she had always dreamed of a college education. She became an icon on campus, sharing her wisdom and experience with everyone. She liked to dress up and reveled in the attention she got from other students. When she was invited to speak at a football banquet, she fumbled and dropped her note cards on stage. Rose apologized to the crowd for being so jittery; she'd given up beer for Lent, she told them, and the whiskey was killing her. The audience roared with laughter. Rose said she would never get her speech back in order, so she would just speak about what she knew.

She told the crowd that people don't stop playing because they are old; they grow old because they stop playing. Her secrets for staying young, being happy, and achieving success were simple. She encouraged people to laugh and find humor in every day. She said to never lose sight of dreams because without dreams, people die. She told them that growing older doesn't take any talent or ability. The idea is to grow up by always finding opportunity in change and having no regrets.

I loved that story. I thought of Rose's sage advice and how it applied to my life. The whiskey and beer didn't fit me, but dropping my notecards on stage...yep, I could see it! I identified with Rose in so many ways. I loved her philosophy and positive outlook. The changes in my life had been many, but I still wanted to grow, to laugh, and continue to dream.

By sharing Rose's wisdom with Sammy, I intended to give him a glimpse of who I was and how I believed that her philosophy, no matter what we have been through, could apply to anyone who chooses to look through her lenses.

"I firmly believe in Rose's theory of life," Sammy wrote in his next e-mail. *"I do not plan on quitting life. I will continue on living and loving; it is what life is about. It is our job."* We were on the same wavelength.

Slowly our friendship was changing. I believed he was an honorable man that I could trust, and little by little, I found myself thinking about him quite a bit after that first phone conversation, but with great caution. Somewhere toward the end of summer, our conversations began to take on little flirty overtones, and part of me loved the excitement I was starting to feel each time we e-mailed. I loved Sam's positive attitude; I always thought I was the most positive thinker around, and I realized I had met my match.

But I also felt a bit guilty. How could we flirt when we had each loved our spouses so much? How could I do this to Tim? There was a constant tug and pull with my feelings. It had only been five or six months since Peggy's death, and it seemed too early. I remembered how I felt half a year after Tim died, so it was hard to consider that somebody else could look at it from a different perspective and have a different reaction.

It was during that time that Sammy and I had long discussions about everyone having different timetables for mourning. Sam explained that he had started feeling a sense of loss and sadness during Peggy's cancer ordeal. In reality, he had grieved for five years already. I totally understood that. When she died, he didn't know how he could continue on. But he also said that he and Peggy Jo had talked openly about his finding someone after her death. She knew that he had terrible nightmares from Vietnam and that he needed someone to be there with him, to hold him. She didn't want him to be by himself; she knew he wouldn't thrive being alone, and she feared that he might start drinking or become a recluse, staying home all the time. He was still young, she told him, and she wanted him to find somebody else.

He asked her how long he should wait. "Thirty days," she quipped. It became a little private joke between them. When he asked her realistically how long she would want him to wait, she told him, "You'll know. Six months would be appropriate, but if you'd happen to meet somebody before then, that's OK, Sam. I'll be gone, and I want you to be healthy and happy."

I had already sensed from what Sammy had told me about Peggy Jo over the previous few months that she had been an extraordinary woman. He talked about her with such respect, and that said a lot to me about both of them. He called her the strongest person he'd ever known, and he told me he didn't think he'd be alive today if she hadn't been there to help him find his way back from the horror of his Vietnam experience.

But my admiration for Peggy expanded when Sammy told me about their conversation before she passed away. I'm not sure I could have been as unselfish as she was. If I had been the sick one, would I have been able to tell Tim that it was OK to find somebody else soon after I was gone? I'm not sure. Maybe when we're close to death, selfishness evaporates. True love means wanting the best for your spouse, even though it means letting go and giving him or her permission to find someone else. Perhaps Peggy was much closer to Heaven than I am now and understood eternity. Maybe she could see more clearly what is important and what is not. She was unselfish and an exceptionally gracious and wise woman, indeed.

I did finally manage to put aside my feelings that it was too soon after Peggy's death for Sammy and me to consider more than friendship. I had already waited four years past Tim's death, and Sam had been grieving for five years. We could choose to live in the past holding on to something we could never have again, or we could choose to live and let the love we had experienced with Tim and Peggy help to move us forward toward a new future. We both had languished in very dark woods, and the e-mails between us felt like a glimmer of light and sometimes maybe just a tiny glimmer of magic.

I wanted to feel that magic, but it scared me, too. Sometimes Sammy would say things that made me feel he was moving a bit too fast, and then I would pull back. He once told me he loved me as a sister, but he thought with the proper motivation that problem might be resolved. Sometimes I'd flirt a little too much, and then I would pull back again.

August 2, 2004, proved to be a very pivotal day in our lives. I think I had finally come to a point where I knew I really liked Sam, and I was ready to see if there was a chance for something more than friendship between us. Eleven e-mails flew back and forth between us, and by the end of the day, we had moved forward in a whole new direction. As we talked about the stages of grief and how long it takes people to plunge back into life again, I told Sam that I'd reached a stage where I might be open to finding a companion again. I never thought I'd ever feel that way, but time and the love of friends and family had helped me heal to that point. I told him that for the longest time, all men paled in comparison with ol' Holiday, but I had come to realize that if there was ever another man in my life, he would have his own special qualities. There would be no comparing. Maybe I had been spoiled by Tim's bigger than life personality and all the craziness of the music business. Most of the men I had come across seemed to be content to be couch potatoes in front of TV. Not for me. I wanted somebody who would be willing to try new things and go to new places. I needed someone spontaneous with a zest for life. I also never wanted to settle for a love that I could live without.

I told Sam about my grandparents and their nightly summer ritual of taking their wicker lawn chairs out to the driveway to visit with neighbors until the 10:00 p.m. news came on. I wanted that kind of relationship, and I wanted somebody to rock with on the front porch when I was eighty. I wanted us to be able to carry on a good conversation about a multitude of subjects and not sit in silence behind newspapers. I also voiced my fears that if I did find someone, how would I know I wasn't making a mistake? How would I know if another person would be of Tim or Peggy's caliber?

One of Sammy's many endearing qualities is his ability to say volumes with just a few words. When I wrote that perhaps my hopes were all a pipe dream, he came back with a single sentence. *"Pipe dreams only require effort to become true."*

I melted when, in a subsequent e-mail that same day, he declared that I was a vibrant, beautiful young lady with so much to offer any man. I knew what I wanted out of life, he said, and I should pursue it. If I followed my pipe dream, at the very least, I would have had a wonderful time pursuing it.

We bantered back and forth all day. By the time we started talking about pipe dreams, I felt like there were a hundred butterflies in my stomach doing the Texas two-step. If high school kids think they have a corner on the giddy market, I'm here to tell them that grandmas know a thing or two about flip-flopping hearts, and I'm not talking about a pacemaker! As those e-mails came in from Sammy, I was in love with the whole world, just giddy about everything, and I was feeling a burst of life I hadn't experienced in years. It was like someone had turned back the clock, the cloak of grief and sadness had suddenly fallen away, and I was sixteen again. Sammy Davis had touched something in me that I never thought anyone could reach again.

Even though I didn't know how to handle my feelings yet, I knew I wanted to get to know this man a whole lot better. I asked Sam if he ever had any speaking engagements in Texas. If he was anyplace near, I would take him to

Mineola to the hardware store for lunch. It turned out that he'd been in Texas a lot, but at that time he was traveling more on the East Coast. However, he hoped he'd get back to Texas, and he would enjoy dinner with me in Mineola. For some time our conversations had been full of little hints of maybe meeting each other someday, until that one fine day in August.

After our e-mail marathon, Sammy called to invite me to Freedom Fest, a veterans reunion in Skidmore, Missouri, in September. Skidmore is a tiny drop of water on the map of northwest Missouri, but the little town of fewer than three hundred people had hosted Freedom Fest, since 1988. The annual patriotic festival was a celebration of America's freedom, an educational event, and a tribute to those who sacrificed for freedom. In addition, there were recreations of historical events and settings to give visitors an experiential interpretation of history. Sammy said veterans and friends with tents and campers gathered from all over the country for reunions, homemade fried chicken dinners, pie auctions, speakers, a veterans roundtable, ceremonies, great music, and lots of camaraderie. There were displays, vendors, crafts, interactive exhibits, and lots of yummy food.

Sammy had been part of Freedom Fest since its inception, and he said he'd seen the healing effect that the town of Skidmore and the festival had on veterans from all over the world. Over the years, soldiers from Australia, Vietnam, Thailand, Germany, and other countries had attended the event. It was a very special place for Sammy, and he wanted to share it with me. I had never been to Skidmore.

Sam e-mailed me the information and all the details. Our meeting was no longer something vague swirling in the air; we were starting to make concrete plans to see each other. The butterflies in my stomach would not line up and fly in formation; I felt light-headed, I was goofy, and I was excited to see where this relationship might go. Still, I didn't exactly say yes, and I didn't say no.

Sam had told me that Tim's singing partner, Michael J. Martin, would perform at the reunion in Skidmore. I knew he still set up Tim's microphone when he did his gig, and I wasn't sure I could sit there with that empty space on stage and listen to Michael sing the songs that he and Tim had sung together. I knew a lot of Tim's friends, as well as our friends together, would be there, and I didn't know if I could handle it. I had been doing pretty well back in the comfort of my Piney Wood Hills, but I knew if I went, it could open a floodgate of very painful memories. Then there was the expense of a plane ticket. I'd finally gotten to a point where I was managing financially, but there was no money tree in the backyard for big expenses like plane fare.

After finally telling Sammy I would go to Skidmore, I found myself having second thoughts. Notes went back and forth about my apprehension, and Sammy said his last date was in 1968, so he would be a little rusty about this date business, too. To make sure I could not hide behind financial considerations, he insisted on paying for my plane fare. I had run out of excuses. Finally, I confirmed my flight information before I got cold feet. After messages back and forth about connections, my apprehensions began to melt when I received a message from Sammy that read, "I AM EXCITED ABOUT LIFE…Thank you!"

I felt right then, at that minute, the possibilities were just endless. I was thinking about something Sammy had said about Dean Martin's song, "You're Nobody 'til Somebody Loves You." How true that was. But even more so, I realized we become somebody when we give love away, without reservation, to someone else. I loved my son that way, my daughter-in-law, my grandkids, all my family, and good friends all around the United States. But I also wanted that special love between a man and woman again. I wanted that special man with whom I could sit on the front porch, rocking and holding hands. I wanted to laugh with him until I couldn't get my breath, I wanted to go on adventures together and see new things through each other's eyes, and I wanted to be there through thick and thin. I told Sammy that much. I also shared with him how truly amazed I was at my feelings. He was the first man since Tim's death that I'd had an interest in. I never thought it possible, and I was almost euphoric. I couldn't wait to see him and talk to him. My heart skipped a beat when Sammy wrote back that he had great respect and admiration for me and agreed that possibilities were indeed endless.

I talked to Michael J. and had told him that Sam was picking me up at the airport so we could spend time together at Skidmore. His reaction was stunned silence; it was the first time I had ever known Michael to be speechless. "If my opinion means anything," he finally said, "you both have my blessing." Michael added that Sam was among the finest, most honorable men that he had ever known and that I was just the same. Then there was silence again. At last he mused, "I wonder if ol' Holiday had a hand in this."

I told Sam I had also touched base with Patty and Colonel Earl Hopper. When I identified myself, she burst out laughing. She said she and Colonel Dad, as we affectionately called him, were just talking about Tim and me. So I told her about Skidmore and dropped a few hints about Sam; she laid the phone down to tell Colonel Dad about our conversation. When she came back on the line, she reiterated Michael's sentiments. "You both have our blessing," she said.

Their approval meant a lot to me, just as it did with Michael. Having the support of people who had known and loved Tim was comforting, and a weight lifted off my shoulders. I was opening up to the possibility of love again. Then she added, "I'll bet that Tim and Peggy had something to do with this."

I mused over that very possibility and shared my thoughts with Sam. Maybe Peggy Jo and Tim had found each other. In our church, we believe that families are together forever, and I find it a comfort to believe our friends on earth are going to be with us in the afterlife, too. I have no idea how things work in Heaven, but wouldn't that be a hoot if Tim and Peggy were somehow orchestrating this new beginning? If they had anything to do with it, I was grateful.

Sammy sent me a photo of a beautiful sunset with a message that read, *"Thank you for putting light in my life again."* His words touched me more than I can say. By then, I was fully aware that he was making my days much brighter as well. He made me laugh. He made me think about the future without feeling guilty about leaving the past. I was amazed that he had shown me that there was room in my heart for more when I thought it was not possible. Although I'd felt pangs of guilt when I realized I had feelings for someone other than Tim, knowing that Tim would have been happy that it was Sammy who had caught my attention helped me a great deal. I came to realize that it was something like having more than one child. When another one comes along, you don't love the first one any less. You have room in your heart for both of them. That's how I began to feel about the love I'd had for Tim and what I was beginning to feel for Sammy.

As the date of our meeting in Skidmore grew closer, I kept wavering between excitement and panic. The very hope and promise that made my heart race also weighed on my shoulders. There was so much at stake. Was what we were beginning to feel for each other the real thing or an illusion? What if the magic we felt over the phone and e-mail vanished when we met face-to-face?

When Sammy told me he had shown my picture to his daughter, Nikki, and said he had invited her and the four grandbabies to Skidmore for Freedom Fest, I became even more nervous. By then Sammy had talked a lot about his kids, and I wanted to meet Nikki and the babies, but I was also having second thoughts about my first meeting with Sam being so public. What initially felt like safety in numbers started to feel like pressure.

What if things were not as we hoped? Or what if they were better? Sam is the center of attention wherever he goes, and I knew people would be watching us and speculating. I knew that under the glare of so many family and friends, I would hold back and probably not be totally myself. At that point I wished that what would be our first face-to-face meeting in years could happen someplace where nobody knew us, with just the two of us.

But every time doubt crept in, Sammy always found the right words to calm my nerves. After a series of pretty romantic e-mails, I playfully wrote back that he was either the most charming and romantic man I had ever met or he was a silver-tongued devil. Which one was it, I asked. His answer took my breath away.

"Dixie, I have never thought of myself being either. I am an old soldier who has learned many lessons in life. The most important one being that you get what you give in this life. I have tried to share with you how I feel about you and our forthcoming rendezvous and all of the emotions that you provoke in me that I had feared were gone or lost to another life…only in a dream, maybe, with reality staring back at me through gaunt eyes. Thank you for making me feel whole again.

It is too early to be able to say I love you, but I can say that I love how YOU make me feel simply by hearing your voice, and that, my dear, is an awesome start of whatever may come next."

That e-mail told me more about Sam than any other conversation or e-mail had. I treasured it. There was an elegant, honest simplicity about Sammy that I adored. He was smart and sharp as a tack, and he seemed to be such a good man. My feelings were growing stronger for him with every e-mail and phone conversation, yet some residual anxiety simmered at the back of my mind. I still feared that our relationship was happening all too soon for him, and somehow it would boomerang on us. I was fretting a lot about it. Once again Sammy found the right words. He told me not to fret; we would have a better idea of where we were going after we spent time together.

As the countdown to our meeting in Skidmore kept ticking away, sometimes too fast, and sometimes as if the day would never come, we kept e-mailing and talking on the phone. At times we got downright silly. We were both so excited about meeting each other in Skidmore. Then I received my airline tickets from Sam, wrapped in a note with his cell phone number.

"Dixie, above all else, we will have fun," the note read. *"Don't worry, it will be OK. I promise to be a gentleman at all times."* The tickets in my hand made it all very real, and I took a deep breath. *Well, this it, I'm really going,* I thought. And this amazing guy really wants me to come! Then came Sammy's final e-mail, right as I was about to leave for Skidmore. *"Dix, it's down to hours now, darling! See you in Skidmore."*

Down to hours. I was so excited and so scared at the same time. I remembered what I'd felt all those years before when I left Freeport and drove to Texas to spend time with Tim. Once again, I was leaving the comfort of my world to face the unknown. Once again, I feared disappointment, but I was so full of hope. And there were only hours standing between me and what could be a whole new future with Sammy Davis.

CHAPTER 6

I Can't Help Falling in Love with You

It was a beautiful September morning in Texas in 2004 when I jumped in the pickup to make the two-hour drive to the airport in Dallas. My flight would take me to Kansas City, Missouri, the closest airport to Skidmore, Missouri.

I was a basket case; it's a wonder I didn't have a panic attack or something worse. In a swirl of emotions, I was giddy, scared, excited, and everything in between. On the way, a hawk flew by the truck, and I wondered if it was an omen. Was I doing the right thing? Should I turn around and go back home? Then I heard a big clunk on the roof of the truck. There were no trees in the area, and I was in the middle of a four-lane interstate highway, so something had to have fallen out of the sky. That got me more rattled. What was it, and what did it mean?

I was anxious, and every little thing felt like a big issue. Would I find a parking place, and would I be at the plane on time? What would Sammy think when he saw me? Maybe he'd realize I wasn't who he thought I was. What would his friends think? What about his daughter, Nikki, and her kids? What kind of impression would I make on them? I worried about Tim's friends. The veteran communities are very tight, and I knew by the time I got to Skidmore, everybody would know that I was coming to meet Sammy. What on earth was I getting myself into?

Where was that confident woman who prided herself in knowing what she wanted and was not afraid to go after it? Maybe this was just some kind of pipe dream after all. At the same time, I couldn't wait to finally look into Sammy's eyes and get that big bear hug he promised. How I even kept the truck on the road that day is beyond me; I was scared to get on the plane and scared not to. I felt like a bona fide nutcase.

Somehow I made the flight. Sammy had called me when he arrived at Skidmore, and the festival committee had scheduled him to speak to a group of students at the time I was to arrive. We were both disappointed that he wouldn't be there to greet me, but he sent a trusted friend, Jeff Hofmeister, to pick me up. Maybe that was good because it gave me a couple of hours to make small talk and get myself composed (sort of).

As Jeff and I drove into the festival area, veterans in caps denoting their branch of service roamed the grounds addressing old friends with "Hooah," a greeting familiar to those in the military. Lawyers in IZOD polos hugged bearded bikers sporting do-rags on their heads. They came from many states. These veterans had served their country, many in the hellhole trenches of war, and for that reason, they considered themselves brothers. Others plunked in lawn chairs or perched on picnic tables with a cold drink, visiting with motor home neighbors. The stars and stripes and black and white POW flags billowed on a soft breeze at many campsites. Mouth-watering aromas of fried chicken dinners from a concession stand saturated the early autumn breeze. A contagious spirit of patriotism and camaraderie pervaded the city park turned into festival grounds.

I hadn't attended any veteran event since Tim died so, for me, it was a mix of coming home, excited anticipation, and sad memories. I needed to pull out my "Rose card" and think positive. I had to concentrate on renewing friendships, on the joy that might lie ahead with Sam, and on keeping myself in the present instead of the past.

As soon as I got out of the van, old friends rushed over to greet me with big hugs. I especially remember Patty and Colonel Dad Hopper and Roger and Sandy Walker from Illinois. Roger and Tim had been very close. It was the first I'd seen many of them since Tim died. I had seen photos of Sammy's daughter, Nikki, and her four children, so I recognized them right away. Nikki came up to hug me, too, and later we got to chat a bit as we pushed the little ones on the swings.

As I greeted folks, my eyes were scanning the grounds. I could hear myself talk, but my mind was elsewhere. Where was Sammy? Then I saw him down by the pavilion, standing in front of Michael J. Martin. He was looking down at his shirt, kind of one of those, "Do I look OK" things. I hadn't seen him in years, but from where I stood, he was looking *real* good. I was trying to be cool and not seem anxious, but my heart just about jumped out of my chest. I could only hope the people around me didn't notice how befuddled I was.

Then Sammy and Michael walked up the hill toward me. They moved as if in slow motion, and it felt like everyone was staring at us, just waiting to see what would happen. I so wished our reunion could have been in private, but instead it was in front of all those people. I might as well have been sitting in a pressure cooker, and I'm surprised that steam wasn't blowing out my ears.

Finally, I got that big ol' hug from Sam that he'd been promising. I was still holding back because we were on display, and it had been so long since I had felt a warm hug. But in Sammy's arms, I felt instantly cherished, and I didn't want to leave his embrace. I felt like it was where I belonged. When I looked in his eyes, I knew he was somebody very special. Throughout all the months of phone and e-mail conversations, I'd gotten to know the real Sammy. This was no pipe dream. He later told me that he knew he would marry me from that initial hug. He was even giddier than I was; we were both like teenagers the whole time we were together.

Programs and activities were planned for the entire weekend, so everything seemed like a whirlwind. There were people around us constantly, well-wishers and those who just wanted to talk to us. It was great seeing old friends and meeting new ones, but privacy for Sammy and me was not on the agenda.

It had seemed like a good idea to meet in Skidmore: if things didn't work out, there would be lots of other people to spend time with. But after that hug, all I wanted to do was be alone with Sam. There was so much to say. I'd come to know the private Sammy Davis throughout all our long-distance conversations, and I suddenly had to confront the reality that Sammy was also a very public figure. I'd had plenty of practice with Tim; his music and activism meant that at times, and I shared him with the world. I had understood and accepted it. In fact, I'd loved that commitment, that sense of mission and service to others. Still, as Sammy and I were realizing the strong connection that was building between us, I wished so much that we had more time for ourselves that weekend. As it was, we stole every moment we could. We did a lot of hand-holding, and finally we managed to sneak our first smooch behind a car, hoping nobody saw us, but not really caring if they did.

Sammy shared a hotel suite with Nikki and the children, and my room was down the hall from them, so we still weren't alone to really talk very much. One night we did make plans to meet in my room later. However, before anyone gets too excited, all that happened was a lot of conversation and laughing.

Happy as we were together, both Sammy and I had our moments that weekend. When it came time for him and Michael J. to pay tribute to Tim on stage, the comments about Tim weren't as hard to bear as I thought they would be. I managed to keep it together. Hearing Tim's music, on the other hand, was heartbreaking. The worst was seeing his microphone set up in its usual place next to Michael's without him standing behind it. In my mind, I could see Tim so clearly standing there with his guitar poised to sing; the pangs in my heart were sharp, and I was reminded how much I still missed him. As I choked back tears, I was glad I was with Roger and Sandy and the Hoppers. We were kindred spirits; they understood and were a great comfort.

As a tribute for festival regulars who had passed away that year, there was a tree planting. A tree was planted for Peggy Jo, and Sammy spoke a few words about her; I knew he was dealing with his own pain as well. He had told me that Peggy helped him to become a better person. She taught him that there were different ways to react to a situation other than with a quick temper, and she taught him the importance of gentleness. I appreciated the way he talked about her. It helped me understand more about the lovely woman she was, and it gave me even more insight about how she had helped mold him into the kind, gentle person who was pulling on my heartstrings. I was grateful to

Peggy, and my heart went out to Sammy because I knew it was difficult for him to face his memories as well.

Despite the jarring moments of memories, most of the weekend was joyful. One afternoon I was sitting with the Hoppers just outside a tent to the right of the stage. Sammy had been up on stage jamming with all of the bands, just making that ol' harmonica wail. I was really impressed that he played by ear and jumped in with whatever song they were doing.

However, at one point he was standing next to Michael in Tim's place playing harmonica. That stirred more conflicting emotions in me, and Sam later told me he felt such a strong presence of Tim standing beside him. He said other people told him that when he stepped in front of Tim's microphone they felt Tim was there, too. Then Sam laid his harmonica down, stepped off the platform, and walked over to where I was sitting.

For a split second, I thought something was wrong because when Tim was sick, if something was wrong he'd come to me. Then I got my wits about me, and I wondered what on earth Sam was doing.

Bowing in gentlemanly fashion, Sammy asked, "May I have this dance?"

I kept shaking my head no; I was so embarrassed. He wouldn't take no for an answer, and grasping my hand, he led me out in the middle of the grounds with all those people watching us. We danced and the crowd applauded. There were whistles and "hooahs" and for us—it was like getting the Good Housekeeping Seal of Approval from all the veteran friends. Despite my embarrassment, I was learning that Sammy Davis was delightfully romantic and wasn't afraid to be spontaneous. How I loved that about him.

I also loved that music was a big part of his life like it was in mine. One evening Nikki, the kids, and Sam and I went with friends to the home of Carla and Russ Wetzel, the festival organizers. We sat around a fire pit, Sammy borrowed a guitar, and he sang song after song. I like to think he was trying to impress me. I was duly impressed, but for some reason, at that moment, I was having dubious feelings.

My thoughts rambled back to my childhood as a Brownie Scout. I was sitting around a bonfire when I got my tennis shoes too close to the flames and smoke started rising from the soles of my shoes. At that moment, I wondered if I was too close to the fire. Was everything happening too soon? I think I was afraid that things were going too well, and maybe it would all go up in smoke. My emotions were so raw, and they seemed to play tricks on me off and on during the weekend.

I had no idea that Sam could play most stringed instruments except a violin. Although I'd already come to realize that weekend that he was a mean harmonica player, I also didn't know that he'd jammed on stage with performers like Stevie Ray Vaughn, Buddy Guy, Carlos Santana, Mike Pinera and the Classic Rock All Stars, plus Larry Gatlin and 38 Special. He was just full of surprises, and I wondered what was next.

That weekend I realized that Sammy had music in his soul. Tim always said that "I don't play the music, the music plays me." I could see that it was the same with Sam. Tim and Sammy both played by ear. The music just seemed to come from somewhere down in their souls, and both were a joy to hear. It reminded me of our family standing around the piano as my mom played. Music has always been important to me, and I knew that if I ended up with Sam, the music would continue in our lives. That was one more thing about him to love.

I learned more about Sammy and his life over those few days in Skidmore as he invited me to be a part of it. I felt privileged to meet Jim Deister, one of the men that Sammy saved in Vietnam. I especially liked Jim; he was a sweetie.

As I listened to Sammy address the crowds that weekend and talk to people individually, I realized what a profound impact he had on them, especially the veterans. He had a special gift of connecting with them, lifting them up, and giving them hope. I was inspired by his message of duty, honor, and country, which resonated with my own values. While he had not yet shared the details of his Vietnam experience with me, I knew Sammy had faced many hurdles in his life. He amazed me with his resilience as he reminded everyone that "you don't lose till you quit trying."

I began to understand why his public speaking was so important. He genuinely helped people and made them feel better about themselves. Sam was America's hero, but with each passing moment, he was becoming my hero as well. Through e-mails and phone calls, I'd seen what was in his heart, and I loved what I had learned. But as I watched him at Skidmore, I was getting an even broader picture of the big heart he has for others.

I was also impressed and touched by how good he was with kids. Each year the festival bussed students from within a forty-mile radius of Skidmore to visit the different booths and to talk with veterans. On Thursday and Friday there were hundreds of young people there. Sammy spoke to them about the Medal of Honor and what it means. Talking to young people is one his favorite things, and I marveled at the way he interacted with them from the stage. He treated each one the same and tried to make them feel special. No one was made to feel foolish because he or she asked an inappropriate question. Nothing was off the table, and Sammy was willing to answer anything. The kids seemed to love him and wanted to shake his hand and hug him after his address.

Long before the weekend was over, I knew I wanted to see Sammy again. He was everything I had hoped he would be. He said I was everything he had hoped for, and before we left Skidmore, plans were in the works for me to go to an upcoming event with him in Blue Ash, Ohio.

On the last day of the festival, Michael J. pulled me aside and asked me what I thought about Sammy. I told him how I felt. He asked if Sam treated me well. I said yes. I really had no hesitation telling Michael; I knew how much he loved Tim and how much he thought of Sam. He had already given me his blessing on the phone, but then he let me know he approved, and he thought ol' Holiday would approve, too. It was kind of like getting a blessing from your dad; I was touched, and it meant a lot to me.

When Sammy kissed me good-bye at the airport, I headed back to Hawkins fairly certain that my world would never be the same as it had been when I left.

Over the next few days, as we started making arrangements to travel to Blue Ash at the end of September, I received an e-mail from Sammy. I clicked on it, expecting some information about flights and schedules. Instead it took my breath away.

Dixie Darling,
I love you so very, very much…so much more than I ever thought would
be possible. I don't really understand how five days can produce all that
has happened…I am just so thankful that when we touched, I found that
the world was revolving around us. I truly need your touch just to keep
me sane.
    Hanging on in Flat Rock.
Your Sammy Lee

I just sat there, reading and rereading Sammy's words. How could such a wonderful man exist, and how did I get to be so lucky? I wanted to laugh and cry at the same time. I wanted to dance and twirl around the house and shout from the rooftop. Instead, I hit reply and typed the following words:

Sammy, did you see the eclipse of the moon last night? It reminds me of
our lives. We went from light and gradually experiencing the darkness—
but in the back of our minds we were aware that the light would gradu-
ally begin to shine again. When the moon came out bright and full again
last night, I thought of you…the light of my life.
Dixie Marie loves Sammy Lee

There was only one fly in the ointment. Back in Skidmore, when we sat around the fire and Sam played music, he lit up and stuffed cigarettes under the strings on the neck of the guitar. I waved the smoke out my face, and whenever a cigarette fell out, I discreetly stepped on it. I told him that I didn't do well with the smoke.

I knew in my heart that before we went any further, I had to talk to him about smoking. As much as I was falling in love with him and admired him and hoped we might have a future together, I just could not go through what I'd lived with Tim all over again. Sam had been smoking for decades, and it put him at risk for throat cancer as well. I knew I would be taking a chance if I told him to choose between me and cigarettes, and I wasn't sure I'd come out on top. What if he couldn't quit? What if he didn't want to quit? But it was immensely important to me, and I couldn't let it go. I had seen what it did to Tim, and I just couldn't bear the thought that it could possibly happen to Sam, too. There was no way around it; we had to have that conversation and the sooner the better.

Later that September, Sammy picked me up at the Indianapolis airport. From there we drove together to Blue Ash, Ohio, where he was to speak at the Moving Wall. In the car we talked and laughed and were having so much fun together, but the smoking issue was weighing on my mind. It had been ever since Skidmore, and I knew I had to confront him about it. At best, I expected Sammy might say he'd work on it, or he'd try to quit. The worst, well, I didn't want to think about it.

I mustered all the courage I had, took a deep breath, and explained my feelings. I have never seen Sammy litter the highway since, but that day a pack of cigarettes went flying out the car window. I know how hard it was for Tim to quit smoking, and I was shocked at how quickly and easily Sam was willing to quit. I was also very proud him, relieved, and deeply grateful he was willing to do this for me and for himself. He has never smoked since.

With that issue resolved, I was over the moon with happiness; now Sammy and I could move forward. I couldn't help but feel I needed to tighten my seat belt one more notch for full speed ahead.

CHAPTER 7

Always on My Mind

To me, Sammy was first and foremost a really sweet, humble guy. It wasn't until we traveled to Blue Ash together that I grasped the full significance of what it meant for him to be a Medal of Honor recipient and the remarkable impact he had on people. I'd caught some glimpses of it at Skidmore, but I'd been too unhinged to take it all in.

It was the first time I heard Sammy address an audience as the keynote speaker. Most of what he said about his Vietnam experience was new to me except for the bits and pieces I had heard from him. I just couldn't believe all he had endured and had survived; I wondered, too, how he experienced such trauma and remained not only human, but possessed the ability to reach out to others the way he did.

Sitting back and watching him interact with veterans in Ohio, I was moved to the core, inspired, and so impressed. Many people seemed awed to be in the presence of a Medal of Honor recipient. Some would cry when they met him. He made time for everyone and listened intently with an open heart. During those few days, over and over I witnessed Sammy's ability to make people feel they are special and that each story is important. He truly cares, and people sense that.

Sam had traveled to Bosnia in 1997 to address the troops, and after his presentation in Blue Ash, a young woman in military uniform who had heard him in Bosnia stepped forward to speak to him. Tears spilled down her face as she explained she had been driving a military vehicle when it was hit by a roadside bomb. Seven of her buddies were killed, and she was guilt-ridden because she couldn't see the enemy and was unable to fire or respond in any way. She told him that she was just the driver, as though her role was not important.

Sam asked her if she did her job and had she not done it to the very best of her ability? He stated that if any one of the soldiers had not done his or her job, no one would have survived. He assured her that her job was immensely important; it always takes each person doing his or her part to get the job done. Then Sam hugged her.

They were talking softly, so I couldn't hear the whole conversation until Sam shared it with me later, but her countenance said it all. It didn't matter that I didn't know what they discussed; I just felt like she needed to know people cared about her story, and I reached out to her with a hug as well. She seemed to really appreciate it.

With each passing day, I knew with increasing certainty that Sammy was an extraordinary man, indeed.

The organizers of the event asked if I wanted to sit on stage while he was addressing the crowd. Before I could say anything, Sam answered, "I would love to have her there." So I sat there, but I was to learn a valuable lesson that day, and I have never sat on stage again unless there were extenuating circumstances. It was no fun having to constantly be mindful of adjusting my skirt so it didn't ride up too high; boy, I could never be one of those models who sit there cross-legged in the perfect pose. Also, I wanted to gaze around the crowd and see how people reacted to Sammy, but it would have looked pretty tacky to be gawking left and right from the stage. To this day, I prefer sitting in the audience and watching others react to what Sammy says. Almost immediately, I can pick out the veterans in the crowd. They nod, laugh, and cry.

Knowing what some of them have been through, my heart breaks for them, so when I can, I talk to them and give them hugs. During the Last Patrol marches, hugging the veterans and their families was second nature to me, and I joined Sammy in hugging them in Blue Ash as well.

When Sammy wasn't in uniform that weekend, we each wore red, white, and blue, and people commented on what a cute couple we were. New friends I'd made in Skidmore were in attendance, and they made me feel very welcome, introducing me to others as though I was their new best friend. It was touching to feel so accepted among Sam's friends. After the years of sadness during Tim's illness, everything felt new and exciting, and it was so good to laugh and enjoy the people and the upbeat atmosphere at the event. Sammy made me feel special just by his attentive gestures, a smile, a touch on the arm, or a little hug for no reason. Just being with him was fun, no matter what we did.

The event organizer took us on a tour of Blue Ash and showed us a beautiful gazebo in their park. Sammy and I were being goofy, holding hands and acting like a couple in love, so the gentleman told us he thought that gazebo would be a great place for a wedding. We weren't making any plans for marriage at that point, but I guess he thought it was a foregone conclusion that we were headed for the altar.

Yet we were soon to hit some bumps on that road. As a Medal of Honor recipient, Sammy was always invited to presidential inaugurations. A few months later, in January 2005, a new president would be sworn in, and Sammy had invited me by e-mail to attend with him. I was very touched. I knew what presidential inaugurations meant to him. He had only ever taken Peggy or one of his kids with him, and his invitation confirmed his feelings for me.

I was also about to burst with excitement. Never in a million years had I ever imagined that I would watch anyone become president of the United States from the front row. During those months when we'd talked on the phone and by e-mail, Sammy had regaled me with all kinds of stories about the inaugurations he had attended, and I was looking forward to balls and magnificent rooms, tuxedos and beautiful gowns, and meeting all kinds of people I'd never thought I would ever talk to.

Shortly my bubble would burst when he called to tell me that his adult children were having a difficult time with the idea of him taking me to the inauguration. For them, it was too soon after their mother's death, and Sam felt that out of respect for his children, I probably shouldn't go with him. He was caught between a rock and a hard place, wanting to take me but not wanting to upset his kids. He was very upset and apologetic.

I wouldn't be telling the truth if I said I wasn't crushed and hurt that Sammy rescinded the invitation; I was so looking forward to the inauguration with him, but I tried hard to understand his children's perspective as well. After wrestling with my feelings, I wrote him the following e-mail.

Dear Sammy,

I thought a lot last night about your children, and I think they have a valid reason about the public appearances. I know that I have conducted myself with dignity when we have been in public but to ensure future family unity, I am willing to wait. As we know, not everyone heals in the same time period. For some, it takes months and for others it takes years. In one of the many books I read about grief, it said that the normal grief period is a year, but again, everyone is different, especially when there is a long illness involved. We had the time to prepare mentally, but again, that is an individual thing.

You and Peggy talked about you finding someone in six months, and it was six months by the time we first saw each other at Skidmore. When you are on the backside of fifty, six months is a very long time, especially when you have seen how fleeting love and life can be. It seemed after Tim died, at first each day seemed like an eternity. Time dragged when I wanted it to fly. After the death of a beloved spouse, time takes forever. You and I both know how six months can seem like it is standing still and will never move forward.

Your children haven't walked this road, so their perspective of time and grief is different than ours. I can understand their feelings and I hope in time they might understand ours.

Sammy, I know that we loved Tim and Peggy with everything we had and never thought we would lose them. The kids don't know that we talk about them as much as we do and that we have cried, laughed and remembered together. We are not trying to forget them—we are just trying to go on. Their influence is with us every day. The good that each of them put into our lives will be what we carry forward. The mistakes we made with them will hopefully be the lessons learned about life, and we can leave those behind. We are both fortunate to have had people like Tim and Peggy. We realize that. I know we talked about the fact that we can still love them and what we have found with each other does not detract from that. I was amazed that a new part of my heart opened up for you and that there is peace with Tim. I feel fortunate.

Life continues on.

Love,

Dixie

When Sammy replied to me with the following e-mail, I could feel the heavy burden shrouding him about the situation with his children.

My Dixie

Everything will be ok, Dixie. I love you so very much and I know we are right. It's just time that we need for my children to heal. I remember when my momma passed away. It messed me up for a while also. I have to believe they will get better with time. I love you, Dixie. It will be ok. I love you, Dixie, it will be ok. I love you, Dixie, it will be ok…I have prayed all night that it will be so.

Your Sammy Lee

That fall e-mails and calls flew back and forth, and I attended a couple of functions in Indianapolis with Sammy. Not being able to be together all the time, trying to be respectful of his children's wishes, and the distance between us was all very difficult. When we were together, it wasn't enough. Time was always too short, and we had a lifetime of catching up to do. Most of the time, there were many people around, and privacy was at a premium. That was frustrating for both of us. I wanted to be with Sammy, to share all the little everyday things with him, and I wanted to feel free to love him, but there was the constant underlying thread of knowing that his children were struggling with our relationship. Why did it all have to be so complicated?

We began to refer to the things we had to deny ourselves and had to wait for as "building character." We were also becoming more and more certain of our feelings for each other. In an e-mail, Sammy declared his intentions toward me.

My Dixie Marie
My intentions toward you are to properly cherish you forever…to love and protect, to be at your side no matter what. You are so very special, and I love you tremendously. I am shameless when it comes to loving you. I am ready NOW for us to be together forever. I love you, Dixie, and I want you to be Dixie Marie Davis.
Your Sammy Lee

From our previous conversations, I thought eventually Sammy was going to say he wanted to marry me, but there it was in black and white. I was thrilled and practically turning cartwheels. I had to tell somebody, and there was nobody around but the cats; silly as it seems, they were the first to know. Then I called my friend Sherry. We had shared so many joys and sorrows together, and I loved that she was always there for me. I knew she would rejoice with me about Sammy's e-mail. I was over the moon about Sam's declaration of love.

In my heart, I knew, too, that it was Sammy I wanted to spend my life with. As we talked about a future, he shared that he was afraid another man would sweep me away. He thought I would get tired of "building character," and he feared the distance between us and not moving forward more quickly might become too difficult for me. Despite my frustrations with us not being together, his fears were unfounded, and I tried to reassure him that I was in love with him and that there was just one pair of big old arms in this world that I wanted holding me. He was the only one I wanted to snuggle with, to share the good times and bad times with, and he was the only one I wanted my grandbabies to call Grandpa.

Sammy and I do a lot of silly things together. So if we were in hurry to get somewhere at an appointed time, I would feed him yogurt as he drove. I reassured him he was the only man I wanted to feed yogurt to in a moving vehicle. I told him he was the one I wanted to live, love, and laugh with for the rest of my life, and even though he belonged to the American people, he was my personal treasure.

Sometimes we lamented about how unfair it was that we couldn't be together right then, but I felt there was one thing that was more than fair. Out of billions of people on earth, we had been able to find each other. That was a miracle. It was true that life is short, and we felt like every day apart was a day we were missing out, but we tried to assure each other that the "character building" wouldn't last forever.

I told him I loved him enough to wait, to keep him happy and content, and enough to get us through the rough times so that he'd never doubt the depth of my feelings for him. I loved him enough to make him laugh and that he could lean on me when he needed to. I loved him enough for eternity.

He thanked me for loving him enough to wait, and he promised he would always do his best to deserve my love and make the wait worthwhile for me. He promised to properly cherish me and called me a wonderful, caring, and beautiful lady. I tingled from head to toe when he said he loved me ferociously and wanted to shout from the rooftops and tell the world of our special love.

I felt the same way about Sam, and I was anxious to introduce him to everyone I loved.

CHAPTER 8

Piney Wood Hills

In November 2004, I invited Sam to come to Texas to meet my family and friends. There were no speaking engagements, no schedules, nobody pulling us in different directions. We would finally have time for ourselves. I couldn't believe I wouldn't have to share him with anyone unless I wanted to. It was like anticipating a huge present wrapped in gold ribbon.

I also looked forward to introducing him to my life in the Piney Wood Hills. I couldn't wait for him to get to know all the people and places I loved so dearly. At the same time, I was a bit nervous. I didn't know what to expect from people who knew Tim and me as a couple. But as it turned out, I had no reason to fret. Some told me later that they were so happy I had found a nice fellow that was worthy of me.

I invited several friends and neighbors for an evening meal. At first I felt a little awkward about having everyone in the home I had shared with Tim, but because of their kindness and happiness for us, everybody was comfortable after the first few minutes. We had such a good time laughing and sharing crazy stories. Sam, with his silly sense of humor, fit right in.

Kathie and Tim Hubbard were neighbors who ate with us that night. Kathie's first husband, Lee, who died from cancer, was one of Tim's first acquaintances when he bought the Texas property. They met when Lee came over to find out who that long-haired hippy in the neighborhood was. He then became one of Tim's dearest friends. Neighborhood friends Becky and Mike Attaway came over, and Mitch Mitchell, who Sam had met previously when Tim and Michael played at veteran gatherings, was there. I also invited John

DeFoore, Tim's lead guitar player. John was a veteran, and he knew all about the Medal of Honor. Also, he already knew what kind of man Sam was. I knew that Tim had asked John to look out for me, and if John had voiced any objection or doubt about Sam, I would have listened. They all treated Sam so warmly and extended a big Texas welcome to him.

Sammy and I also ate out with other friends, and because we were on neutral ground, that was easy, too. Others just stopped by to meet Sam. It reminded me of the first few days I had been in Texas years ago. All of Tim's friends came by to meet me, and I was the one who had to pass muster. Now it was Sam's turn. We laughed a lot about that later.

My friends' approval and blessing was important to me, and watching them welcome Sammy the way they did was heartwarming. This felt like a big step, and it gave me extra reassurance that I was doing the right thing. Welcoming as they were, my friends also looked out for me. Sam told me later that he got the "You had better treat her right" talk from more than one of them. This extended beyond Texas, and one of the funniest moments included my dear friend Sue Eisenhower from Freeport, who stands five foot two on a good day. She marched up to six-foot Sam and poked her finger in his chest. Looking him right in the eye, she declared, "If you don't treat her right, I will kick your butt." Sam answered with a resounding, "Yes, ma'am!"

I enjoyed every minute of having Sammy to myself during his visit to Hawkins without constantly being at someone's beck and call. We finally got to relax, and it was a time for lots of talking and discovering more new things about each other. That's when I found out that Sam was such a good cook, nothing fancy, but just good old home cookin' like I grew up eating. He fixed bacon and eggs and toast and threw in leftovers as he cooked. He was a great homemade soup maker, and I baked the bread and deserts. Tim had liked to cook, too, but we never really cooked together. He made the meals, and I was always the dessert girl. During Sam's visit, he and I discovered we really enjoyed conjuring up food together in the kitchen.

He shared an amusing story with me about Peggy Jo not knowing how to cook before they were married. With four girls at home, they couldn't all fit in the narrow, little kitchen at their house, so rather than teaching them to prepare food, Peggy's mama ran them out of the kitchen. When Sam and Peggy moved to Texas, her mom wrote a big portfolio of recipes with the most basic instructions—get a saucepan out of the cupboard and fill it with water. She had written everything step-by-step.

Sammy, who knew how to cook, found it hard to keep a straight face as Peggy painstakingly followed each step exactly as it was written. She once made biscuits from scratch that were pretty on the top but black on the bottom and hard as hockey pucks. They tried to cut the tops off to eat them but ended up throwing them out to the armadillos. The critters wouldn't even eat them. Sam said with practice, she did become an awesome cook, but it took some time.

Somehow it seemed so natural to be in the kitchen in the house I had shared with Tim, cooking with Sam, and talking about Peggy. I loved that we felt so comfortable talking about the ones who had been so much a part of our lives before.

Sammy wanted to know more details about my family, and he wanted to see what I looked like as a little girl, so we spent hours going through picture albums. He wanted to see where I lived and where I went to school. It was fun to revisit my childhood with Sammy, and I found that at this stage in life, it helped me to understand how I got to be who I am and how I developed deeply held values. I'd really never stop to think about my family in that context until we started talking about it out loud. As my sister, Roxie, suggested, it's also important to remember and to pass those values on to our children so they understand who they are and why.

I told Sammy about my parents' lives and marriage; family-owned farms were a way of life, and each generation continued on as their parents before them had done. When my parents got together with friends after chores for card games, we were never left with babysitters. We kids, a pack of boys and girls age six on up, were free to play with little supervision.

The upstairs bedrooms became our playground where we jumped on beds until one of our parents yelled upstairs for us to stop jumping. We dressed up in our parents clothing and played house. Our imaginations were limitless. It was also delicious fun to spy on the adults through the heat grate in the floor. You could hear every word they said, which was especially useful at Christmastime!

The word bored was not in our vocabulary because when there was a lull, one of us would always think up something to do. Nobody had to be in bed by 8:00 p.m. When our parents saw that we were tiring, they'd put us into whatever bed was available, and we'd all fall asleep. Many times our folks carried us out to the car and then into bed at home.

If the weather was nice, we were outside playing kick the can, hide and seek, badminton, croquet, or baseball, and we roller skated with those old clamp-on skates that we had to tighten with a key. Catching fireflies and putting them in mason jars was a favorite summer evening pastime. Many times at our house we followed cow paths through the woods, played with baby animals and rode ponies, or played across the road at the Black Hawk Monument. We climbed trees and rode bikes, and in winter we delighted in sledding at breakneck speeds down Monument Hill. When our parents would allow us to go, we loved ice skating on the Mill Pond in Pearl City or at the baseball field that was flooded by the fire department for ice skating. As we got older we entertained ourselves with board games and were pretty good at cards as well. Looking back, I think those were times of learning how to get along with others, no matter our ages, and we learned how to work out our differences when we didn't agree with one other.

Saturday night was about friends and fun. Sometimes we went fishing for bullheads. Other times there was a picnic at the Owl's Club or dinner or a sandwich at the Flying Cloud, a restaurant/bar owned by Helen and Spud Becke, good friends of my folks. Most often we'd just gather at someone's home to have a good time.

When Roxie and I got old enough to date, there were no honking horns at our house. The young man came to the door to pick us up. When we got home from a date, we could sit in the car for one minute, and then the yard light would be flicked off and on a couple of times. We had one more minute to get into the house. The Blackhawk Monument across the road from our house was known far and wide as the prime high school necking spot, and we couldn't even use it. What good was that going to do anybody?

Our family went to church on Sundays, and we always stopped at Ide's Market for the Sunday paper. Sometimes we'd have dinner with grandparents, and occasionally we'd take a family drive and end up at Sunnyside Grocery for an ice-cream cone.

Those were wonderful times, and I got nostalgic talking to Sam, thinking about how things have changed. It seems that childhood is now so scheduled, supervised, and overly organized. Families revolve around running kids to this or that game or sport instead of sharing time as a family. Is there ever any downtime without technology to play and use the imagination? The more the world changes the more we lose the old ways, and for me, that is sad. I truly believe that too many of our young people are losing out on the treasures of childhood.

Sam had already heard about my dad's crazy sense of humor, but it occurred to me that it was my dad, Howard Busch, who taught me about the responsibility of doing my chores before play, about caring for others, respect for the land, and the value of laughter. One of Dad's rules was that we do not eat until the animals are taken care of. Everybody in the world loved my dad. He worked hard on the farm and played hard as well. I learned from him that if a neighbor needed help, you stepped up to the plate and tried to make the world a better place for one other.

I was truly fortunate to have two wonderful sets of grandparents for mentors, as well. After Grandpa Busch sold the farm to my dad, he started a feed store in Pearl City and built a lovely house in town. He always walked the three blocks to work and stopped for his one glass of beer on the way home. Like clockwork, Grandma had supper on the table when he walked into the house.

Grandpa was kind to everyone, and as rambunctious kids we never heard him raise his voice, even when we climbed on the feed bags in the store after being told not to.

After we were old enough, he let us cut his grass with a motorized reel-type lawn mower. For this chore we received fifty cents. We didn't know he was teaching us about a strong work ethic and the importance of paying attention to details. Of course, he would first make a couple of rounds to be sure we didn't demolish the shrubs or Grandma's flowers. He showed us patience, taught us about kindness, and made us feel important.

Grandma Flory Busch was round and fluffy. She dusted on Wednesday and Saturday, and her house was immaculate, even in the attic. She loved cross-stitch, needle punch, crocheting, quilting, and sewing. Is it any wonder I learned to love stitching, as well? I still have two little aprons she made me before I started school. I think I take after Grandma Busch the most with my love of gardening, beautiful flowers, baking, desserts, and needlework. I can also thank her that I love a clean and orderly house.

Grandpa Lester Fehr, my mom's dad, had a great sense of humor, and like most men in our area, he was a farmer. Grandma Bessie Fehr was a home-maker. She had been a teacher, but in those days when you got married, you had to give up teaching. She loved poetry, and at Christmastime the family would give her poetry books as gifts. She was the refined one in our family.

In addition to keeping house and putting up food from the garden, she kept a flock of chickens for eggs and a flock of mean geese! They were hateful things and delighted in chasing us and giving us a flogging when they could catch us.

Grandma Fehr was also a great baker and could make a mile-high angel food cake from scratch. She had a gift for making everyone feel welcome. Like many from that era, she made sure everyone else was fed and content before she would take care of herself. I learned a lot about hospitality from her.

Everyone has certain teachers who inspire them, and Mrs. Widmer, our first grade teacher in Pearl City, was a favorite of many students. She praised us for everything we did well. She once called me to the front of the class to show how well I colored. I was so proud, and I learned that if you do some-thing carefully and to the best of your ability, you will be recognized for it. Of course, the same happens in a negative way for poor behavior and sloppy work. I wanted to be in the good group, the Bluebirds, in her class, and I have always strived to be in the Bluebird group all my life. On second thought, maybe I wasn't quite as diligent with schoolwork when I discovered boys and got involved with cheerleading and other school activities. I may have lost some Bluebird feathers here and there, but somehow I still managed to make the honor roll and was a member of the National Honor Society in high school. Mrs. Widmer's Bluebird lesson has served me well in life.

I told Sam how grateful I was for my family and others who taught me solid standards and laid a firm foundation for me to go forward into this world. The wonderful love they showed me continues to live with me every day of my life. They would have loved Sam, and I wished he could have known them all. In reality, we're the sum of all the people we have ever met and the lessons they've taught us, and I also treasure others who, just by being who they are, have touched me in a special way. I shared the hope with Sam that I can always share those blessings with people I meet along the way.

As we continued looking at the album, Sammy knew a lot of the people in photos with Tim, so that was an added connection that helped to make everything feel right about Sam.

While I knew the story in a nutshell about how Sam earned his Medal of Honor, he had not been forthcoming with intimate details, and I didn't ask. I wanted him to tell me when he was ready. That didn't happen in Texas, but I was just dumbfounded when, during our conversations about our lives, he revealed the extent of his injuries from that dreadful night in Vietnam.

Sammy took about thirty beehive rounds (metal darts) in his legs, buttocks, and lower back, his back was broken, and his ribs on the right side were crushed. In addition, he had an AK47 round in his right thigh, burns over his face, hands, and neck, and numerous shrapnel wounds all over his body. Tears filled my eyes as I tried to grasp the gravity of what he had suffered. How did this man I loved survive, let alone save three other people under those circumstances? What if he hadn't survived and I had never known him? That thought made me feel sick to my stomach. I knew he was a walking miracle and that somehow God let him survive for a purpose. If I had been grateful for the gift of his love before, I was thankful tenfold after discovering part of what he had been through.

On a beautiful autumn afternoon, Sam and I sat on Tim's memorial bench in the backyard, sharing thoughts about him and Peggy Jo. While I knew Tim wasn't really there, it was a touchstone where I felt close to him. I told Tim I was happy and explained that the love I had in my heart for him would always stay there. It would never diminish. I told him that my heart had room for loving Sammy, too, and I believe Tim would have understood that. Sammy had his own private chat. He told Tim that he loved him and promised to take good care of me. In the Lakota tradition that was so important to Tim, Sammy and I burned sage, offered prayers for our future together, and gave thanks for the past that we had shared with our spouses. We both shed some tears, and it was very healing.

I had the feeling that Tim was right beside me on that bench and that he was pleased. I knew he wouldn't have entrusted my care to just anybody, probably to no one except Sam. I could imagine him smiling, and I felt happy and content. Sitting there with Sam, feeling as though Tim had given his blessing, was a pivotal and powerful moment for me. I knew I really was ready for the future with Sam. I made a commitment that day, and I was ready to do what it would take to care for Sam as I had for Tim.

In addition, I took Sam to a very sacred place to me, in a grove of sassafras trees near Tim's bench. It was my special place where I had spent many hours thinking about Tim and pondering my life. It was important for Sam to be there with me. I wanted him to know how much Tim meant to me and that I was making a very significant step into the future. I wanted him to know that I was putting a lot of trust into his hands. I felt like Sam understood the gravity of all I said to him.

Also, I finally got to take Sammy to eat at Kitchen's Hardware Store in Mineola. Even though I'd spent so much time there with Tim, it wasn't hard to take Sam to the place I associated with Tim. A lot of changes had taken place in the store in the years since Tim died. They had built on a new section, and my and Tim's stools were gone. That made me sad for a minute or two, but it was OK. There was still an old-timey atmosphere with the picnic tables and mismatched chairs, and I was glad they still sold the hardware along with the food. An ice-cream counter had been added, so it was the same, yet it wasn't. Perhaps, in a way, those changes made it easier for Sammy and me to make our own memories at Kitchen's.

Even more momentous was our visit to Wimberley, Texas, for Sammy to meet my son, Tony, his wife, Christie, and my six grandkids. The whole family came running out to the car to greet us and made Sam feel very welcome. One of the first orders of business was to gather around the trampoline outside to watch the kids jump. There were lots of shrieks and giggles, and if there was any ice to be broken, the kids took care of that. We all talked and laughed, and the grandkids wanted to know everything about Sam. That made the initial meeting very easy.

Since Tony and Sam were both in the 9th Infantry Division of the army, they had a lot of common ground for conversation from the start. They discussed weapons, knives, animals, and kids, and the conversation flowed easily. I could see that Tony was warming up to him right away, and that made me very happy.

Tony is my only child, and it was so important to me to have his acceptance. He was my rock, living next door to us, during Tim's illness. He helped me many times when I had to lift Tim, change his hospital bed, or get Tim into the car for doctor appointments. Tim wasn't Tony's biological father, but the two of them had grown very close. So when Tim passed away, Tony was the one who looked after me and gave me emotional support. I thought I was looking after myself, but it was a great comfort knowing he was next door if I needed him. When Tony and his family moved to Wimberley for a job promotion a couple of years after Tim's death, Tony still called almost every day. He was very protective, and I think because he didn't live near me anymore, he was a little apprehensive about this new relationship. He didn't know Sam and, after all the pain with Tim's illness and death, he didn't want to see me hurt again.

The little ones thought it was something else that Grandma had a boyfriend. The girls asked if we kissed, and when Sammy said yes, they smiled and said, "Aawww." Zac, on the other hand, expressed his disdain on the matter in typical boy fashion with "Ewww."

Sam and I both spent a lot of time playing with the grandkids. He loves children and is always gung ho to do anything they come up with. We visited a park where the scouts set up Christmas displays and sat around the campfire and drank hot chocolate. We all went shopping in Wimberley, a small, artsy town with shops full of handmade crafts catering to tourists.

We both loved the whimsical items, and Sam and I bought a carved wooden pig bread bowl that got lots of laughs from the family. After our visit, when Tony and I had a chance to talk later, he gave his approval and said he was happy for me.

After Sammy left Texas, I was even more head over heels in love with him than I thought possible. I had such a wonderful time with him, and my mind was filled with dreams of the future. I busied myself with the Avon route and my shaved ice business. Those businesses had helped me when Tim wasn't there; once again they were helping me keep it all together when I couldn't be with Sammy.

Then suddenly, without warning, life cut to the core once more. A day before Thanksgiving in November 2004, one phone call sent my sister, Roxie's, life crashing down around her. In a freak accident, her husband Phil hit his head on the wall while playing racquetball at the YMCA, and he never regained consciousness. He died the next morning. They had just built a beautiful new home, and life was good. Just like that, it was all gone. When Roxie called me, I packed a few things in the truck and headed to Dallas to catch a plane to Illinois. My mind could scarcely let me believe the truth of what had happened. How was it possible? Hadn't there been enough death in our family? My heart just ached for my sister. I knew what she was going through. It was sad beyond belief, and suddenly I was face-to-face with Tim's death once more.

I knew there was probably little I could really do for her, but I also knew how much it means to just have family surrounding you for support. Roxie already had all the food for Thanksgiving purchased, and with a lot of family there, we had to eat. A friend and I took over in the kitchen to prepare the turkey dinner, and we all tried to surround Roxie with love. At least I had Sammy and a future to look forward to, and he was constantly on my mind that weekend, but I knew what she was going to face. It was a delicate balance for me to try to reach out to her yet protect myself from slipping back into the pain that engulfed me when Tim died. I called Sam as often as I could because just talking to him calmed me, and I was able to continue on. My heart physically hurt for all of us, especially Roxie. I discovered that weekend that grief can rear its ugly head again years later, even when you think you have healed.

I didn't expect to feel almost strangled in the clutches of grief again when I returned to Texas, but Phil's death and watching Roxie's sorrow had just transported me back to all that pain again. I needed Sammy so much at that time, and I wrote him about how much I needed his strength and comfort. I wanted to think about something else besides death and grieving, and I knew that I would find peace in his embrace. I needed him to make everything all right again, to put some sense into my world when loss seemed to happen much too often.

With an aching heart, I tried to force myself to think about our upcoming reunion in Vermont in December. Those first days and nights back home seemed endless, but Sammy comforted me as much as he could by phone calls and e-mails. I needed the light of his loving spirit, and I needed to be with him permanently. Humor has always been a shield for me when I hurt, so I tried to make jokes and told Sam I was just in a Poor Pitiful Pearl stage. As the days went by and I got back into my routine, I was thankful that the sad veil began to lift. The Vermont trip in December was the only thing that made being apart from Sam bearable. I knew I would see him soon and that he would make me smile again.

CHAPTER 9

Take My Breath Away

Sammy had received a speaking request from a captain who was arranging the annual Saint Barbara's Celebration for his unit, the 1-86 Field Artillery. The event was scheduled for December 11, 2004, at the Essex Inn in Burlington, Vermont.

Saint Barbara, a martyred Christian saint, is the patron saint of artillery-men, military engineers, gunsmiths, miners, and other who work with explo-sives. She is invoked against thunder and lighting and all accidents arising from explosions of gun powder. The US Army Field Artillery Association and the US Army Air Defense Artillery Association maintain the Order of Saint Barbara as an honorary military society, and Saint Barbara's Day is celebrated in December with numerous events, including parades, balls, dinners, and special honors.

Half of the 1-86 Field Artillery Battalion had been serving in Iraq, and because the unit had finished its rotation, this would be a welcome home event as well. While it would be a festive celebration in many ways, four brave soldiers from the battalion had lost their lives that year, and it would also be a time to pay tribute to them. The captain wanted someone who had been through some rough times and had met life's challenges head-on to speak encouraging words to the soldiers and to the Gold Star families who had lost a son or daughter in the war. As much as I looked forward to a festive celebra-tion, the recent sting of Phil's tragic accident and Tim's death lingered in my heart, and I felt great empathy for the grieving Gold Star families that would be in attendance. I knew there would be moments I would need the tissues in my purse.

However, this would be the first formal event I would attend with Sammy, and I couldn't wait. After years of gray clouds, it had been so much fun to shop for a new dress and dream of such a special night. I felt like a teenager looking for her prom dress, and I found the perfect black gown with lots of glitter and sparkle. It reminded me of the sparkle I felt when I was with Sammy.

We had been trying to see each other about once a month, and this event worked out because it was between my work schedule and family Christmas events. I adored adventures with Sammy, and he loved to see things through my eyes that he had experienced before. He had filled me in on details about the traditional Saint Barbara's Day Celebration, and I looked up a bit more online. I was so excited about the trip.

Finally, the big weekend arrived. I had only seen pictures of Vermont in the winter, and it truly looked like a painting on a postcard. The mountains and the snow were gorgeous, and being there with Sammy made it even more breathtaking. With woods and mountains as a backdrop, the Essex Inn was a welcoming haven after a long day of travel. The elegant resort complex consisted of stately white structures topped with gabled dormers, double brick chimneys, and shuttered windows. To me, it was a sprawling estate fit for royalty.

By night, thousands of twinkling lights transformed the inn, decorated for the Christmas season, into a romantic fairytale setting. The New England air was crisp, and the holiday spirit was everywhere. I had previously been to Vermont about thirty years before, driving through the countryside during a summer vacation, but I had never been to a black-tie event in a beautiful Vermont hotel in the wintertime that reminded me of the castle in Oz. Everything was beyond beautiful, and I was so happy being reunited with Sammy after five weeks apart that I could hardly contain myself.

The night of the Saint Barbara dinner, we were escorted into the glass atrium to tables covered with linen cloths and crystal stemware. The vaulted ceiling was strung with greenery and twinkle lights, and evergreens outside the bank of windows glowed with tiny, white lights. A soft, falling snow cast a silvery shimmer, creating a glittering winter wonderland reflected in the glass. Military men and women in dress uniforms, men in tuxedos, and women in elegant floor-length gowns comprised a crowd of about five hundred people. Everything around me dazzled with magic, and I felt like Cinderella escorted by her handsome prince.

I was also excited because we had invited some friends who lived fairly close to Vermont. Ron and Carolyn Smith, who had been with me in Texas when Tim died, and Chuck and Jayne Harvey, were going to share a table with us. I had met the Harveys through the hospital corpsman group, the Few, and neither couple had met Sam before. Sammy's friend, Medal of Honor recipient Tom Kelley, and his fiancée, Joan, were there to join us as well. They all came with cameras ready to capture the festivities, and I was elated to introduce them to Sammy.

I was proud of the soldiers in the room, and I felt privileged to be part of their night. For me, the time-honored Saint Barbara's grog ceremony and the mixing of artillery punch was most fascinating. The honorary stirrer constantly stirred the mixture with the artillery saber while the eighteen ingredients were poured into a metal cauldron. A number of alcoholic beverages were added, and each ingredient represented something special. Deep red wine represented the "Bloodshed of Our Brothers," and gold-colored rum signified "Hope of Victory." Then they added everything from spring water to molasses, coffee, chocolate-covered cherries and even a horse shoe to "Honor the horses." My favorite was rose petals representing "Love for our Women." The final ingredient was a wool sock, dusted with powdered sugar, representing the dust of the march. The commander came forward to taste it then invited everyone to partake.

Then officers welcomed the troops, and my heart went out to the Gold Star families when they were introduced. As a parent, I could scarcely imagine how one could deal with losing a son or daughter. I blinked back a lot of tears.

There were at least two other speakers, but my attention was on Sammy, who looked so dashing in his dress uniform. He proceeded to the stage to share the experience of how he earned his Medal of Honor, and he told the crowd it is our duty to stand up for what we believe in our hearts is right. He finished with the story of how he learned to play the harmonica in Vietnam.

Not wanting to write home to his mother about the war that was really going on around him, Sammy just didn't write to her. Becoming concerned, his mother went to the Red Cross. One thing led to another and the Pentagon contacted Sammy's captain. As a result, Sammy was approached by his captain early one morning and told, "You *will* write home to your mother every day."

It was unheard of for a captain to come out at that hour to talk to the men, so Sammy was afraid he was about to receive bad news regarding his family. With a great sigh of relief that it was nothing serious, he decided right then that he would find something to write home about.

So Sammy wrote his mother and told her about the unusual fruit and huge bugs he encountered. He would draw pictures of the bugs and tell her about the bananas that grew in six hundred pound bunches. He talked about the monkeys and the elephants, and he even tried to describe how a baby elephant's breath smelled, anything to keep from worrying her with the truth about a soldier's life in Vietnam. After reading all of these letters, Sammy's mother assumed he was bored, so she sent him a harmonica to help pass the time.

When his sergeant heard that Sam got a harmonica, he asked him to play "Shenandoah." Sam didn't know how to play that song or any other, but he quickly learned "Shenandoah," and he would play it in the foxhole for Sergeant Johnston Dunlop. While the sergeant was attending college, when the world got too much for him, he would go to a quiet place on the Shenandoah River. When Sammy played "Shenandoah," it reminded him of his tranquil oasis, and he told Sam it helped him rest from the stresses of Vietnam.

Sergeant Dunlop never made it home from Vietnam. Later Sammy went to the Wall in Washington, DC. and in the deep of night, at panel 50 East, twelve down; he touched the name of Sergeant Johnston Dunlop. One more time Sammy played "Shenandoah" and bid his friend to rest in peace.

That night in Vermont, Sammy played "Shenandoah" for the families of the fallen soldiers. I needed those tissues in my purse, and it's doubtful there was a dry eye in the room.

As Sammy neared the end of his speech, he began to talk about us and the death of Peggy and Tim. He talked about life and how we had to carry on. What was going on? This wasn't part of his usual address. I tried to catch Carolyn's eye, but she was ignoring me. Then Sam reached in his pocket and pulled out a white Faberge-style egg. The pearlescent glass ring box was trimmed in rhinestones and silver filigree that glittered in the soft light. My heart was in my throat.

Slowly he opened it, and I could see the sparkle of a ring inside. "Dixie, will you marry me?" he asked from the stage.

I can't remember saying anything; it was the only time in my life that I was speechless. We had talked about marriage somewhere in the future, but I wasn't prepared for this. My heart raced, I was shaking, and I could hardly catch my breath. The wonderful thing was that my entire being was flooded with joy. I knew in my heart that this was right for both of us.

The whole room fell silent, and I felt five hundred sets of eyes focused on us. Sammy tucked the microphone under his arm and walked over to our table. He got down on one knee and repeated the question with the ring in his fingers. I still couldn't utter a single word, so I put my arms around him, crying and laughing at the same time. People were up on their feet, applauding, and cameras were flashing all around us.

My entire life had just changed within minutes. My first thought was, *I guess everything that has happened in my life has led me to this point.* I felt ready and was willing to learn what I would have to know to be to be a complement to my future husband. Then as funny as it might sound, I thought, *Well, I guess this will not be my one and only Saint Barbara's Day ball.* I know the stars in my eyes were as bright as the diamond on my finger. I'd thought the night had been perfect, but Sammy's proposal made it magical. There were no words to express the happiness in my heart at that moment.

Although I had no idea about Sammy's plans that evening, I found out later that everyone at our table knew ahead of time. Sammy had, in fact, asked permission from the event coordinators. He had also reached out to the Gold Star families to ask if they would mind if he proposed to me that night; he wanted to make sure he wouldn't add to their grief. Later, I saw photos of the table where the moms and dads who had lost their sons or daughters sat. They were also standing, clapping, and crying. Some of them told us afterward that seeing the happiness on the faces of people who had survived a tragic loss was just the uplift they needed at that particular time in their lives. That our happy occasion had brought solace to people who had lost so much touched me very deeply. Their presence that evening meant so much to us. Their sacrifice means that people like Sam and me are able to live freely in the greatest country on earth, and I am immensely grateful that they found in their wounded hearts the strength and generosity to be happy for us that evening.

This new beginning in our lives would mark the onset of a mission that Sammy and I would embrace together. He had been inspiring hope in the lives of others for a long time. It would become the shared mission that would underpin our lives.

I left Vermont with my mind in a whirlwind. I had come there to experience a wonderful time with Sammy and good friends, and I was returning to Texas as Sammy's fiancée. I was on the loftiest of clouds. There was so much to think about as we moved forward as a couple, and I had also been touched deeply by the people I met at the Saint Barbara's celebration. In a single moment my life and its purpose had taken a turn; I could scarcely imagine what might lie in store as I anticipated what it would mean to be Sammy's wife and a Medal of Honor wife. Leaving Sam was bittersweet; I wanted the weekend to last forever, but reality took me back to my work in Texas and Sam back home to Illinois to tend to speaking engagements. Still, there was so much to look forward to, plans to make, and I couldn't wait to see what the coming year would bring.

CHAPTER 10

Making Memories of Us

At the end of December 2004, I was back in Texas, and Sammy was at home in Flat Rock. I was still on a high from our trip to Vermont, but I missed him so much. I had to keep looking at that shiny ring on my finger to be sure I hadn't dreamed the whole thing, yet once again we were miles apart from each other. It would be close to mid-January before I would see him again.

On my birthday, the sting of our separation weighed heavily on my heart. I wanted to be with my future husband more than anything in the world, but I spent the day quietly at home receiving calls from friends and family and smiling at the cards that were in the mailbox. Mostly I spent the day dreaming of a future with Sammy. When his name popped up in my e-mail inbox, it felt like instant sunshine on a dreary day.

My darling Dixie,

HAPPY BIRTHDAY! I did not send a card. With your permission, I will spend the rest of our lives making up for it. I did not forget; I had hoped that somehow I would be able to be there with you to wish you Happy Birthday in person. At fifty-eight, you put most thirty-five-year-old women to shame, Dixie, with your striking beauty, your wonderful poise, your energy for life. I love you so very, very much. Thank you for returning that love to me. I will have the rest of our lives to EARN it every day.

2005 is our year, baby! It starts the rest of our lives together.

Yours, 'til butterflies no longer flitter over beautiful flowers.

Sammy Lee

Our year! That thought gave me butterflies. How wonderful those words were to my ears, and we had so much to look forward to. As we welcomed the year 2005, Sam and I started to make plans for our wedding, including trying to figure out the logistics. One thing I knew for certain, I wanted a minister rather than a judge to officiate. I would have loved to get married in Texas because it had become my home and so many friends were there, but no matter where we chose, it was going to mean long travel distances for family and friends. We finally decided that we wanted to get married in Skidmore, Missouri, at Freedom Fest where we had first fallen for each other. That choice might have seemed a bit strange to some people, but for us, there was also great significance in getting married among veterans. It was an extension of our lives together and our commitment to veterans, and it would be like having extended family surrounding us for our special day.

At the same time, we were trying to do the right thing by Sammy's children, who were still mourning the loss of their mother. Sam had told his kids that we were engaged, but they had little to say. Sammy and I felt that waiting until September to get married, a year and a half after Peggy Jo's death, would respect their feelings and would be appropriate. But all of these considerations came with a lot of conflicted feelings. We wanted to be together much sooner.

Sammy attended the January 2005 presidential inauguration with his son Blue and his new wife, Carrie. Of course, I would have loved to have been at Sammy's side, but as his future wife, there would be other opportunities to attend an inauguration, so it wasn't something I dwelled on.

Sammy is on the road speaking some two hundred days per year, and starting in January 2005, he asked me to accompany him. Knowing that some couples could not happily spend time together twenty-four seven, we seriously had to ask ourselves if we felt that we could. The answer was easy for us. By then, we had come to relish each other's company and had both learned the hard way how precious time is. After losing our spouses, we knew it didn't matter if we spent time sitting in airports, in hotel rooms, attending functions, and even eating restaurant food all of the time. It was not about *where* we would spend our time together. That didn't matter. Just being together did. We're best buddies, and to this day we still do almost everything together even when we are at home—shopping, haircuts, groceries, and errands. Sam once asked if I wanted to ride along while he got the oil changed in the car. I didn't particularly feel like driving to the garage that day, so I said no, but his feelings were hurt. I asked him why he always wanted me along, and he simply replied, "You're fun!" Sheez, how can anyone resist that?

As we prepared for me to travel more and more with Sam, there was much at home in Texas to consider. I had to make sure there were people I trusted to care for the dogs and cats while I was gone. By then my concession business consisted mostly of three-day weekends twice a month, so I had to hire someone to run it if I wasn't there; I tried to schedule around those weekends when possible, and I delivered Avon when I was home. Each time I was away, I missed my home, my animals, and my life in Texas. I was glad to get back to them after each trip, but I was always sad to leave Sammy. I just knew somehow we were going to work it all out so we could be together, and I could have the animals with me as well.

More than anything, I wanted to spend time with Sammy; we'd been apart so much, and I longed to start our lives together. Yet a little voice in my heart kept reminding me that traveling with him while we weren't married was not right. Yes, we had spent time on the road together in 2004, but in truth, I was growing increasingly uneasy. I wasn't brought up that way, and numerous Scriptures in the Bible make it clear that following that route is not honoring God. The stronger my walk with God grew, the more I knew that, for me, it wasn't right.

For a time, I thought I could ignore the little voice, and I made plans to go with Sam to the United States Naval Academy in Annapolis, Maryland. In Annapolis, I was still in awe watching the impact Sammy had on servicemen and women. The midshipmen were so respectful, and they seemed to hang on his every word. We watched the impressive courtyard drills, when four thousand midshipmen lined up for lunch. A loud bell rang, signaling that it was time to eat, and it seemed like they'd all eaten in the five seconds it took me to fill my water glass. As Sammy prepared to walk across the stage to address the students, the midshipmen were all in place, and the spotlights turned up. He looked so handsome in his uniform, and the applause was deafening. Then he stepped forward, I heard a thud, and Sammy had disappeared. He had fallen off the stage.

For a moment, I panicked. I rushed to him, along with everyone else. In true Sammy fashion, he said he was fine. I wasn't so sure; the man would still claim all was OK if both his legs were broken. But he got up and delivered his address to thunderous applause. He wasn't hurt, but he sure scared all of us for a few minutes. Looking back, I can now laugh and see the funny side of it. It was pure slapstick. Kind of like "now you see him, now you don't."

Sammy's stumble on stage was not the only memorable episode during our visit to Annapolis. He fell for a navy captain's little, sad-eyed terrier. Unfortunately, the little dog did not share the feeling; as Sammy bent down to kiss it, the terrier bit his lip and continued hanging off his mouth while blood spurted everywhere. Between the fall and the bite, it was a heck of a way to start the New Year. If there was ever any doubt that spending two hundred days on the road with Sammy would ever get boring, our visit to Annapolis put my mind at rest: life with Sammy was never going to be boring. However, I found myself hoping that future trips would be a little less dramatic.

Luckily, the next event we attended together was far easier on my heart. In mid-January 2005, we headed to the veterans annual Winterfest in New Glarus, Wisconsin. I was ecstatic. New Glarus is close to my hometown of Freeport, Illinois, and it was to be the first time that many of my family and friends would meet Sammy. I also looked forward to spending time in New Glarus again and to sharing that magical place with Sam. Founded by emigrants from Canton, Glarus, Switzerland, in 1845, New Glarus is a picturesque, old-world village nestled in the rolling hills of southwest Wisconsin.

Alpine chalets with shuttered windows, lace curtains, and flower boxes line the streets of the small downtown area. Where else would one find life-size fiberglass cows painted with Swiss designs along the streets? The locals are adamant about keeping their Swiss heritage and culture alive, including the unique architecture, music, festivals, and food. I've always been crazy about the springy, rubbery texture and mild, salty taste of cheese curds—also known as "squeaky cheese"—the delectable Swiss pastries, and the homemade

Swiss sausages sold at the local meat market. Not to mention the Swiss chocolate shop and locally brewed beer. I love the chocolate!

My sister, Roxie; my nephews, Brett and Brandon; Brandon's fiancé, Kara; my great-nephew, David; and my friend Sherry were there when we arrived. Several friends from the Freeport Chapter of VietNow also came up to be with us. Many of the VietNow group already knew Sammy, and it was wonderful to introduce him to the rest of my family and friends. He was immediately adopted into the fold, as I knew he would be.

Sammy had been invited as the keynote speaker for Winterfest. In a stirring speech, after telling about his Vietnam experience, he asked everyone to make sure they let returning soldiers from Iraq know that we appreciated them. Later, he pulled out his harmonica and jammed with the band. Evening events included an outdoor burning of the "greens," a large pile of dried-out Christmas trees from the community. As a group of men played traditional Swiss music on long-necked, wooden alphorns around the bonfire, the haunting notes resonated in the frosty night air, and wood smoke curled toward the stars. I could have sworn we had magically been transported to the Swiss Alps. Later, we all joined in for a walking parade to the firehouse, and folks who'd ignored the advice to bring long johns wished they had them. If you have ever experienced a January in northwest Illinois or southern Wisconsin, no explanation is needed.

Winterfest was also the start of a tradition that almost caused us to build a special room in our house. One afternoon, Sammy, Sherry, and I wandered into a little Christmas shop full of enchanting decorations. Sammy and I were so happy that we started dancing among the shelves of Christmas villages in the back part of the shop, and Sherry caught us on her camera. We were laughing about that when we heard unexpected yodeling coming from the front of the store. As we headed back that way, we were surprised to hear the traditional Swiss music coming from a stuffed goat perched out on the front counter. This happy little creature with a smiling face cocked its head from side to side as it yodeled "The Lonely Goatherd" from *The Sound of Music*. It went on and on and on, sending us all into gales of laughter. Unbeknownst to us, Sherry decided then and there that she would order one for us as a gift.

When we attended Winterfest the following year, the goat traveled back with us to New Glarus. We'd place it in the hotel elevator, singing at the top of its music box lungs, so it would startle people with its song as the door slid open. It always guaranteed interesting conversations and laughter. On occasion, we'd sit the singing goat outside the door of a friend staying in an adjoining hotel room to yodel at the crack of dawn as an alarm clock. The goat started a tradition of wind up, push button animals as gifts for Sammy, who had endless fun with stuffed turkeys, chickens, cats, pigs, and who knows what all. In fact, Sammy filmed a hilarious video of some of these critters singing, squawking, and dancing, which ended up on YouTube.

As inspiring as Sammy was to veterans, and as serious and committed as he was about his mission, I quickly realized during those early days of our engagement that his spirit, humor, and zest for life would continue to make traveling with him a joy for me.

I was ready to hit the road with him for the next adventure.

CHAPTER 11

Did I Make a Difference

After New Glarus, we flew to Las Vegas for the annual Shot Show at the Sands Expo and Convention Center, the largest trade show of its type. The event is not open to the general public but restricted to professionals involved with shooting sports, hunting, military ware, law enforcement, and tactical products and services. Sammy had been involved with the show for a number of years, and in 2005, he was sponsored by Gerber Knives. His job was to talk with people who visited the company's booth and autograph his official Medal of Honor photo and citation. We sat at a high table so we could be at eye level with the person in front of the table. I still wasn't clear what my role was to be.

Sammy and the other Medal of Honor recipients consider themselves ordinary people and don't want anyone to put them on a pedestal. However, it happens everywhere they go. In Las Vegas, veterans immediately fell back into a military mode and addressed Sammy as a superior; the respect they paid him was amazing. As he was chatting, I also noticed that some people were intimidated and seemed afraid to speak to him directly. I decided I couldn't just sit there, so I started visiting with folks as well. I tried to make them feel more comfortable and to add some humor to Sammy's seriousness. Most people wore nametags with their place of residence, so conversations were easy to start.

"Are you Mr. Davis's wife? Do you think Mr. Davis will let me have a photo with him?" people asked me over and over. Many wanted to know if we'd been married when Sammy was presented with his Medal of Honor.

They asked if we had children, how often we traveled, and if I always traveled with him. They were curious about the man behind the medal, and whether part of our lives bore any resemblance to theirs. I believe that some people found it less intimidating to talk to me first. I did all I could to make them understand that we were regular folks like everybody else, so they would relax. I tried to find some common ground with anyone who stopped at our table. The Shot Show was the very first time I stepped into that role and answered those questions. I still get these same questions today everywhere Sammy speaks.

That very first time—and time and time again ever since—I also faced really serious questions about post-traumatic stress. I was surprised at first because I hadn't expected that. Sam would be talking to the husband, and the wife would talk to me on the side. I was asked if Sammy had any trouble adjusting after Vietnam, or if he had any health problems. Did he still have any problems? The answer is yes on both accounts. After nearly fifty years, he has the same reoccurring nightmare about Vietnam almost on a nightly basis.

Even that first time at the Shot Show, I answered from the heart. I am not a trained counselor, but I have been married to combat veterans who suffered from varying degrees of PTS. I've also spent much of my adult life with friends whose husbands or wives had been in combat situations, so I understood the questions.

I've met wives whose spouses with PTS suffered from extreme anger issues and would lash out at them or their children with the slightest provocation. These women spoke of their spouses yelling and screaming or throwing and kicking things. I have also known some women who have suffered physical abuse from husbands with PTS. I've personally known veterans who simply could not deal with authority, others with deep depression, and those who couldn't hold down a job. I've heard stories from both veterans and their spouses about alcohol and drug issues that have destroyed their families. Others have talked about flashbacks, problems relating to their spouses and children, fear of loud noises, avoidance issues, hypervigilance, depression, and suicidal thoughts. I especially think of the veterans who told me after Tim died that they had once planned to take their lives, but hearing Tim and

Michael's message in music made them change their minds. As I've heard these stories over the years from friends, people I met on the Last Patrol walks, and at veterans reunions, little did I know that I was being prepared to understand the plight of many people I would meet with Sam.

Because spouses and children may receive the brunt of their partner or parent's PTS, they are affected as well. More than one wife has shared with me over the years that the father in the family ruled with a heavy hand, belittled the kids, and never said a kind or encouraging word to them. The children were not validated, felt unloved, and they avoided their father at every turn. Consequently the children grew up never having a relationship with their dad. Like the soldiers, they need to know that they are not alone. Healing can start to take place with a talk to clergy, a trusted friend, or a therapist. It's also helpful to talk with other spouses or children who have had similar experiences.

Spouses sometimes ask where they can get help, and I tell them what I have learned from others. VA hospitals have programs, and there is a lot on the Internet. Joining a veterans group like the VFW or American Legion is also a good way to find support. Those who are on military bases usually have spouse support groups. If one seeks a therapist, be certain that person has a good understanding of PTS. It's also important to know that it is not just people in the military who suffer from PTS. Anyone who has suffered a traumatic experience of any kind may be affected. It goes without saying that it's important for those with serious problems to consult a trained professional.

That day at the Shot Show, it just felt natural to talk with people about PTS. I was thankful I knew what they were talking about and could relate. I remember, after hearing one woman's story, just putting my arms around her and holding tight for minute. I tried to offer encouraging words so she might walk away from the table with a little renewed hope.

On the other hand, because Sammy has talked about his experience for so long, he's probably one of the most well-adjusted Vietnam veterans I've ever met. Telling his story was very difficult for him in the beginning, but forty years of talking about it has helped him immensely. That said, there are tens if not hundreds of thousands of veterans who are not dealing with PTS as well as Sammy has. I believe we have an obligation as a country to help them.

Sammy remembers clearly when the late John Finn, at that time the last surviving member of fifteen Medal of Honor recipients from the Japanese attack on Pearl Harbor, gave this advice. "You have to find a way to move the war from in front of you to beside you in order to move forward."

Sammy likens all our life experiences, whether good or bad, to tools. They are life lessons, and we have to decide how we are going to use them. We can either learn from them or let them impede us. We each carry our own toolbox. Sometimes he says his toolbox is as heavy as a Mack truck, and if he doesn't carry it to his side instead of in front of him, he will trip over it and will not be able to move forward. In order to heal, it is so important for soldiers to talk about their experiences to someone they trust. They have to get their stories out in the light of day and decide how they can use their tools to move forward, or that part of them stays in the dark and will never heal.

When asked about Sam's issues from Vietnam, I also related that he suffers numerous health problems from exposure to Agent Orange, including diabetes. Someone asked how we handled that out on the road. My Grandma Fehr was diabetic, so it wasn't all new to me. For me, if it wasn't cancer, it could be managed. That's how I looked at everything after Tim's illness.

The first thing I did when I learned Sam had diabetes was to try to encourage him to change his eating habits; I wanted him around for a long time. He loved rich deserts, bread, and mashed potatoes. It was important for him to closely monitor his sugar and carbs. Sam loves to cook, and deep-frying was his specialty. There were a lot of eating habits that he needed to change. Of course, my advice didn't go over so well at first, but he has learned to make substitutions that are still tasty.

Our biggest dietary challenge occurs when we are traveling. It is difficult to know what goes into recipes. Hors d'oeuvres are sometimes loaded with sugar, and they are often the worst. If there is a choice at mealtime, Sammy orders fish. The fact that I love to bake is our challenge at home. I wish I got as much joy from making salads instead of breads and cakes. I end up giving away a lot of the breads so Sam can stay healthy.

Sam uses insulin pens containing slow-and fast-acting insulin, which thankfully do not require refrigeration. That sure makes traveling easier. He always carries a sugar tester that he uses six to ten times a day, and he doesn't eat anything until he tests his sugar. The tester indicates how much insulin he needs to take and whether or not he needs to wait awhile to eat.

We also have to make certain his sugar level doesn't get too low. Too much physical exercise will cause it to fall and also speaking on stage can contribute as well. Amazingly, speaking uses a lot of energy. Normally he'll check his sugar right before he goes on stage, and if he's not had a chance to eat, he'll have a dinner roll. Ordinarily I carry breakfast bars for him, too, and because of the carbs, they will usually carry him through an event.

One time we were shopping at Lowes where Sam had to walk a long distance, and suddenly he said he had to sit down a minute. I took one look at him and got him to an endcap to sit down. I was scared, and I asked one of the clerks to watch him because something was wrong. When Sam gets like that, he doesn't always understand me, so I just yelled, *"Don't you move"* and ran to the car for the sugar tester. His skin below his eyes gets really white when his sugar is low, and he breaks out in a sweat above his lips. That time we had no bars or candy with us, so I ran up toward the register until I saw some Little Debbies on the shelf. I grabbed a box, telling the checkout girl that I would be back to pay for them, and I ran back to feed the cakes to Sam. It didn't take long for the sugar to make him feel better, and within a few minutes, he was just fine. But it was very scary when it happened. Low sugar can have very dangerous side effects for a diabetic, and now I always make sure I have mints, hard candy or bars in my purse.

I have also learned to watch for signs that Sammy is getting overtired or is in pain. Walking long distances causes him pain as well as possible diabetic problems. I can always see it in his eyes. Sam will never say a word; I guess it is just a macho man thing. At some events the organizers have us hopping from one thing to another, and I try to take care of that up-front so that Sam has sufficient time to rest a bit. Organizers, for the most part, are very understanding after they are told and will build time into our schedule.

In addition, Sam has severe back problems, and he's undergone numerous surgeries on both knees. He has a hearing disability, and he's also had skin cancer removed, all as a result of his experience in Vietnam. Our daughter-in-law

Carrie is a dermatologist, so she takes excellent care of Sam with the skin cancer. He goes for a checkup every three months; we are very lucky to have her. There was a time when Sammy was very sick in his younger years after Vietnam, and he didn't think he would live very long. Thank God the mysterious fevers he suffered gradually disappeared in the 1990s. The doctors never could pinpoint a specific reason for them until it became clear later that they were the result of dioxin poisoning from Agent Orange.

Sam protects me, and I protect him; we just naturally look out for each other, and I knew that staying on top of Sam's health issues would be one of my many roles on the road with Sam. I also make sure that he keeps appointments with our family doctor because if something comes up, it's a lot easier to fix early on.

Sometimes after answering the questions, I would see a visible sign of relief on the face of the person who had asked. Often the wife would tell me that her husband was a veteran. What she really wanted to know, by asking about Sammy, was that she wasn't alone in dealing with a spouse with PTS or war-related illnesses. That scenario has happened over and over as I have traveled with Sammy, whether it involved veterans from Vietnam, Desert Storm, Afghanistan, or the Iraq War. Hearing that Sammy has dealt with PTS and health issues often provides an opening for the spouse to tell me her story.

In this new journey with Sam, I was trying to find my place. How could I do the most good in the life we would live together? I wanted to do something more than sit and smile; I wanted to make a difference. I wanted to shape a vision that would complement his so we could work together toward the common good and always find strength in each other. I could fill in Sam's blanks, and he could fill in mine. If we were on the same page, we could help each other in an unobtrusive way. We could keep each other on track. It became clear to me at that Shot Show what my job was to be in Sammy's life work. I would listen with an open heart and try my best to offer encouragement and hope to those who were struggling.

We have since realized that our common goal is pretty simple. We want to help people to discover the best about themselves, whether it is with a hug, an encouraging word, a gesture, Sam telling his story, or by just letting people know they are not alone in what they are going through. We also let people know that all of our strength comes from our faith in God. We can't do it alone. No matter who we are, we all need spiritual strength. Everybody needs somebody to lean on.

Sometimes, we don't immediately understand why we go through certain things in life, but I believe there is a reason for everything. Because of what I have lived through and encountered, I am able to understand what others in similar situations may face. I believe God is allowing Sam and me both to use our experiences to connect with others. Sam can tune in to the hearts and souls of combat veterans, and I to their loved ones. I also pray that our stories and our bond provides some solace and hope to those with tragic losses, like it did for the Gold Star families the night of our engagement, and that it is a testimony to faith in God and the power of second chances.

I had no idea at the Shot Show that I would soon come to an even deeper understanding of why the aftermath of war is so traumatic for veterans and their families.

CHAPTER 12

The Last Firebase

In February, we flew back to Indianapolis and made the two-and-a half-hour drive to the little rural town of Flat Rock, Illinois, Sammy's home. I was to meet Sammy's family. The pressure was on, and I didn't know what to expect. Dinner with his sisters was planned at a small restaurant, and his daughter, Nikki, whom I had already met, was to join us. Later that day, I met Sammy's oldest son, Beau, who was living with his dad at their home in Flat Rock.

I had only heard wonderful things about Peggy Jo, and I hoped I could live up to her character. I wanted to be myself and liked for who I was. I wish I could say that everything felt comfortable in those first meetings, but it wasn't easy.

I'm sure it was difficult for Sammy's family to accept someone new into the fold; his sisters and Peggy Jo had been friends since high school, and I didn't have that history with them. Sammy came from a very tightly knit family, and when people are so close, it sometimes makes it hard for someone new to fit in. I wondered, too, if things would have been easier had I come into the picture much later. They were all still mourning Peggy Jo. I felt like the outsider, and I wished I could do something to make the climate feel a little sunnier.

I loved Sam so much and just wanted us all to be a family, but sometimes in life our wishes take a long time to materialize. I just hoped someday his sisters and children would accept me as part of their family.

During that visit to Flat Rock, Sammy and I sat on the couch in his living room holding hands. He had decided the time had come to tell me more details about his life with Peggy and his Vietnam experience. Each time I heard him at speaking engagements, it seemed I learned a little bit more, yet there were many details I still didn't know. Perhaps it was because we were at his home where he felt entirely comfortable that so much came tumbling out of his heart that day.

Tears filled Sam's eyes as he told me about sitting by his wife's bedside in March 2004, at Crawford Memorial Hospital in Robinson, Illinois. Sammy knew she was losing ground. Even though he was a national hero, he always felt like Peggy Jo was the most courageous person he'd ever known. During her fight with cancer, she tried hard to stay upbeat, and would always tell him, "We'll get through this, Sam; we'll get through this."

Sam said throughout their marriage, Peggy Jo had always been the wind beneath his wings. As she held on to life by a thread, he was already grieving; he was terrified of losing her and scared of being alone.

How well I knew those helpless feelings as I thought of my last moments with Tim. The sadness threaded with panic, wondering how I could possibly survive without him, had closed in like a black shroud around me.

Sammy remembered nurses pushing medicine carts with wiggly wheels that rattled through the hall. The swinging doors to the nursery were a short distance from Peggy Jo's room. Their oldest daughter, Nicole, was born before they'd moved to Flat Rock, but it was in that same nursery where Peggy Jo had given life to their two boys, Beau and Blue. Sam thought of that each time he came to visit her.

In a blue-gray room, Peggy Jo was hooked to tubes and IVs. Morphine eased her pain, and she would occasionally open her eyes and look up at him. Sam held her hand and kissed her cheek. His gaze turned to the window where a robin perched on a low bush outside. A few yellow daffodils were just starting to show color. As spring and new life announced its arrival, Peggy's life on this earth was ebbing away. The thirty-six years since Vietnam, his marriage to Peggy, and their lives together rolled like a video through his mind.

He told me that when he came back to Flat Rock from Vietnam in March 1968, he had seen things that totally changed his perspective about life. People would get angry and excited about something as mundane as a family member returning the car without filling up the tank. To him, if there was nobody shooting at him, why not take it with a grain of salt?

Yet, at the same time, like many of the guys back from Vietnam, he had a short fuse. He wished he could change it, but it was part of the PTS a lot of veterans had to deal with, and nobody understood it at the time. He didn't look at much of anything the same way he had when he'd left home to serve his country.

When Sammy returned, the young lady he'd been writing to while he was in Vietnam had a six-month-old baby, and he knew it wasn't his. Sam's experience in Vietnam had made his heart hard, and that revelation further dashed any romantic hopes about life.

However, he went with his sisters and one of their friends, Peggy Jo Martin, to a 1950s sock hop at the school. She was only seventeen, but Sam said she acted much older and seemed so responsible and grown up. After that date, he realized something was happening to the scrap heap of a heart he had brought back from Vietnam. She didn't know it, but already she had touched something inside of him that he thought had died.

When Sam realized he loved her, he knew she had to know what happened in Vietnam, and he told her just like he was telling me that day. On the night of November 18, 1967, Sammy was an artillery man, and his unit was in a no-win situation. They had been airlifted to Firebase Cudgel in the Mekong Delta of Vietnam on November 17, and the next day a helicopter flew in. The major onboard told them there was a hundred percent chance they would be attacked that night. He got back in the chopper and left. *A hundred percent chance.* There was no turning back, and Sam's unit prepared for the attack.

With a faraway gaze in his eyes, Sam recalled how the night air was heavy with dampness and mosquitos, and the jungle smelled sweet and musty. Squishy mud that oozed near the water smelled like poop, he told me. The soldiers learned to pay attention to the bird and monkey sounds because if somebody was walking through the jungle, the animal noises would change to an agitated pitch, and then they would get very quiet. Everything was quiet that night, eerily quiet.

Sam made it all so vivid, and I couldn't imagine trying to focus in that humidity where mosquitos swarmed all around him. Sammy and his buddies had to stay quiet so the enemy didn't know where they were plus endure the misery of mosquito bites, leaches, mud, and sleep deprivation coupled with the fear of an impending attack. I felt my muscles tighten as I tried to understand the stress that each soldier must have experienced.

Suddenly mortars started coming in, and the soldiers heard the enemy screaming orders in English from the other side of the river, "Go kill the G.I." Somebody played a bugle charge, and then an onslaught of enemy soldiers came crashing out of the jungle, heading straight for their position. There were forty-two young soldiers in their Battery C, as well as infantry guys guarding the perimeter and Battery D fighting the offensive that night. They were vastly outnumbered against a reinforced battalion of about 1,500 North Vietnamese soldiers. Sammy, as well as his friends, never thought they'd make it out alive.

I sat next to him in disbelief. I thought of the terror that must have gone through Sammy's mind that night. The courage it must have taken for all of them to hold their ground; what is built into the soul of humans that gives them that kind of resolve in such an impossible situation?

I knew Sam was badly wounded that night; he had previously told me about his injuries, but not in the detail I got that day. Hearing the whole story helped me connect the dots as he painted word pictures about the thirty beehive darts imbedded in his flesh from mid-thigh all the way to his lower back. I could scarcely let myself imagine Sammy being blown into his foxhole face down when a rocket-propelled grenade hit the shield of the Howitzer. It knocked him out for a time, causing a traumatic brain injury. I could almost smell the smoke from the burning wheel on his Howitzer that scorched his face, neck, and arms. I understood so much more about the excruciating pain he still endures; the two-ton Howitzer rolled back on Sammy, crushing his ribs, splintering a vertebra, which in turn caused spinal nerve damage that affected his legs. With those injuries and an AK 47 round in his right thigh, how could he have even moved, let alone made his way to help others? I couldn't comprehend that kind of courage and resolve; it didn't seem humanly possible. In my heart, I knew the angels were with him that night.

Sam said through divine help, he somehow managed to get across a river twice with a life raft and dragged three of his wounded brothers from the infantry back to our side. His mom and dad always told him, "You don't lose till you quit trying," and Sam knew he couldn't leave them there. He described the agonizing groans and screams of his buddies, the graphic bloody scenes of battle, the faces of the enemy, the explosions from the Howitzer he fired and the tracers that looked like fireworks. Sam was running on adrenaline and never realized how badly wounded he was until later.

I just sat there and looked at him. It was all so surreal. Every time I thought he was finished with his story, there was more. Hearing what his eyes saw that night, the terror he experienced, plus the physical trauma of his wounds, I understood in a way I never had before why Sammy and other veterans suffer from flashbacks and nightmares. If there was ever a description of a living hell, Sammy and his unit experienced it that night. How did they endure? Sammy's prayer to God that night was, "Please, sir, just let me do my job, just let me do my job." I silently thanked God for answering Sammy's prayer and for saving him as well.

I couldn't wrap my mind around all that he'd told me. It was like watching a terrifying movie about the Vietnam War, only this time the man I loved was the main character in that movie. This was real life, and I was horrified as each scene unfolded; I sat in stunned silence, not really able to articulate my feelings. As much as I tried to comprehend everything, I had no real point of reference to remotely understand what it was truly like to experience what Sammy had been through. I had talked to many veterans who had described their war experience in very general terms, and Tim had shared bits and pieces of his time in Vietnam, but nobody had ever talked to me in detail like Sam did.

After the battle, Sam somehow found the strength to help get the wounded on choppers, and then he passed out. In the end, only twelve out of the forty-two men in his artillery Battery C were left standing the next morning, and most of those twelve were wounded in some way. It wasn't until the after-action reports came out that Sam found out about the miracle; none of the forty-two from his battery died that night. Most were wounded, but by the grace of God, they all pulled through. Sadly, a number of the infantry soldiers were killed.

Waking up in Dong Tam hospital, Sam was in bad shape. His left kidney, perforated by beehive darts, had been exposed to human waste in the canal and to Agent Orange, which had been sprayed to defoliate the area. That caused him to go into toxic shock. He was severely dehydrated and in and out of consciousness; the doctors had really given up on being able to save him. Sam needed blood that the hospital didn't have. Gwyndell Holloway, one of the men Sam had saved that night, was recuperating in the same hospital, and miraculously he and Sam had the same blood type. Gwyndell insisted that the doctors give Sam his blood; it was a direct transfusion from Gwyndell's body into Sam's. The man that Sam saved was responsible for saving the man I loved. I am thankful to God they had the same blood type.

Each time Sam woke up with a nightmare after our conversation about Vietnam, I wanted to hold him a little tighter and make sure he never had to wonder if he was alone. He had always talked about the need to be with his brothers, and I understood so much more clearly why he had made it his life mission to serve veterans. It strengthened my resolve to be a part of Sam's mission, and it reminded me how important it was for us to spend our lives together encouraging others.

On November 19, 1968, at a White House ceremony, President Lyndon Johnson presented Sam with the Medal of Honor for his courage.

Five soldiers were presented with the medal that day; each was the first from his field in Vietnam. Sam was the first artillery man, the chaplain was Angelo Liteky, Gary Wetzel was a helicopter door gunner, Dwight Johnson represented Armored Vehicles, and James Taylor was from First Armored Cavalry Division

After the ceremony, Sam remembered his mom saying, "Son, your legs were shaking so badly I could see your knees knocking."

Ever since Vietnam, Sam had unexplained bouts of fevers, and it didn't help that he was running a 101° F fever that day. He was also so scared of meeting the president and receiving the medal that he was just lucky to breathe.

President Johnson took all five of them in a little room just prior to the ceremony where he stepped in front of them individually to talk to them. Sam said it didn't take the commander in chief but a minute to realize that he was just an old country boy, so they quickly started talking about catching catfish and crawdads. That impressed Sam to no end. The president tried to make them feel comfortable and talked to each recipient about something he could relate to.

One of the things Sam recalled most that day was General William Westmoreland telling him, "You need to always act right, son, because everyone is going to be watching you."

After Sam and Peggy were married, he would wake up with nightmares every night, and Peggy would hold him and assure him it was OK. He said she would always lead with her heart and constantly assure him it was all going to work out. He didn't think he would be alive today if it wasn't for her. In Sammy's words, "Peggy Jo took a hardened, battle-bruised heart and a mean, young soldier and taught him how to love."

She knew what was really in his heart even though he had a hard façade and had turned into a bitter person after he came home from Vietnam. Sam said she would take him aside and remind him that he should be a loving person, not sharp-edged with a short fuse. He resisted at first, but he said with her constant prompting, he learned how to be kind and gentle again. With Peggy Jo's love, he got his life back in order.

I thought about Peggy at eighteen, just out of high school, dealing with Sammy's experiences. One minute she was going to sock hops and enjoying the carefree life of a teenage girl, but in a few short months, with her vows to Sammy in December 1968, she would hear all the dreadful things about war that Sammy had told me. By the time Sammy and I were together, he'd had years to round off the jagged edges of his experiences, but Peggy was thrown into a role far removed from the life that was familiar to her. She had to live with Sam as he struggled to deal with all that was fresh in his mind, as well as his severe health problems, which back then had no answers.

The fevers, coupled with pain, continued to hit him off and on, and doctors couldn't explain what caused them or why they would come and go. By the 70s and 80s, Sam began to feel tired, old, and really sick. He didn't know it at the time, but Agent Orange was taking a toll on him. The illness made it hard for him to be the dad and husband he wanted to be, and he started having to miss work.

An ATV accident in 1978 further complicated their lives. Sam was driving with his little brother, Johnny, in the front yard at his parent's house. A hard rain left a deep puddle in the yard, and he flipped the ATV and tore his knee apart. The only thing holding it together was the skin. Following surgery, Sam was put in a cast, then his knee became infected, and he started running high fevers again.

Peggy was pregnant with their youngest son, Blue, and she had to wait on him because he couldn't get around by himself. It was hard on her as well as him. Then another surgery was required to clean out the infection in his knee. Sam worked for Central Illinois Power Service Company, but he was off work for a year. When he went back, he tried to do his job, which required climbing lots of stairs at the power plant. His supervisor even changed his bandages so he didn't have to take time away from work. The company doctors looked at him and finally decided to put him on disability. It helped, but it wasn't like getting a full paycheck, which added to their struggles. Sam's health declined so much that finally in the early 80s, he was put on full government disability.

Dr. Kinman, his orthopedic surgeon, was a Vietnam veteran, and he talked to Sam's family doctor. After blood tests, Sam's doctor asked him how much whiskey he was drinking every day. Sam told him none, and the doctor wouldn't believe him. Sam was thirty-two years old, and he was told that his liver was like that of seventy-year-old man. He wasn't drinking, but he had cirrhosis. Sam had so many internal problems, and the doctors really didn't give him much hope at that time. That led to more testing, and about two years later Sam's doctors sent him to Dr. Bertram Carnow, a leading expert in environmental health at the University of Illinois in Chicago. He was also associated with Woods Veterans Hospital outside of Milwaukee, where Sam met with him. Dr. Carnow was one of the first to start testing for Agent

Orange, and he suggested Sam start drinking Clamato juice. The Japanese had used clams for thousands of years to help liver problems. Nobody should start drinking large quantities of it without asking his or her doctor, but Sam started drinking at least a quart a day, and it began to flush his body of the toxins. In time, his health, on some levels, began to improve.

When he was thirty-six, Sam was included as a test subject in the Point Man Project in conjunction with the New Jersey Agent Orange Commission. The Clamato juice had helped cleanse his body, but the damage from Agent Orange still affected him on a cellular level. His lungs were affected, and for a long time he coughed up terrible-looking stuff. He later developed diabetes (with no family history of it), and he was diagnosed with kidney damage, all thought to be effects of dioxin poisoning.

Sam and Peggy had three kids, and during his times of sickness, it really hurt him that he couldn't get out and throw a ball with them and do things he normally did. Some days he would feel better and would try, and other days he just couldn't do it.

Once again he was in an accident in 1992 that crushed his good knee and put him even further out of commission. A truck belonging to Sam's son Beau was on a hill and the emergency brake started to slip. Beau was trying to hold the truck back as it started to roll down the hill, and he couldn't get out of the way. Sam made a running tackle and pushed Beau out of the way, but the truck rolled over his leg. He was in a wheelchair for months. Peggy Jo was working at the sheriff's department as a dispatcher, so Sam took care of himself as best he could. Once again, normal life was on the back burner.

Life was no easy task for Peggy Jo and all the young brides who had no manual to teach them how to deal with PTS or health problems that plagued their husbands. I was grateful for all that Peggy did for Sam, and I had the greatest respect for her.

Peggy's last wish was to hear her grandkids playing and laughing, so Sammy took her home where they had a bed set up in the very living room where we were sitting. He got the little ones down rolling on the floor and giggling just like she wanted. On March 12, 2004, Peggy went home to Heaven.

All I could do was squeeze Sam's hand in support as he relived that sad experience all over again; I knew too well what he was feeling.

As I listened to Sammy's story, he seemed like a cat with nine lives. He had miraculously defied the odds so many times through combat, illness, and accidents. He had known the deepest grief. I believed then as I believe today that he was spared because God had something very important left for him to do.

So much had happened in Sam's life and mine, and we pondered the reasons for all that we had experienced. We both believed there was a reason for everything, both the heart-wrenching experiences as well as the good things. We would never know all the reasons this side of Heaven, but Sam knew his journey to serve others would never have happened if he had not been at Cudgel that fateful night. We both believed that it had taken everything we'd been through to bring us together to love each other and to blend our experiences into a mission to love and encourage others.

We covered so much that day, hours and hours of conversation. I was truly thankful that he wanted to share everything with me, but it was draining for both of us, especially Sam. That conversation in Flat Rock was a pivotal point in our relationship, cementing an even stronger bond between us. Still, my heart was heavy because Sammy's family was not yet ready to fully accept me. That was a constant source of stress for me, and it was hard for Sammy. We were only in Flat Rock three or four days, but with the exception of seeing Beau at the house, we never saw the rest of the family again during that visit.

Sam took me back to the airport in Indianapolis for my flight to Texas, and on the way he told me he wanted me to hear the song, "Total Eclipse of the Heart" by Bonnie Tyler. In fact, he played it over and over as we drove. The lyrics touched both of us to the core, and I think at that moment, we both knew what we had to do. I accepted Sammy's invitation to return to Flat Rock in March.

CHAPTER 13

Chapel of Love

There was so much on my heart when I got back to Texas, and Sam and I were on the phone back and forth several times a day. We talked a lot about the song "Total Eclipse of the Heart" that we listened to in the car and how it seemed to describe much that we were feeling. By waiting to marry, we were trying to respect his children, yet day by day life was passing us by. We knew how precious time was; at our stage in life, there was no promise of years and years together. We wanted to make every moment count, and it was painful for both of us to keep putting off what we felt was right in our hearts. Our September wedding was still months away, but we both wanted to be married, and we didn't want to wait.

In addition, the closer I drew to my Heavenly Father, that still, small voice that let me know it wasn't right for Sammy and me to be traveling together as an unmarried couple kept getting louder and louder. I wanted to set the example for our grandkids, for the young women in our church, and the young veterans we spoke to on the road. It wasn't right to talk the talk and not walk the walk.

Also, Sam continued to have some silly notion that somebody would steal me away, which didn't hold a grain of truth, but in the end there was no question as to what we should do. Guess what? Older folks elope, too.

I told my family because we knew they would give their blessing. I would have loved for Tony to be there, but taking his six kids out of school and the long trip from Louisiana would have been very hard on his family. Sammy knew the news would not be welcomed by his children, so he felt it would be better to tell them after the fact. Nothing would have made both of us happier than to have all our families there with us, but it just wasn't going to happen that way. However, we had each other to share in this monumental day in our lives, and that was what mattered most.

I had returned to Flat Rock, and after a three-day wait for the marriage license, on an overcast morning on March 29, 2005, Sammy and I drove to Olney, Illinois, to the Church of Jesus Christ of Latter Day Saints. As we walked up to the brick building with white pillars and a stately white steeple, to me, Sammy looked like the most handsome man in the world. He wore a navy-blue suit, and my skirt and paisley, sequined jacket were a soft pink. Yellow jonquils and daffodils, the happy, little flowers of spring, were popping up, and the grass had changed from winter brown to a verdant green. Robins were singing, and spring was in the air. Even more, spring was in our hearts; this was our new beginning, and I thought I would burst with happiness. At 10:00 a.m., as I tried to blink back the tears of joy, two church members witnessed the brief ceremony in which the minister pronounced us Mr. and Mrs. Sammy Davis.

Sam and I chose words from 1 Corinthians 13 from the Bible as the Scripture reading. The apostle Paul told the Corinthian Church that of all the gifts from God, love was the greatest gift of all, a gift that goes on forever. He said that love is patient, kind, and is not jealous or proud. It is not selfish or rude and does not keep a record of wrongdoings. He continued that love doesn't demand its own way nor does it hold grudges. It rejoices when truth wins out, and it never gives up on the loved one. With love, there is faith and hope, and love is eternal.

This was not just a reading; they were words we both believed in and wanted to live by.

When I talk to my grandkids or young people anywhere about marriage, I tell them, "Don't settle. Be in love—really. You must like someone before you can love them. I believe it's important to have the same values and to be going in the same direction with similar goals. A couple has to really have things in common, not just a physical attraction."

For me, it was important to share the same faith as well. Sam and I had to decide early on, if there were things we couldn't change about each other, would we still be happy in ten years? We had to talk about finances and make sure we were on the same page. We both believed it's important to be mannerly and courteous to each other and to never make fun of each other in order to make ourselves look better. We also talked about how crucial it is to never say anything negative, biting, or critical, especially in public, to intentionally hurt the one you love. Words can crush one's spirit. We believed that if we tried to put each other first and thought about how our actions would affect each other, then we would have a good foundation for marriage. Certainly Sam and I aren't perfect, and like any married couple, we have our differences. Occasionally we are a little unhappy with each other, but it never lasts long. Life is too precious to spend quarreling.

It's also important to continue courting each other in marriage. Courting is such a nice, old-fashioned word. It's all about still doing those sweet things for each other that we did in the beginning when we were trying to win each other over. Sam and I still try to surprise each other with little gifts. For instance, he might come back from a dental appointment and bring me bananas, ciabatta rolls, and yogurt, my favorite breakfast. One time he bought me a beautiful baby doll that I had admired. I may surprise him with a new shirt for traveling that doesn't wrinkle. Recently I had all of his boots resoled because I know he loves those boots. Sam is also great at sending me e-mails or text messages; maybe he'll surprise me with a simple "I love you" or a funny photo he found or something with cats. For him, I pretend I really love reruns of *Bonanza* or *Gunsmoke*, and he turns the TV to *Dancing with the Stars* just because he knows how much I enjoy it. It doesn't have to be a birthday or Christmas for gifts; thoughtfulness reigns every day.

For us, touching is very important. Sammy says just touching me calms his soul. People will see us holding hands in public, and they are just as likely to see us hugging or dancing in the aisle at Walmart or the grocery store. Besides making us happy, it makes people smile and hopefully encourages them to rekindle a little romance in their lives. Life is too short to live any other way.

After the ceremony, we drove to the Dairy Queen and ordered foot-long chili cheese dogs and ice-cream sundaes to celebrate. There were no tin cans rattling from the back of the car to announce our marriage, but we were as happy and giddy as teenagers. We couldn't quit smiling and looking into each other's eyes, even with chili and cheese smearing our faces. Sam and I realized there would be hurdles to jump and storms to weather in the coming weeks and months, but for that moment, all was right with the world. We would still have the wedding in Skidmore for family and friends, and we couldn't wait to share our happiness with those we loved, but on that beautiful day we had each other, and 2005 had truly become our year.

There was no time for a honeymoon. In fact, the next day, March 30, Sam was contacted by the media in Indianapolis and told that the national Medal of Honor Memorial in that city had been vandalized. We immediately drove to Indianapolis, and I think that may have been the first time it really hit me that my life with Sam would not be my own. As his wife, I would go with him wherever he was called to go. I didn't mind; I had already committed to being Sam's helpmate, but I was finding out firsthand, very soon after our marriage, what that meant.

I'd been to Indianapolis with Sam on numerous occasions, but it was always to catch a plane, or we were at a hotel preparing for him to speak someplace. I had never seen the impressive Medal of Honor Monument on the north bank of the Central Canal, adjacent to Military Park. Curved, green glass panels set in concrete bases were arranged into fifteen walls, each representing the conflict from which the Medal of Honor was awarded. The name of a recipient was etched in each panel, and there were 3,456 names. Sammy's was one of them.

It was a strange feeling to see his name there in writing, almost surreal. I don't know what it was about seeing it written, but I felt like, "Oh, wait; I'm married to this man depicted on this memorial." To me, he was my husband, not this name on the glass. Perhaps because I hadn't known him when he was a soldier, nor was I in his life when he received the Medal of Honor, I had no way of connecting with his experience except for what he had told me. Never once had I felt that way before, but I think I was overwhelmed with the American history and honor of so many men that the memorial represented. And Sam was one of them. It's one thing to know it and to have been with

Sammy at various functions, but I couldn't quite wrap my mind around seeing his name there. Somehow his name inscribed on that glass made it different. I have no idea why; it was the weirdest sensation and totally unexpected.

The park like area along the canal is beautiful, and the monument is especially stunning to look at from a distance. A TV screen set in a cement pillar played looping videos of the recipients, and I couldn't believe that when we walked up to it, we were greeted by a video of Sammy playing "Shenandoah" on his harmonica.

Then we saw the vandalized panels. One was shattered, and one looked like it had been gouged. Also, beneath a bridge over the canal, vandals had spray-painted a peace symbol, a heart, and an anarchy sign. They had written obscenities about America, President Bush and the Indiana governor. It was heartbreaking to see. I could only shake my head, and I wanted to cry. Only a person without a moral compass could have desecrated a memorial and park of such honor. The news media interviewed Sam, and when he introduced me as his wife, they started asking me questions like how I felt and my impression of what had happened. I was shocked. Why did they want my views? Once more it hit me that as Sammy's wife, I would be expected to play more roles than I ever anticipated.

I went back to Texas as Mrs. Sammy Davis, but I still had my jobs and animals to care for, and I continued traveling with Sam around my schedule. The difference was that with our marriage, I no longer heard that nagging little voice, and Sam and I both knew we had done the right thing. Sometimes we would meet in Indianapolis for a short getaway, and it was as right as right could be. We were so happy together, and we talked a lot about September when people we loved would join us for the ceremony at Freedom Fest in Skidmore.

Meanwhile, in April, I was excited to accompany Sam to Fort Sill, Oklahoma, where he had trained as an artilleryman before going to Vietnam. He was only twenty years old at the time. Sam showed me a Howitzer that was like the one he fired in Vietnam, and we watched young soldiers in Advanced Individual Training in artillery undergoing a confidence course. Utilizing teamwork, they were trying to walk across logs carrying large, heavy packs on their backs. I knew I sure couldn't do that, and I tried to visualize a young Sam out there on the field. He said it didn't look nearly as intense as the training he'd gone through, and then he grinned and admitted it was because he wasn't involved in the efforts we were watching. I didn't like thinking of Sam having to endure such stress even before he left the States, but I also knew that his training is what helped keep him alive that night in Vietnam. It was also an eye-opener for me to get a glimpse of what present-day soldiers endure in training to serve our country.

Sam told me that Geronimo died in 1909 at Fort Sill, and he took me to see his gravesite alongside those of other Native Americans. Tim would have loved looking at the pyramid monument made of round stones topped with a huge eagle that honored the Apache warrior. Even with Sam, Tim continued to be with us. I loved knowing that Geronimo had walked the grounds at Fort Sill and that we were experiencing Native American history.

Eating in the loud, bustling mess hall was quite the experience, too. Trays clanking, TVs spouting the news, and soldiers talking and laughing, all the while trying to choose food that looked appetizing. I closed my eyes and tried to see Sammy as one of those soldiers. It sure wasn't mama's home cooking, and I know he must have missed that.

It was also special to see the Sammy L. Davis Howitzer Crew Training Facility at Fort Sill, known as the Home of Artillery. Since Sam had trained there—and fewer than one hundred artillerymen from the Civil War through Vietnam have received the Medal of Honor—the building was named after Sam. I realized I was going to have to get used to seeing his name on monuments, buildings, and signs. I didn't have the same feeling about seeing the writing on the building as I'd had at the Medal of Honor Memorial, and I felt very proud to know that folks at Fort Sill had honored Sam in that manner.

Toward the end of April, we headed to Melbourne, Florida, to attend the city's annual veterans reunion at Wickham Park and to visit Sammy and Peggy Jo's friends, Buzz and Diane Cipola. Sammy took our marriage license along, and they were the first friends to find out we had tied the knot. He wanted them to know since we would be staying with them and sleeping together in the same bedroom. It was the first time I had met them, and they were thrilled for us; we have remained close friends through the years.

The Cipolas were members of the Nam Knights, a national motorcycle club comprised of veterans and police officers. Sammy was also a member and had ridden with them for years as the club escorted the moving Wall to the reunion. We were given the use of a motorcycle during our stay in Florida, and that year I would have the privilege of riding in with Sam for opening ceremonies where he would speak.

I had been on a motorcycle a few times before, but these were serious bikers who took long trips together. There were a lot of biker vendors at the veterans reunion, so I splurged and bought a black leather jacket with Native American beadwork and fringe. I was determined to look the part of a Harley biker. With a borrowed helmet, my cowboy boots, and gloves and a scarf I bought, I thought maybe I had captured a little bit of the look. Then Sam gave me a pair of big, old, bug-eyed yellow glasses to wear, and that blew my whole image up in smoke! I found out that riding bikes is all about the clothes—and I'm not talking about fashion. It can be ninety degrees out, but once you get the speed up on a bike, the wind will freeze you to death if you don't have on plenty of clothes.

Route 4, the main highway in the area, was closed to accommodate an estimated one thousand bikers from all over the country headed for the reunion. Our group from the Nam Knights was in the lead, and I road on the back of Sam's bike, sometimes holding on for dear life. I was a little nervous in all that traffic, but I just had to depend on Sam. He had been on motorcycles all of his life and even raced them for a while, so I knew I was in capable hands.

A huge garrison-size American flag fluttered in the breeze attached to two high ladders from fire trucks on either side of the road. What an impressive canopy to ride under as we roared into the park. Because Sam was speaking, fortunately we were able to park near the stage, but it was quite a sight to watch that many cycles trying to park out in an open space on the grounds.

After we got off the bike, a woman who had ridden behind us came up to visit. She told me that she had been watching me behind Sam, my head turning from side to side taking in every new sight. Suddenly I thought of how General Westmoreland had told Sam that he needed to always act right because people would be watching him. Her comment made me realize in a very real way that as Sammy's wife people would be watching me, too.

I thought of how I had been taught the very same words the general told Sam. "You are to act right," I could hear my mom saying, and at that moment, I was thankful for my upbringing. I knew I would always try to do my best to respect Sam and the awesome honor that he represented. While I was still in awe of all the new things I was privileged to experience with him, I was also becoming increasingly aware that my life as I had known it, and my privacy, would never be the same as it had been.

That day Sam talked about the casualties whose names were on the Wall and about the ones who had not yet been accounted for. I was touched when he quoted from one of his most well-known speeches, "The Promise." He spoke about our blessings as Americans who are born with an inherent promise of freedom and the pursuit of happiness. He said it is our duty to be vigilant, to be keenly aware of our blessings, and to protect and preserve our country that has given us this promise. These liberties must be passed on to our children, and no enemy must be allowed to ever deny the promise to the people of America. I was constantly amazed at how eloquently Sammy was able to deliver what was in his heart.

Our visit to Florida was full of new experiences, and while Diane and Buzz were working, Sam took me deep sea fishing. Never again! With each choppy wave, my stomach got queasier, and the dizziness made me so ill I couldn't stand up. I stretched out in the boat and tried to shield myself with a jacket from the blazing sun. Even breathing made me feel like I had to throw up. I was so sick I think they could have thrown me to the whales that day and I wouldn't have cared. Poor Sammy was trying so hard to show me a wonderful time, but it was one of the most miserable experiences in my life. The dizziness didn't go away for a while, and I couldn't walk straight for two days.

On the other hand, I just adored the lumbering manatees when Sam took me to watch them swim. Later we were sitting in Buzz and Diane's living room when I happened to notice a magazine rack. I glanced at it then looked back quickly. The top of a booklet was sticking out, and it read *Manatee*

Cookbook. Manatees are a protected species, and I didn't know what to think. I was shocked. Who were these people? They didn't seem like the type that would poach and cook manatees, but it really worried me. Once when they went out of the room, I whispered to Sam about the booklet and that I wondered if they were poaching manatees.

When everyone was busy and not paying attention, I quietly slipped back in and took a peek at the cookbook. As much as I hated the idea, I wanted to see the recipes and understand how they could cook such a big creature. Then the thought occurred to me that they must only eat the babies. That was awful! I carefully pulled the book out and saw the front cover that read *Manatee High School Cookbook.* After a sigh of relief, I laughed myself silly, and I couldn't help but tell the others about it. That was Buzz and Diane's first experience with "Dixieisms" as some of my friends call it. Goodness knows what they really thought. I've been known to come up with some pretty off the wall ideas, but they shrieked with laughter, and I will never live that story down.

It was only April, and I couldn't believe all the places that Sammy and I had been together, the people I'd met, and all the firsts I'd experienced in just a few short months. Sammy had opened doors to so many new experiences for me, and every day with him was an adventure. I was also learning much more about what it meant to be married to a public figure. I had become Mrs. Sammy Davis, and I was unbelievably happy. Every night with him was the honeymoon we hadn't had in March, and all those frustrating months disappeared when we melted in each other's arms. Life was good.

In the meantime, Sammy and I had numerous events to attend over the summer, and our Skidmore wedding to plan. Little did we know that we were about to step into a raging storm.

CHAPTER 14

Walking in the Sunshine

Before the summer of 2005 tested our mettle seven ways from Sunday, the spring kept showering us with moments of lighthearted joy. In May 2005, sandwiched between Sam's events, we headed to northern Illinois for the wedding of my nephew, Brandon, and his fiancée, Kara. However, I just have to preface the sharing of that happy occasion with our infamous chicken tale.

About five miles north of Freeport, Illinois, lays the small village of Cedarville whose most famous citizen is Jane Addams (1860–1938). Jane was a pioneer leader in women's suffrage, an author, a philosopher, a sociologist, and the first woman to win the Nobel Peace Prize. In 1890, my great-aunt, Mary Fry, at the age of twelve, went to live at the Addams's household in Cedarville. Aunt Mary became the companion and housekeeper to Jane's stepmother, Anna Hostetter Haldeman Addams.

In the book *Generous Spirit: The Life of Mary Fry,* by Mary's nephew, Paul Fry, Mary was portrayed as a selfless and devoted individual who took care of everyone. However, there was a photo in the book of Aunt Mary wearing an outrageous hat almost as tall as her head, and it looked like a full-grown chicken was perched on top of the hat. That picture made me wonder if there was another side to this great-aunt. Apologies to Aunt Mary, but that photo had always sent my friend Sherry and me into shrieks of laughter, and for years, we referenced that chicken hat any time we got a chance. Anything that had to do with a chicken sent us rolling in the floor.

The year after Tim's death, I had gone back to Illinois. Sherry and I attended the annual veterans reunion at Lake LaDonna where I had first met

Tim. Michael J. Martin was to perform that weekend, and many of our friends were coming. It was difficult to be there, yet comforting in another way. A storm had blown in, so rather than Michael singing from the stage, he set up in a shelter area with picnic tables. After he had finished a song that was particularly difficult for me, one that he and Tim had sung together, Sherry stepped up to the microphone. She was holding a beautifully wrapped package, and in a serious voice, she called me to the mic. She said she had something very special to present to me, and she wanted to be sure our friends were there to share it with me.

I was sure it had something to do with Tim, maybe some sort of tribute, and I was wishing I had some tissue in my pocket. Listening to Michael sing the songs that he and Tim used to sing together was hard enough. Whatever it was, I hoped I wouldn't cry.

Slowly I unwrapped the package and lifted the top. What in the world? Inside was the dumbest looking chicken hat I had ever seen. It was made out of some kind of flimsy white cloth, and when I put the cap of it on my head, the long, skinny chicken legs with yellow talons dangled off my ears. The gangly neck of the thing with its red crest and black, beady eyes fell down over my face.

All seriousness instantly evaporated from the atmosphere and silliness took over—exactly what the chicken gift was designed to do. I wore it over my cowboy hat, Michael had it on while he played guitar, and it got passed around to everybody in the place. The chicken hat made its appearance on various heads throughout the weekend, and the chicken story took on more momentum.

In the latter months of 2004, when I first started telling Sherry all the wonderful things about Sam, she sent me an e-mail. *"He sounds great,"* she wrote, *"but the real question is—will he wear a chicken hat?"* She knew I needed someone spontaneous with a sense of humor. I immediately sent her a crazy photo of Sam dressed in a complete chicken suit riding a motorcycle! He passed muster with flying colors.

I don't know how it is in other parts of the country, but in northwest Illinois, it is an unwritten rule to play music for the chicken dance at wedding receptions. With Brandon and Kara's wedding coming up, we couldn't pass up a chance to move the chicken saga to even greater heights. Theirs was a traditional church wedding in every sense, except that Kara wore Cinderella glass slippers that blinked and flashed neon colors with each step she took down the aisle in her gorgeous gown. The wheels were turning in my head as I thought of our upcoming wedding. Hmmm, I remembered that Kara and I wore the same size shoe.

At the reception, Sam and I slipped out to the car for a few minutes and stepped back in without being noticed. We headed to the restrooms for a quick clothes change, and if anyone had come in and seen bright orange webbed feet under the bathroom stall, I'm not sure what would have happened. Sammy had talked with the deejay, and he was privy to our little plan. As the guests were flapping to the chicken song, we both jumped in. Dressed in bright yellow chicken getups, we started flapping our wings and wildly shaking our tail feathers. Those chicken costumes were so hot that I thought Sam and I were going to suffocate, but the crowd thought it was a hoot, and how many people can say a pair of chickens danced at their wedding reception? Aunt Mary's chicken hat lives on!

Following the wedding, our traveling schedule brought more heartwarming joy. Later in May 2005, we went to Salina, Kansas, where we attended a Purple Heart Banquet and spent time with Jim Deister and his wife, Rita. Jim is one of the men that Sammy rescued in Vietnam; he had been shot in the head and left for dead. His hearing was seriously impaired, but he could read lips. There was a humbleness and gentleness of spirit about Jim, and I was so honored to be with him and Rita. We also met their friend Jim Cole, who often interprets for Jim when he doesn't understand someone. The conversation centered on kids and grandkids, and there was a lump in my throat as I looked at Sammy. Without his bravery that night in Vietnam, we would not have been sitting with Jim and his wife having that conversation.

It was one thing to know the story, and yet quite another to sit in the company of a man who was still alive because Sammy had saved him, knowing that one single act of valor had a ripple effect that continues to touch many who we will never know. Not only is there another generation of Deisters who would not have been, but Jim worked for the Kansas Department of Rehabilitation where he assisted others with disabilities. When he talked to them, they knew Jim had been there himself. He understood their needs, and he cared deeply. It was like a huge circle of love that started, despite all the horrors of war, that fateful night in Vietnam. I thought about the Scripture from Romans 8:28, which tells us that all things work together for good to them that love God, to them who are called according to His purpose.

We seldom see the big picture when tragic things happen to us, but I am reminded of a story I read long ago. Life is like a tapestry in which we only see the top side. We don't see the tiny, golden filaments mingled with the dark fibers underneath the tapestry. It takes all of them woven together to create the light and the shadows of a beautiful scene. Sometimes the dark threads, which by themselves are dismal, become the foundation for something more beautiful than we can imagine. Because of Sam's love for his brothers, Jim Deister lived to extend that love to others. Spending time with Jim and Rita during those few days really brought that home for me, and I will never forget the emotional power of that experience.

In June, we headed back to Indianapolis for the Miracle Ride, a fund-raiser for Riley Children's Hospital, one of the top children's medical facilities in the state and in the country. Sam had long supported the annual event for kids that attracted some five thousand motorcyclists. Little did we know then that one day we would come to personally rely on the expertise of doctors at Riley Hospital. In March 2013, eight years after Sammy and I first attended the fund-raiser together, our thirteen-year-old granddaughter Katelynn Smith was diagnosed with leukemia and spent several months at Riley's undergoing chemotherapy. Her care was excellent, and we have the highest regard for the doctors and nurses there; they were wonderful to our entire family. We are grateful that Katelynn was back in school in December 2013. She ran track the following spring and played summer league softball. Thank you, Riley Children's Hospital. We were glad we'd had the privilege of being involved in their fund-raising events.

While spring brought sunshine, a gray veil of clouds was starting to grow darker as summer approached. I was still trying to tie up loose ends in Texas. Even though Sam and I were married, I didn't move to Flat Rock, Illinois, until July 2005. Making the decision to move was one of the most bitter-sweet events of my life. I would have loved to stay in Texas and make our home there, but Sam had built up a large network of referral contacts in the Midwest for his speaking engagements, and he knew he would have to start all over in Texas. He felt that travel would also be much easier from a more central part of the country. In addition, he didn't want to leave his family. With Tony in Wimberley, Texas, I no longer had family in Hawkins to hold me, so with a heavy heart, I agreed to move. The one consolation was that we were planning to keep my home and spend part of every month there.

As I took my daily walks, I knew I would miss the beautiful Indian paint-brushes and Texas bluebonnets. They didn't grow in Illinois. I couldn't bottle the pungent smell of the pines or the sweet fragrance of Carolina jessamine to take back with me to Illinois. All of the natural beauty of East Texas had been such a source of comfort for me through the difficult times when Tim was sick.

Where would I find friends like those sweet Texas souls who lived in our neighborhood? They had been so good to Tim and me and had been there for us through thick and thin. There would be no Piney Woods Pickin' Parlor or a funky little restaurant in an old-fashioned hardware store. There would be no more fishing at Lake Fork. There would be no more, there would be no more. Those words kept echoing through my head.

It was time to move on, but it was hard to hold back the tears when I thought of leaving the little home that held so many fond memories of my life with Tim, even in difficult times. I walked through the rooms, each one filled with recollections that swirled and drifted through my mind. I was leaving everything that was familiar to go to a place where the only person I really knew was Sammy. Even though I was going back to Illinois, my friends and family would be six hours away. Why did it all have to be so heart-wrenching?

The emotional part aside, the logistics of selling the concession business, packing up my things and putting most of them in storage, and finding someone to stay at the house and take care of the animals until I could bring them to Flat Rock was overwhelming. Just as I had all those years before when I left Illinois for Texas, I would once again uproot myself and move toward a new life. I loved Sammy dearly, and I wanted to be with him, but leaving the Piney Wood Hills and the life I had known in Hawkins, Texas, was a pain worse than I ever imagined.

Initially, I found someone to temporarily take care of my two cats, Annie and Hobbie, and my one remaining dog, Cheesi, in exchange for living at my place. The other dogs, which had come as strays, were old when Tim was alive, and sadly by that time, Cheesi was the only one left. I truly wanted to take the animals with me, but there was nobody to care for them in Flat Rock. Our plan to return once a month to check on things and spend time in Texas didn't work out. With Sammy's schedule, we were only able to get back on three separate occasions that summer, each time for just a week. I missed my pets so much; I just had to find somebody in Flat Rock to take care of them while we traveled.

Maybe my move north would have been easier if I'd felt more welcome in Flat Rock. Also, I was moving into Sammy's house, which had been the home where he and Peggy Jo had raised their family. In fact, it had been Peggy Jo's parents' house as well. Looking back, the whole plan was a recipe for failure, and it is only by the grace of God that Sammy and I weathered the storm.

Perhaps some couples succeed in creating a new life in the home where a beloved spouse has lived, but from our experience, I wouldn't recommend it. I was a decorator, and I longed to create a cozy home that reflected both Sam's personality and mine. All of my furniture and most of my personal belongings were in storage in Texas. I didn't feel like I belonged anyplace. Even when we made simple updates like painting and changing the carpet in Sammy's house, I knew it wasn't accepted. It was clear to me that house belonged to Sammy's family. It housed their memories, it was their touchstone, and they were not yet ready to accept that Sam had moved on in his life. I knew that was not a place that I could ever really call my home. Sammy said, too, that if he had it to do over again, we would have found a different place to live where we could have started to create our own memories.

In addition, Sammy's oldest son was living there with him. We were newlyweds trying to make the usual adjustments of living together, and having an adult child in the house meant we had little privacy at a time we craved it. I'm sure, too, that it wasn't easy on Sam's son to have to deal with his dad bringing a new woman into their family home.

Looking back, I don't know what we were thinking when we made the decision to move to Sammy's house. It ended up being very hard on our marriage. If I hadn't loved Sammy so much, more than once I would have jumped in my truck and headed back to Texas. I wanted to sit down with the kids to talk and bring things out in the open, to give them an opportunity to try to understand our feelings. However, Sam was afraid of losing his kids if there was any kind of confrontation, so any time we were together as a family, there was always an elephant in the room. He continued feeling like he was caught between a rock and a hard place, and that was a source of contention between the two of us. I think being on the road so much was the only thing that saved us. We had privacy and times together in planes and hotel rooms, and we had interesting things to look forward to that kept us from dwelling on the problems at home.

Dealing with the move from Texas and the difficulties in Flat Rock, the summer had turned very stressful for both Sam and me. Our vows for better or for worse were really being tested. I didn't think things could get any worse.

CHAPTER 15

All Shook Up

On Friday, July 15, 2005, Sammy was scheduled to speak at a United Auto Worker's event in Indianapolis. Whenever he has a morning speaking engagement, we usually go the night before so we don't have to worry about potential travel issues that could cause us to be late. With that in mind, we drove to Indianapolis on Thursday and checked into a hotel not far from the Indianapolis airport. Arriving early, Sammy and I went shopping for a little while. I was excited about some area rugs I thought would go nicely in the house, so we bought them and left them in the trunk of the car. It was such a treat to have some free time together, and we had a good time poking around the shops in Indianapolis. Sammy is actually much better at shopping than I am. It's not on my list of favorite things to do, but I always have a great time with Sammy, no matter what we are doing. We ate dinner at the Bonefish Grill, one of our favorite restaurants, where they provide pens for you to doodle on their white paper tablecloths. The food was delicious, and Sammy drew a little heart and wrote "Sammy loves Dixie" inside it. It was going to be a great weekend.

The next morning, as we were getting ready for the speaking event in our hotel room, Sammy realized that he couldn't find the watertight briefcase in which he always locked up his Medal of Honor. The FBI had advised him that the safest place to keep the Medal of Honor when traveling was locked in the trunk of his car, so usually that's where we left the case. Occasionally, however, if Sammy was going to need something out of it, we took it to the hotel room with us. The briefcase had been a gift to Sam from the Pelican Company, which manufactures watertight equipment and technically advanced gear for law enforcement officers and the military, and it was our traveling safety deposit box. In addition to the medal, that is where Sammy kept his speeches, our personal papers, photographs, mementos, and anything we might need.

We headed out, but went back to the room just to check one more time. No briefcase. Concluding that we had left it in the trunk of our car, we walked to the hotel parking lot. Sammy opened the trunk, and our hearts sank. There was no Pelican briefcase, and Sammy's new Craftsman toolbox was gone as well. Two cases of harmonicas were missing, and my new rugs had vanished. We had been robbed! For a few seconds, we were both numb. It couldn't be; there had to be some mistake. Then reality hit and an overwhelming, creepy feeling engulfed both of us. There was such a sense of being violated and having our privacy invaded.

The magnitude of the loss then dawned on us. Tears filled Sammy's eyes. The Medal of Honor had been stolen on his watch, and he felt like he had let his brothers down. Sammy has always felt that the medal belonged to them and to America, not to him. Awarded for his service, it also represented the gift of life and the death he'd cheated. Now the most salient reminder of the entire Vietnam experience was gone.

Out loud he voiced the bewilderment he was feeling. "What would make somebody do something like that? How could they? Was it for drugs?" He hoped if they found out there was no money in the case, they would throw it in the Dumpster and somebody would find it. But mostly, Sam lamented that nothing would ever be the same without his original Medal of Honor, and he was filled with overwhelming grief and loss.

He grew very quiet; Sam internalizes his feelings when something hurts him, and I could see intense pain and emotion in his eyes. Then I watched his face get red, and I knew he was ready to explode. When he gets angry, his military training kicks in, and he is ready for fight or flight. He said at that moment if he had found the thieves, he would have cleaned their clocks. At the time, I was so angry that I was glad I wasn't face-to-face with the perpetrators, or I don't know what I would have done.

At the hotel office, we found out that several cars had been broken into. Sam figured the thieves had not taken time to open the briefcase, so at the time they probably didn't know his Medal of Honor was in it. It was a small consolation to know that we hadn't been singled out. The county sheriff was the first one on the scene. Sammy immediately called a friend, Detective Alan Jones, at the Indianapolis Police Department as well as FBI agent Tom Cottone, who was assigned to cases involving stolen Medals of Honor and their recipients. The investigation was underway.

When the authorities were finished questioning us and fingerprinting the car, Sammy still had a speaking engagement to fulfill. It wasn't going to be easy. We arrived late, so Sammy explained to the UAW members what had happened. A growing sense of outrage spread throughout the room. Many in the audience were veterans, and everyone was shocked that someone would steal Sam's Medal of Honor.

Throughout the day, Detective Ron Gray from the Indianapolis Police Department called periodically with updates; that sparked a little hope and helped assure us that the police were doing all they possibly could to track down Sammy's medal. Those calls were so appreciated. So much support and empathy came from the UAW workers; we felt like everybody circled the wagons around us, and it meant the world to both Sammy and me.

By the end of the day, nothing had turned up, and we were still in the dark on the whereabouts of the medal and our belongings. There was nothing we could do, so we drove back to Flat Rock and waited. We spent Saturday and Sunday on the phone with the media, the Indianapolis Police Department, the FBI, and our insurance company. The insurance company wanted details that we had never even considered, such as the value of Sam's speeches and the various autographs we had. Who would even think of that sort of thing? We were calling all over the country trying to figure out the answers to their questions.

On Sunday after the theft, we were sitting at home in our living room when the phone rang. We had been watching TV, and the news had reported torrential rains in Indianapolis that had left the White River, which runs through the city, swollen and raging.

Detective Gray had previously told us that he was following up with a person of interest named Bradley who had connections with a suspect they were looking for. We always have the speakerphone on when somebody calls, so when I heard Detective Gray's voice, I nodded to Sam to listen. Bradley had told Detective Gray that the briefcase had been thrown in the White River.

I felt a knot in my stomach, and I got up and started pacing back and forth as we talked. Sam fidgeted in his chair. Because a Pelican briefcase floats, it could have traveled downriver to the next county very quickly, but Detective Gray was trying to organize a dive team to search for it. While Sam continued to agonize about his Medal of Honor, with this call, our hopes of recovering the briefcase and its content were fading fast.

As we awaited word from Indianapolis, Sammy's mind was racing about the significance of the medal he'd worn for nearly forty years and those who were forever connected to it. The government could issue a new medal, but it would never carry the same history. He had taken that medal around the world with him to honor his fallen brothers. It had gone through the hands of Presidents Johnson, Reagan, and Bush, father and son.

Pope John Paul II and Mother Teresa had also held it in their hands. In 1993, Sammy had been privileged to have an audience at the Vatican. He was an advocate on behalf of prisoners of war and had been seeking information about reported live prisoners still left in Vietnam. At that time, Catholics were not allowed to openly practice their faith throughout Vietnam, and the Vatican invited Sammy for a visit so he and Pope John Paul II could share information.

On July 15, 1993, Sammy met Pope John Paul II, who he found open and friendly. Sam sat on a step below the papal chair. Holding Sammy's medal in his hand, His Holiness asked pointed questions about what had happened in Vietnam. As Sammy told his story, he looked up and saw a tear rolling down Pope John Paul II's face. The tear trickled off his cheek and pooled onto the face of the Minerva embossed in the Medal of Honor. That moment touched Sammy profoundly and will always be etched in his heart. What a strange coincidence that the Medal of Honor was stolen on July 15, 2005, exactly twelve years to the day after Sammy met with Pope John Paul II.

Rome was also where Sammy met Mother Teresa, who was invited for an audience with the pope as well. Sammy had been invited to go with Vatican members to the airport to pick her up. During the week, Sammy had three occasions to talk with Mother Teresa. A tiny woman, her hands were large, gnarled, and had the rough look of one who had been working out in the hay field, yet Sam said they were beautiful hands. During one of their conversations, she held Sammy's Medal of Honor and turned it over. Sammy was touched to tears when she lifted both hands and held his Medal of Honor to her heart. She had given Sammy a small, silver medallion that day. It was also in our missing briefcase.

Sammy's medal had been in the hands of celebrities like Clint Eastwood and the late blues guitarist, Stevie Ray Vaughn. The night in 1988 when Stevie Ray held the medal, he had invited Sammy up on stage to play harmonica with him on "Pride and Joy." Then there were the rapt faces of thousands of school kids over the years that were eager to hold this piece of history. Sammy also kept seeing the pain-filled eyes of wounded warriors who had clasped the medal. Thousands more veterans and many others had touched this sacred memorial to fallen soldiers with great reverence and respect.

Sammy had always encouraged people to hold the medal because he believed it helped them feel more connected to its true meaning and values. Each time someone held that medal the men who had died in Vietnam were remembered and honored. Each time it laid in someone's palm, Sam hoped the one holding it would have a keener understanding of service to his or her country and to each other. The Medal of Honor was about love and honoring all of those who had served, and it was as though the people who had touched Sam's medal throughout the years had endowed it with a soul of its own. None of that could ever be replaced, and it crushed Sammy's heart to even consider that his original Medal of Honor could be gone for good.

The missing harmonicas meant a lot to Sam as well. Fortunately, the original harmonica that Sam's mother had sent him in Vietnam wasn't in the stolen briefcase; it was already in the Medal of Honor Museum at Patriots Point in Mount Pleasant, South Carolina. A couple more that Sam's mother had given him, however, were in the case. Several others also carried great sentimental value because Sammy had played them on stage with many noted musicians and performers. They were also the ones he played each time he spoke of his experience in Vietnam. They were his personal tribute to Sergeant Dunlop, and now they were gone.

Sammy was heartbroken about the missing Medal of Honor, the harmonicas, and other irreplaceable items. Over one hundred of Sammy's original handwritten speeches were in the briefcase, some signed by the likes of Mother Teresa, General Westmoreland, Willie Nelson, Martha Raye, General Al Haig, Lee Greenwood, Donnie Van Zant, and others. They, too, were gone. I couldn't bear to see him in so much pain. During that weekend, we hugged each other a lot, held hands, prayed, and shed lots of tears while we waited for news.

As the hours passed I grew angrier; angry that someone would steal the Medal of Honor and our other belongings and angry for the anguish they were causing us. Dealing with insurance kept us busy, and in some way that was a blessing. Our greatest hope and encouragement came from the numerous calls from Detective Gray. He was like a junkyard dog, and he wasn't going to back down until he found Sammy's Medal of Honor. We wanted so much to believe that he would find it, but the raging White River made it seem like an impossible mission. Was there the vaguest possibility that the authorities could find Sam's briefcase with the medal under such adverse conditions? The waiting and not knowing was taking its toll on both of us.

We held our breath each time the phone rang, and sleep didn't come easy. Detective Gray had notified us that a dive operation for Sammy's briefcase was scheduled for Monday morning. The Amish clock in the living room chimed on the hour, and I think we heard every chime that Sunday night. All we could do was hold each other tight and pray for a miracle.

Sam and I wanted to be at the river for the dive operation, but for security reasons, we were not allowed to, so we waited it out at home. We are early risers, and that Monday morning was no different. But we were so tense that it was hard to focus on anything. Sometime around ten o'clock the phone rang. I answered and heard the emotional tone of Detective Gray's voice. "You are never going to believe this," he said. "I'm standing on the bridge holding Sam's briefcase. Sam's Medal of Honor was still in it."

I started shaking, and I screamed for Sam. "They found it! They found it!" God had answered our prayers, Ron's prayers, and the prayers of many others for a miracle.

Sam rushed to the phone, but he was having a hard time wrapping his mind around what I had just told him. How was it possible? He let out a deep breath of pure relief, and all he could say was "Happy, happy, happy." We were both just babbling away as Detective Gray was trying to give us details. When we hung up tears of happiness and relief flowed. We just kept hugging each other. How could we be so blessed? We were immensely grateful to the countless people who put in so much time, effort, and commitment to find the briefcase and Sammy's Medal of Honor.

Still reeling from the good news, we called family and friends, the FBI, the insurance company, and those who had supported us through this trial. As soon as word was out that the medal had been recovered, we started receiving calls from newspapers and TV stations requesting interviews. I don't think our feet touched the floor for a week.

On Thursday, July 21, 2005, Sam and I went back to Indianapolis on the steps of the Indianapolis War Memorial for a ceremony to return his medal. We thought just a few people would be there, the police would return the medal, and that would be all there was to it. We were both taken aback when we arrived to a crowd of about three hundred people, TV cameras, and journalists everywhere. Sam was amazed and humbled by how many friends, veterans, and people we didn't know who turned out for the event. Throughout the ordeal of the theft and investigation, we knew people cared, but every step of the way we were overwhelmed to see an ever-growing outpouring of love. That day we saw it once again.

A number of dignitaries made emotional speeches, and I blinked back tears as I watched the intent faces of a group of firefighters and policemen pass Sam's medal from one hand to the next before it was presented back to Sam. These were the people who had demonstrated such faith, commitment, and perseverance, and some had put their lives on the line in the effort to get Sam's medal back.

Detective Ron Gray's hands trembled as he placed the recovered medal around Sam's neck and told the crowd, "If I could give anything back to all of America and the people here, I wish you could have been on the bank when that briefcase came up."

Sammy wiped away tears. It was all he could do to hold himself together and not break down. Overwhelmed and humbled are words that are overused, but that's what we felt, and we were both about to break down at that point.

Gathering his resolve, Sammy said, "The reason I earned this medal on November 18, 1967, although it was in time of war, was because of love, because I loved my brothers, and because I did my job. The reason the medal is back around my neck is for the same reason, love."

When Sammy originally received his Medal of Honor, he felt deep sadness that his brothers from Cudgel were not there to receive it with him. That day it was different.

"I feel so fortunate this time that I can have my brothers and sisters with me who are responsible for me having this medal back around my neck," he added. "That's such an awesome feeling."

With his Medal of Honor safely back around his neck, Sammy thanked Mr. Turner, the director of Public Safety, and with a catch in his throat, he continued, "You get what you give. You all have given everything. I'll sweep your floors for you if you need it."

Neither Sam nor I were prepared for the heartwarming climax after the ceremony. Detective Ron Gray escorted us to a room inside the War Memorial. It was a private time with no audience and no media. In an emotional conversation, Ron had previously told me he'd salvaged several papers and photos from the briefcase, but he wanted to keep it a secret to surprise Sam. I just couldn't believe when he told me that he'd taken the contents of Sam's briefcase home with him, and he and his kids used tap water to carefully wash each piece separately. They were lying out to dry everywhere, draped over chairs, and he told me his house looked like a history museum. He said it made him so nervous to have all those things, and he wouldn't let them out of his sight, not even to put them in a safe.

Two long tables were covered with our belongings. There were photos, some of Sam and Peggy and some of Tim and me. Most special to me was our marriage license and a photo from Vermont with Sammy kneeling in front of me with the crystal egg containing my engagement ring. The first card I ever gave Sammy was there along with our passports, newspaper clippings, mementos, and numerous other papers. While there was some water damage, most of what we saw was in remarkable condition. Sam and I both broke down and cried, and then we laughed, and then we cried again. There were not enough words to express our gratitude to Ron and his kids.

Sadly, when the rocks were put in Sam's briefcase to weigh it down, Sam's original speeches with autographs had been destroyed. Also, we never found the little medallion from Mother Teresa. However, there was a small card in Italian with a picture of the Madonna and child that Mother Teresa had given Sam. So much would have been lost if it had not been for the efforts of our junkyard dog Ron Gray to salvage each piece. Then Ron gave Sam his dad's briefcase so he would have something to put all the items in.

From this incredible experience, Ron became not only a friend but a brother by choice and a member of our family. How do you thank someone for the kind of love he showed to us? We came to know his family, and they even helped to do concrete work when we later built our house. When Ron's dad passed away, Sammy was most honored to be asked to speak at his funeral.

I also learned that no matter what trouble comes into our lives, Sammy and I will always be there to support each other. In a 1985 article from *Ensign Magazine* entitled, "Courage Counts," President Thomas S. Monson of the Church of Jesus Christ of Latter Day Saints said, "To live greatly, we must develop the capacity to face trouble with courage, disappointment with cheerfulness, and triumph with humility."

This chapter in our lives that started out in such an agonizing way ended up as a story of faith, real miracles, and selfless love. We were so blessed.

However, it took nine years before we were to learn, as commentator Paul Harvey used to say, the rest of the story. Being involved in a stressful and heartbreaking situation—like we were when the medal was stolen—it is easy to have tunnel vision and view everything from your own perspective. Yet there was so much more.

In 2014, vivid and emotional details about the investigation that we weren't aware of were revealed in exclusive interviews with three individuals who played key roles in solving the crime and recovering Sam's medal. They were Detective Ron Gray of the Indianapolis Metropolitan Police Department and Captain Jerry Martin and Lieutenant Michael Scott, both of the Indianapolis Fire Department. Up until that time, we had not fully realized the extent of the dedication and tenacity of these three brave men. Indianapolis and America can be very proud of these public servants for the diligence and heart they displayed. What we discovered profoundly touched us.

Reliving the story through their eyes added a much broader dimension and made us believe even more in miracles. We are grateful beyond words for their selfless acts of love, courage, and sacrifice. These are individuals who exemplify many of the values that Sammy talks about when he shares his Vietnam experience. They went far beyond the call of duty, and they put others before themselves. They are patriots who understand that the Medal of Honor belongs to America. They understand that love requires sacrifice, and they don't give up.

From their narratives, Sammy and I got an even greater sense of how much the city of Indianapolis was pulling for us, just how much people cared about us, and how much they love our country. It has truly been heartwarming for Sammy and me to realize that their experiences further expanded the aura of love that has always been part of Sam's Medal of Honor story. It is only fitting that each of these men shares his account of events in his own words.

CHAPTER 16

Bad Boys

Detective Ron Gray, Indianapolis Metropolitan Police Department

Somewhere around 2003, I first met Sammy Davis at the Slippery Noodle, a blues venue in Indianapolis where he was playing the harmonica with a band called Big James. I was with my brother, James Gray, who is on the Indianapolis Metropolitan Police Department (IMPD) SWAT team. James had previously met Sammy at a SWAT function where Sammy was the speaker, and that night he introduced me to Sammy.

Sammy was at the next table, and he invited us to sit with his family. We talked for a couple of hours, and that was the first time I ever held the Medal of Honor. For me, holding the medal was a very serious and humbling thing; I could almost feel the electric charge and the respect that it was due. The feeling is not something you can put into words. To me, it was not about the medal, event, or person. It was much bigger than that. I kind of compared it to the feeling you get when you stand at the rim of the Grand Canyon the first time and can't breathe...there was a sense of awe, honor, and respect. Sammy and his late wife, Peggy Jo, treated us like family. Peggy Jo was like an incarnation of Sammy, so likable and loveable, and Sammy was the real deal, just humble and sincere.

On Friday evening, July 15, 2005, I was in my car on the way to Louisville when one of the officers from the Indianapolis Police Department called to tell me that Sammy's Medal of Honor had been stolen. My first question was whether it was stolen in Indianapolis. It was. Then I wondered if a detective was assigned to the case and if so, who?

Being an investigator, I worried about those things to make sure that initially as much as possible was being done. Those steps are what we normally take in these situations. The Medal of Honor was already taken, so now the question was could we recover it and possibly charge the persons involved.

Then there was the emotional side of knowing how heartsick Sammy must have felt and how the hopes of getting the medal returned diminished as the hours went by. Thieves had broken into several cars at the Indianapolis hotel where Sam and Dixie were staying and had taken Sammy's Pelican briefcase containing his Medal of Honor. I told the sergeant that I'd be back as soon as I could and would be available to help with the investigation.

Even though I knew what the Medal of Honor was, I don't think I really got the full significance of it until I became so connected with it. I thought I knew, but I found out I really didn't. At that time, it wouldn't have mattered if it was a Purple Heart or a Navy Cross or a watch given to Sammy by his father. I thought of my dad, a veteran from the Korean War, and some of the things that happened to him and some of the other military people I've been around during my career working as a police officer. I knew that certain mementos meant so much to them.

This one was really heartbreaking for Sammy. It represented all of his brothers in the battle that night in Vietnam and all who have served in the military in any capacity. Sammy has referred to the Medal of Honor as their medal, and he is just the caretaker. In Vietnam it was about love, sacrifice, and service to our country. I knew I had to do something to try to find it.

As an investigator, I get so used to doing stuff for people who really don't care; they just want you to do something for them. This was much different. Along with notifying the sergeant, I contacted the detective assigned to the case and volunteered to assist in any way I could.

When I got back to Indianapolis about ten o'clock that night, I started pulling police reports to get an idea of what was going on. There was not a lot of information on the case yet, maybe a person seen in the area was about all.

Nobody had heard anything yet about Sam's missing briefcase with the Medal of Honor in it. One thing I knew—if a burglar or thief ever sees something extremely identifiable, they'll get rid of it right away. So I found out which hotel the thefts had taken place and headed out there.

A witness had seen one guy with a lot of tattoos near Sammy and Dixie's car. The description matched that of an individual who was staying at the hotel the night of the thefts. That man's room had been searched by police and cleaned by the hotel personnel, but I wanted to look at it anyway. I noticed a mirror was loose from the wall, and when I looked behind it, a kid's knapsack fell out. It was one of the missing items from the vehicle thefts. More and more it appeared that the person who had stayed in that room was my suspect. I now felt I had enough to at least interview and possibly obtain a search warrant if I located the suspect.

When I checked reports at the communication center, I also ran off several computer-aided dispatches of each run. Sometimes those hold information that is not in the reports. They did. I found information that associated the suspect with a kid named Bradley, and I stuck that away in my mental file cabinet just in case. Bradley dealt marijuana and also did other drugs.

Several officers and I began a search of the hotel and immediate area for any stolen items out of the vehicles and any other evidence that might be there. Our search included every outside trash can, and I climbed into a Dumpster while a lieutenant assisted me as I combed through everything in it. It was a hot, sultry July night, and it wasn't the most pleasant place to be, but it had to be done. My biggest fear was that the trash would all be thrown away, and we would never recover the medal, so we had to secure the area first. By that time, between what they saw on the media and by word of mouth about the theft, twenty or more officers had called in wanting to help and asked what they should do. The department referred them to me.

I gave them a description of the alleged suspect's truck and told them to start driving around and especially to check the motels. The guy we were looking for was on parole for dealing in cocaine, so he would have to find a place to stay where he thought we wouldn't be looking for him.

I went back to the communication center and followed up on things, organized what I had, and rechecked the reports like I normally do in an investigation. By the time I finished, it was probably six or seven o'clock on Saturday morning of July 16. I had been up twenty-four hours with about three hours sleep the previous night because I had been called out. I talked to a couple of the guys, and we had nothing, so I said I'd hit a few of the motels on the way home. I knew the odds of finding something as identifiable as the Medal of Honor was slim. Because of its uniqueness, it couldn't really be sold. So many people were saying we were on an impossible mission, but as worn out as I was, I was even more focused on the case. Somehow I seem to function better when challenged by people who don't believe our efforts could succeed.

As I drove by Beech Grove, just south of Indianapolis, I saw a Motel Six. When I pulled in, low and behold, there was the truck I was looking for. I couldn't believe it. I called in a couple of Beech Grove policemen and told them what items were taken from the cars that had been broken into. We were going to try to locate the suspect and with some luck maybe recover some items taken from the cars. We also had to obtain consent to search from the occupant of the room. Otherwise we would have to get a search warrant.

We found out which room the suspect was in, and the officers and I went to the door. A guy covered in tattoos opened it and was trying to play real cool. I recognized the individual as the suspect from a mug shot I had. I asked if he minded if I searched his room, and he said no. So I got the consent to search, and I found four or five little items like a paperweight and other things that were on the stolen items list. Then I knew I had a couple of theft charges on him. I placed him in cuffs and took him back to the Beech Grove police station to conduct a formal interview. After a few hours I told him my main concern was to get the medal back.

He said he didn't know what I was talking about, but he finally saw I was being pretty persistent, and I wasn't going to give up, so he said, "Why don't you go ask Bradley?"

I knew that name sounded familiar, so I was thinking and thinking, and I went back outside and flipped through my notes. I saw a Bradley who had been arrested two weeks before. Son of a buck! That was it!

I called a couple more officers, and immediately ten or fifteen more volunteered to try to find this Bradley guy. By then it was one or two in the afternoon, and I was running on nerves and sleep deprivation, but I couldn't quit. How many times had Sammy said, "You don't lose until you quit trying?"

I found out this Bradley kid was nineteen, and he had some minor charges, but nothing too serious. We got to his neighborhood, and I put on my raid vest.

I told the sergeant and eight other guys, "Here's the deal. I don't have a warrant to get in the house, but just play along with me and surround the house like we've got a warrant. I'm going to try to BS my way in, and I'm not going to kick the door down unless something bad happens."

The mom came to the door, and behind her I saw this nineteen-year-old kid with a bunch of tattoos who obviously lifted weights. I told her I was there for Bradley.

Bradley looked up at me, and I saw his head drop. I told him I wanted to have a talk with him, and we needed to go sit on the curb. I could tell when he dropped his head that it was almost like a form of submission; I thought it would be best to try a softer approach in the interview. I told the other officers that only two guys needed to stay with me. You never know if you are safe, but just reading the actions of Bradley, his mom and dad, and him being respectful, I did not want to disrespect his family with a bunch of uniforms in the yard for the neighbors to see.

We sat down, and I started explaining to him about the medal and what it meant. I was getting pretty weary by then, and I said to Bradley, "I'll be honest with you, kid, you know, I don't care anymore. The only thing that means anything to me is to get this guy's medal back to him. This means so much to him, and if I have to kick your butt to do it, so be it. I promise if I can get the medal back you won't go to jail."

Bradley's dad was standing there by us and heard everything.

Bradley sighed and looked up. He said, "I met Sammy when I was in sixth grade."

My heart stopped. I didn't really know Sammy very well at that time, and I thought what have I gotten into? What is going on here? After that, Bradley told me that Sammy had come to his school to talk to them. Then the kid clammed up.

I looked up at Bradley's dad, and he looked at his boy. He said, "Son, I'm telling you now, this man is sincere. If he says you're not going to jail if you give up that medal, you're not going to jail. Now you tell him the truth."

Bradley raised his eyes up at me and said, "Sir, I'm not a sinner."

I told him, "Well, everybody is a sinner."

He said, "No, sir, I'm Catholic, and I don't steal."

In his world of faith, the whole thing about drugs was OK, but the stealing part wasn't.

Finally he opened up and began to talk about being in the hotel room when the suspect came back to the room. They had been partying in the room that evening, but witnesses only stated they had seen one tattooed man by Sammy's vehicle, and he didn't match Bradley's description.

Bradley said the suspect had several items with him when he returned, one of which was a hard, black, plastic briefcase. This individual began showing Bradley everything and placed it out on the floor. When the briefcase was opened and Bradley saw the medal, he knew it was Sammy's. Bradley recognized the paperwork and medal from when he had met Sammy at his school. Sammy would pass the medal around when he told the kids his stories at the schools. It would always come home. Sammy believes that through the years over a million kids may have touched the medal, and Bradley was one of them.

Bradley told the guy in the hotel room not to throw the medal away, that if the police ever figured out who took it and they didn't get it back, he and the suspect would be in major trouble.

Then Bradley told me that they threw the briefcase with the medal in it off the Harding Street Bridge over the White River. My heart stopped again. I just had a sick empty feeling, and I felt lost and deflated. I knew that Sammy would be devastated.

So I immediately took Bradley up to the bridge above the White River on the south side of Indianapolis. He pointed to a specific spot in the river and said that's where the suspect threw it. I said, "What do you mean there?"

He said, "Right there," and pointed to the same spot.

I asked how he knew, and he said he was in the car and saw it in the rear-view mirror when the suspect threw it over. I asked how he could see where it landed when he was a hundred feet in the air. I played along with him for a while, and I finally took him home and told him I'd get back to him later, adding that he'd *better* answer his phone.

He replied, "Yes, sir."

He did answer his phone, and we talked more about what happened. Bradley was truly sorry about the medal, and I could see that he really cared. He was worried about Sammy not being able to get his medal back. Bradley agreed to cooperate and said he would do whatever he could to help out.

I knew we had to get some divers down there, so I started making calls. The sergeant of the dive team wanted to meet the CI (confidential informant) Bradley to speak with him. I had promised Bradley that I would not reveal him to anyone, and not yet knowing for sure whether or not he was telling the truth, I wanted to make sure that I could keep that trust. I explained to the dive commander that I had interviewed him thoroughly and even tried to triangulate what Bradley had said about the location off of landmarks on shore and the bridge as best we could. I was hoping to at least get a small boat, and they could check the banks in the area in the event the briefcase got hung up in brush. The sergeant stated that he could not provide a boat until Tuesday. The Indianapolis Police dive team was busy at the time and could not offer to meet and check out the scene. I was very nervous that with the storms that were in the forecast, if I waited until Tuesday, the briefcase could be washed away.

Then I called Sammy and told him that we had an idea where the medal might be but not to get his hopes up. We were trying to line up a dive team to look for it in the river. As we kept in touch back and forth, some of those conversations were also conducted through an officer that knew Sammy.

By that time FBI Special Agent Tom Cottone was involved. Tom called me and said, "You don't understand, man. Do whatever it takes to get that medal back! This is a big deal."

Then it was starting to really hammer on me. I was thinking, *Son of a buck, what have I fallen into?* I understood that the medal was very important and special within itself. But working burglaries and robberies helps teach a person how a material thing that might not be worth much in monetary value can be priceless. Example: a piece of porcelain and some ashes. However, when it's an urn with your husband in it, and burglars take it, you are devastated. I was doing this for someone who had given so much to everyone, someone who continues to give even long after his initial actions. It's not just about love for humankind or your oath; this was my time to give back to a great person, and for me, personally, finding Sammy's medal would be one of the few accomplishments I could reward myself with that no one could take away.

I knew a Pelican briefcase would float, but there was a lot of stuff in that river. People threw all kinds of junk in there; there might even be cars for all I knew. That case was either going to be hung up on something or somebody would find it five miles downstream. With the heavy rains forecast for that night and the next day, the outlook wasn't good.

We had permission from the FBI and Southern District of Indiana US Attorney for a dive. I had spoken a lot to my brother, James, during this event, and he had helped search the motels throughout that first night. During efforts to find a dive team, my brother called a medic with the SWAT team who was instrumental in coordinating with my hero, Captain Jerry Martin, dive team commander of the Indianapolis Fire Department. Jerry said they would set up with a dive team at 9:00 a.m. on Monday morning.

On Monday, July 18, 2005, I took Bradley and my children and met my brother, James, Captain Martin, and a couple of other officers up on the bridge. For a while Bradley and my kids were off to the side where nobody would notice them. Later I brought Bradley over to point out where he thought the briefcase was.

As far as I know, even to this day, it was just the main suspect that actually took the briefcase. I was very quiet about Bradley; no one knew much about him. For the most part, this is the first time this part of the story has been told. Bradley kept insisting the briefcase was in that same spot. He even threw a rock in the water at the location where he said it was.

The torrential rains had come over the weekend, and the river current was swirling, the kind of current that moves rocks and objects. You couldn't see anything through the murky water, and there was a lot of area to cover. Logically thinking, I couldn't imagine there was any way we were going to find that briefcase with Sammy's Medal of Honor, but we all stood on that bridge and prayed together to find it.

Even knowing the slim odds, I was involved so deep that the only choice was to keep going forward. I did not want to live with the thought that we had not given everything we had. Everyone else involved in this was giving everything, and I had to give my all as well.

Sometimes in an event you end up with the best of the best for whatever reason. You don't know it at the time, but it just happens. I have to bring faith into it; you have to give God his due. When God slaps you in the back of the head to go forward, you just shut up and do it. He'll be there with you.

We watched diver Private Michael Scott from Fire Station 14 go down on his very first official dive. In just a short time, a fist shot up out of the water and the brief case was in his hand. It was like something out of the movies. I couldn't believe what I was seeing. Everyone on the bridge erupted into cheers.

In an investigation, I try to keep an open mind, separate my emotions, and keep moving toward the goal. But this was different. When I saw that case, I collapsed on the bridge and just sobbed.

There really aren't words to explain what I was feeling. It wasn't exactly relief, but it was extremely emotional. I think that is when I realized that it all had come together, and a burden had been lifted and given to someone else, kind of like my responsibility was over. I had done my part. It hit me way hard; maybe it was just God hitting the release valve for me.

What we didn't know was that holes had been drilled into the briefcase and rocks put in it for weight so it wouldn't float. Duct tape was wrapped around the case.

We took the duct tape from around the briefcase and water and mud started running out through the holes. When we opened it, the first thing I saw was a certificate, and the name Lyndon B. Johnson stood out from the muddy muck that covered the paper. I didn't know if it was Sammy's original Medal of Honor citation or a copy. The gravity of everything dawned on me one more time. We started going through things in the case, and there it was,

Sammy's Medal of Honor. I just kept thinking, *We've got it, we've got it. Thank God we've got it.*

Some investigations take months or years, but in a few days we'd had so many volunteers who came forward to help, we'd found the guy who broke into the cars, he'd led us to Bradley, Bradley had met Sammy and knew what the medal was, and he led us to it.

Even though Bradley was involved with the alleged suspect, without his help, I know Sammy would have never seen his medal again. The kid had never had too many positives in his life, and it was the boy's proudest moment when that brief case came up out of the water. God blessed us with a rookie diver on his first dive in dangerous currents, and against all odds, he had found the case with Sammy's medal. I couldn't believe how the pieces fit, and it was clear to me that someone much bigger than all of us had pulled this thing together. There is no doubt in my mind that God had heard our prayers. It was all pretty overwhelming.

Everything in the briefcase was nasty, so I submerged it in a bucket of water to preserve everything and keep it in the environment it was in. We retrieved the Medal of Honor, Sammy's Vietnam ring, and some other metal objects from the case.

I called Sammy and Dixie while I was still at the bridge. It was pretty hard to talk about it. I just told Sam that we got it; everything was a blur. I just remember us being silent on the phone for a while, immersed in the moment. Then he told me that he wanted me to hang on to his Medal of Honor for a few days until he could get over to Indianapolis to get it back. That was most likely the most scared I had been, me holding the medal for a few days. I could barely hold it in my hand without being nervous. Honestly I slept with the dang thing! I was so scared to lose it.

While still at the dive site, I got a call that I was to go to see Robert Turner, the director of Public Safety, at his office. When I got there, he started talking about this big ceremony they were going to have to return the medal, and he said I would be the one to present it to Sammy. At that time, I was literally numb. I knew it was a big deal for Sammy, but I still didn't quite realize how big a deal it was for everyone else. Just for the moment, in my exhausted emotional state, I really didn't care. We'd gotten the medal back, and all I wanted to do was be with my kids.

My sergeant told me to take the medal to a jeweler to have it cleaned up.

Looking back, it is amazing how the whole life circle thing comes around. Jerry Martin and I later figured out that we were actually in the academy training at the same time. The suspect who took the briefcase went to jail on theft charges.

Bradley made some positive improvements in his life and started to head down some great paths. He had gone back to school and really wanted to turn his life around. Sadly Bradley passed away a few years later. I received a call from his father and mother and was able to assist them with a friend that ran a funeral home. Jerry Martin and I went to Bradley's wake at his family's home.

At one point we had taken Bradley to meet some Navy SEALs, and Bradley's family had the Navy SEAL sniper hat that Master Chief Jay Manty had given Bradley sitting next to a picture of Sammy, Bradley, and me at a Vietnam veterans reunion. His mother said that being involved with the Medal of Honor and the positive things that came out of it were the best thing that ever happened to Bradley and to them as a family. Sammy and Dixie were out of town but called and spoke with Bradley's parents. Jerry made Bradley an honorary fireman dive team member and gave his mother the insignia pin.

We have all enjoyed a great bond together. Sammy and Dixie have invited me and my family to be part of their family. Everyone involved has become one as it should be. Life is pretty complex because we make it that way, but really life is about having a good heart and surrounding yourself with solid friends. They don't have to be innocent, perfect, or good-looking (unless they are firemen or Navy SEALs), but they have to have a heart…and as Sammy says, "You don't lose until you quit trying!"

CHAPTER 17

Bridge Over Troubled Waters

Captain Jerry Martin, Dive Team Commander, Indianapolis Fire Department

About three days prior to receiving the phone call to assist with the search for the Medal of Honor in July 2005, I had been home watching the news. I think every Hoosier in the state of Indiana knows who Sammy Davis is, so seeing Sammy on the news so emotional about the theft of his Medal of Honor about brought me to my knees. I couldn't believe someone would actually steal a Medal of Honor. I remember feeling so horrible about it because I served in the Marine Corps from 1983 to 1987. I knew exactly what Sammy was referring to that the medal was for the guys that died over in Vietnam.

As I watched the news reports about somebody breaking into Sammy and Dixie's vehicle, I also kept thinking, *Why Indianapolis of all places for this thing to be stolen?* It was heart-wrenching to me. My emotions were high.

Two days later I was sitting in an Italian restaurant with my family when my cell phone rang. It was Detective Ron Gray from the Indianapolis Police Department.

I didn't know Ron, but he said, "Hey, I need your men, your dive team, and I need you to command this operation to find the Medal of Honor. We think we know where it is in the White River."

I couldn't believe he wanted us involved, but I said, "Buddy, we will be there in the morning! Just tell me when and where." The dive team was to be at the Harding Street Bridge at 9:00 a.m. Monday, July 18.

I couldn't even concentrate on my dinner, and I couldn't sleep that night knowing we were going to look for Sammy's medal. I remember feeling what an important part of history this was, and our dive team would be part of that. I kept thinking that Washington, D.C. would probably be paying attention to us, the whole city, the mayor's office, and maybe even the FBI were going to be down there. I didn't know for sure. I had been told there were even some Navy SEALs who had volunteered to come down if we weren't able to find it. This was a huge deal, and the pressure was really on.

With less than two hours sleep, I remember so clearly putting on my uniform, sliding into my boots that morning, and then meeting Sergeant Gray down on the White River at the bridge.

I had checked with my superiors, and they were all double thumbs-up, telling me, "You go do this, Jerry; just do the best you can."

We have two dive teams, one at Station 7 downtown and one on the north side at Station 14. I selected the team at Station 14, and those guys loaded the tactical vehicles, all the dive gear, and they met us at the bridge. I don't know why I remember these details, but it was such a beautiful day, about seventy-five degrees and sunny.

Up on the bridge, Ron and I talked, and I made an unusual request. He had mentioned that there was a person of interest who said he knew where, from the bridge, the briefcase had been dropped.

I asked Ron if he could go get him and bring him to the bridge because I wanted him to throw rocks in the water to show us exactly where he thought that case was. Ron left and pretty soon he was back with this guy named Bradley.

I asked our guys not to look at Bradley to kind of give him some privacy, and Bradley threw rocks in the water to pinpoint the spot. We put a buoy in to mark it.

I went down to meet with the members of Station 14 dive team. My primary diver was Private Michael Scott. He was a rookie diver, and this would be his first official dive. A lot of people asked me why I would put a rookie diver into a swollen river, in a dangerous situation, especially for this valued piece of American history.

The reason I did that is because I wanted the more experienced diver, Don Brunson, a twenty-year diver, to be ready to jump in if Michael ran up against entanglement issues or something.

All of the divers were really honored to be part of this operation. Everybody knew the significance of the Medal of Honor and about the fallen men it represented. It was stolen in our city, which gave us a black eye, and everyone was just passionate about trying to find it. I wish you could have seen the looks on the faces of the divers. To a man, they all said they would stay all day at the swollen White River until they found it. These firefighters said, "Let's do it." You've got to understand type A personalities; they will get in there and do the job whether it's rushing into burning buildings or diving in a swollen river. They don't quit.

So I went back up on the bridge, and my heart was beating out of my chest. I was thinking there were so many things that could go wrong, but I knew it was the right thing to do. I also knew I was putting Michael in harm's way, but I'd seen his skill in dive school, and I felt confident he could do it.

There were some who told us that we would never find that medal in the river. With obstacles like huge rocks, tires, and everything that had been thrown in the water over the years, it really was going to be like looking for a needle in a haystack. With the added hazard of a rapid current and zero visibility, we knew the odds were pretty much stacked against us.

If you can think about being put in a room completely blindfolded, trying to find this briefcase in twelve feet of debris while fighting the current, that's what Michael was going to be up against.

Just before the operation started, Ron said a prayer asking for safety for the divers and to be able to find the medal. Looking back on everything, I've always felt like there was divine intervention in all of this; it was just an amazing feat.

Tensions mounted as Michael Scott dropped in the water. I would say that in less than fifteen minutes he radioed back that he had found the case. I'll tell you what; it had to be the happiest day of my life. I just remember jumping for joy and the tears were flowing. Ron was crying, people were cheering, and the divers were jumping up and high-fiving one another. It was like a big victory celebration.

We went underneath the bridge and popped open the case. The Medal of Honor was there. We'd found it! Everybody was just in awe at that moment. Ron let a few of us hold it, and just holding that thing, I'm not trying to be overdramatic, but it is a piece of American history. That's what I felt I was holding. I reverted back to seeing Sammy so emotional on the news.

Here was this guy who went to the extreme above and beyond the call of duty, not only to save three men while under enemy fire, but to swim across the river twice when he was already wounded himself. I was holding the medal that represented all of that, and I just can't tell you what was going through my mind. It was just one of the greatest achievements of my life to know that we were part of being able to get that medal back to Sammy.

It was also one of the finest moments for the fire department dive team. In addition, it was a great shot in the arm for them because we'd had two divers drown, one in 2000 and one in 2002, while on training missions. Finding the medal was a great morale booster for the guys, and the city rallied around us. The divers just did a wonderful, wonderful job, and Michael Scott really knocked it out of the park.

But not one of those divers would have said no. I mean, it was next man up if Michael hadn't found it. It would have been the next guy and the next guy; we would have kept rotating divers. We were just that determined to find the medal. What a great day for Sammy, for the fire department, the police department and Ron Gray's spectacular detective work, and what a great day for Indianapolis.

The things I think about when I look back on that day are first and foremost getting the medal back to Sammy, but it also forged a great friendship with Detective Ron Gray and me. We are still in touch today. I could call on him for anything, and he would be there to help. He knows it's the same with me. Also, Michael Scott and I have become very close, and I'm grateful for those friendships.

I was privileged to have lunch with Ron and Sammy one day, and Sammy spoke at my son's school, Saint Theresa. Sammy called my son out in front of the whole school in the gym and told him that his dad helped to find his stolen Medal of Honor. What a day that was for my son! On two occasions, I've gone to hear Sammy speak, and I hope to hear him again because his account of his actions that night in Vietnam is such a powerful story.

CHAPTER 18

When You Believe

LIEUTENANT MICHAEL SCOTT, INDIANAPOLIS FIRE DEPARTMENT

In July 2005, I was a private at Fire Station 14, the Northside Water and Rope Rescue Station, when Captain Don Brunson took a call. We heard him say, "Absolutely, we're packing up now."

Sammy Davis went to school in Indiana, and he's very popular in Indianapolis. Everybody had heard the news about his Medal of Honor being stolen. It was a really big deal, people hurt with Sammy about it, and we all were keeping up with the story. The captain told us they thought the medal was at the bottom of the White River, and we were going down to try to find it. I'm sure he knew about it before that call, but it was the first I had heard about our dive team involvement. I think we were all blown away to be asked to dive for it because we knew how significant the Medal of Honor was.

There were ten firefighters working that day, and all of them are on the dive team with different roles to play. Three certified divers are required to be on shift each day at each dive house. Fortunately we're not utilized a lot, and I say fortunately because that means there are not a lot of occasions where we've been called in to rescue people from the river. Our team mostly deals with life safety. Each dive team member has a function. Two are in charge of equipment, two men man the boat, and there are two line tenders, one witness interviewer, and three certified divers.

During a dive there is the primary diver, a backup who is ready at an instant to relieve the diver if there is a problem, and a third diver who is also ready to come to the rescue if needed.

I was thirty at the time, and I had not made an official dive with the department after completing dive school.

That day Captain Brunson said to me, "Hey, it's your time."

I'm sure Captain Brunson and our dive commander, Captain Jerry Martin, had discussed this before I was told that I had been selected. I was going to be the one to go down as the primary diver, but all the guys were as much a part of it as I was. Knowing that I was going to be looking for Sammy's medal was pretty overwhelming. I really wanted to find it.

The White River is probably a hundred feet below the Harding Bridge and maybe 150 yards across. On the best day, everybody who dives knows there is a risk, especially under a bridge that size. You might find bikes, rebar, concrete, fishing line, and who knows what else that has been thrown off the bridge. Visibility is never good in the White River unless it's in very shallow water, and this area was maybe eight feet deep. We'd just had huge rains a couple of days before. On the morning of the dive, currents were rushing, and visibility was down to zero in the swirling, muddy water. There were dangers involved, and if I was going to find anything, it would have to be by feeling my way, not by seeing it.

Detective Ron Gray of the Indianapolis Police and Captain Jerry Martin, dive commander with the Indianapolis Fire Department, had done a spectacular job. Without their work, we probably never would have found the briefcase with Sammy's medal. They brought the guy to the bridge who knew where the case had been thrown, and I think he threw a rock in to show them the location.

We knew it was killing Ron. He wanted the medal back so badly for Sammy. We knew the pain Sammy was going through, and all of Indianapolis was mourning for him. It was also a black spot on our city that it had happened here.

I just hoped and prayed that we'd find it. Yet in the back of my mind I knew this was going to be tough. In reality, it was unlikely that we could locate that briefcase. As I got ready to dive, there was a lot going on at the bridge and in the area, but our job is to go where we're told to go. I was focused on what I was about to do and wasn't really aware of too much else that was happening above me.

The water was murky when I went under, and I couldn't see a thing. I just started feeling around for anything like a case. I don't remember if it was seven minutes or twelve minutes that I was in the water, but what always replays in my mind is the moment I felt this square object. I felt along the side, and there was the handle. I couldn't believe it. I just knew I had found Sammy's briefcase.

We have communication equipment in our dive masks that transmits to the guy in the boat. I said to Dennis Ford, who was in the boat, "You are not going to believe this. I've got the case."

He came back with, "No, you don't."

I told him, "I'm coming up."

That's when I lifted the case up out of the water. I remember Dennis letting out a loud "Whoohoo!" The smile on his face when I got to the boat and handed over the case is a picture I will never forget. It was like time stood still. I just couldn't believe it. It was just remarkable; there aren't really words to describe it.

I got the credit, and the feeling of being able to help was great, but there were so many people involved. I was just the guy who got in the water, and it was hard to take credit for it. It was such a huge honor for our fire department and our city to be part of retrieving the Medal of Honor.

It was at the ceremony to return his medal on the steps of the War Memorial that I first met Sammy. He is the nicest, most sincere person, and his heartfelt thank you really brought home to everyone what that Medal of Honor meant to him.

About six months later my wife and I got to attend an event where Sammy told his story, and it was such a huge honor to talk with him and Dixie. I got to hold Sammy's Medal of Honor. When I think of the history behind it and what it stands for, and the people who have held it before me, even Mother Teresa, the whole experience was just so overwhelming to me.

I will always have the photo that was taken that day on the riverbank, and I treasure another picture in which Sammy was talking to my son, Andrew, who was just a little guy then. The pictures hang at the top of the steps going upstairs where we see them every day.

We also have a singing Christmas card that Sammy and Dixie sent us along with a thank-you note. It was so neat to get that from them.

My life has been changed knowing that I was a part of that experience and that our city, our firemen, and others here are forever linked to the Medal of Honor and to a true American hero. If there is anybody to look up to, Sammy Davis is the one. I so often think about everything that happened that day.

CHAPTER 19

Holding Out for a Hero

After Sam's Medal of Honor was returned in July 2005, it seemed like every minute was jam-packed. There were still speaking events in August, and we traveled back up north twice to see my mother.

I was also trying to put together a wedding that would take place six hundred miles from home; the singers, the songs, the wedding party, the cake, gifts for everyone, and so many more details. With six children, three of whom were in school, my son, Tony, couldn't be there to walk me down the aisle. Of course, it made me sad, but we were the ones who chose the September date for our wedding, so that was something I had to accept. That also meant I had to find a stand-in for Tony.

Among the lengthy list of unknowns, we had no idea how many guests would be at the wedding. It would be open to everyone attending Freedom Fest. I kept worrying I'd forget something. But I just had to have faith it would all work out. By September I was ready to let pomp and circumstance, organized details, and anything serious fly out the window. After the stress of the summer, our wedding was a release for both Sam and me.

We had chosen Freedom Fest 2005, in Skidmore, Missouri, as the place where we would share our marriage vows with family and friends. This would be the eighteenth year the little town of fewer than three hundred people had hosted this patriotic festival to salute veterans and honor those who had sacrificed for our freedom. It was a place of celebration, and that's what we wanted our wedding to be; a great celebration of our love.

Sam had his own way of de-stressing. When we roared into the Freedom Fest parking lot, the car windows were rolled down and the sunroof was open.

"Holding Out for a Hero" by Bonnie Tyler was blaring as loud as the volume would go from our tape player. Sam was ready to celebrate, but I have to admit, I was a bit embarrassed at his grand entrance.

Across the grounds, the chant of a tongue-tangled auctioneer filled the air as he raised the stakes at the homemade pie auction. A band checking sound equipment on the stage cringed at the earsplitting squeal of a malfunctioning microphone. With that problem fixed, guitar licks from "Sweet Home Alabama" blared through every backyard in Skidmore. Once again, we found ourselves among many friends in a festive atmosphere. This was the perfect backdrop for our wedding.

For us, this was a very special place. Just the year before, we had met each other again on those very grounds for the first time in years. Skidmore was also where I'd realized that I really liked Sam, and that maybe there could be a future for us. It was where I knew for sure that I had reached a place where, after losing my husband to cancer, I was ready to find joy in my life again.

I had recently read an *AARP* magazine article in which Maria Shriver said, "You have to be willing to let go of the life you had all planned out in order to make the life you are meant to lead." Back in 2004, I had come to realize it was OK to let go of the life I had planned, because something new and beautiful was about to unfold.

When our special day arrived on September 10, 2005, I was so excited and rattled that I didn't know what the heck was going on in Skidmore. During the ceremony, the preacher could have been reading from *Moby Dick* for all I knew. At the Freedom Fest grounds, our longtime friends Colonel Earl Hopper and Patty kindly opened their motor home to us. We especially appreciated it because it was the only cool place on the grounds. Sam said all the songs sung on stage that weekend seemed to have special meaning; he thought it was probably because his heart was so full of love. The best part of all was getting to share our happiness with others.

What I remember most was the laughter and so many people hugging us. They truly seemed happy for us. There were many dear friends, and we tried to make time to speak to each one. Marrying Sammy Lee Davis before family and friends made me the happiest woman in the world. Of course, Sam and I were already legally married, but this ceremony meant so much to us.

I was so glad when my sister, Roxie, Sherry, and my nephew Brett Farnsworth and his girlfriend arrived. After warm greetings, I had to hear all about "Who-in-the-world-gets-married in-Skidmore," a place just about further from home than the moon and back. They assured me they had seen nothing but hours and hours of cornfields on the long drive, but it was worth it to see Sam and me so happy. It was also a joy to see my other nephew Brandon Farnsworth and his wife, Kara, from Illinois.

I have to admit that the attire specifications for my bridesmaids had been willy-nilly at best. First it was a dark blue dress, then jeans, then it was a denim skirt—maybe. Red, white, and blue were our colors, but the rest was kind of up for grabs. As one of my bridesmaids, Sherry was getting nervous about it, so when they stopped along their long journey at a little home-and-farm store, she decided that she'd better buy a denim skirt, just in case. Doesn't everybody get bridesmaid attire last minute at a home-and-farm store? It was late in the week until I even knew what I was wearing. Loosey-goosey is not my usual style; I pretty much like to have things in control with details all in tow, but that all seemed to fly out the window in Skidmore.

On Thursday night, people were coming in to set up campers. Because there weren't a lot of activities going on at that time, several folks gathered around where Sam and I sat at picnic tables and brought wedding gifts for us to open. There were original poems, plaques, mirrors, beautiful handmade afghans, and a gorgeous quilt. The presents kept coming, and we could see the love in the eyes of those who gave them. Our invitation had requested no gifts, but people put so much time, effort, and heart into the gifts they brought. Both Sam and I were very touched by their thoughtfulness and generosity.

That evening was also emotional; it was the first meeting between Sammy and his captain, Dennis Schaible, since Sam received the Medal of Honor in Washington. The captain had salvaged a piece of the Howitzer that Sammy fired at Firebase Cudgel. He had it sprayed gold and mounted on a tray as a gift to Sam. Captain Schaible also gave Sam a photo he took when President Johnson presented him with the Medal of Honor. It felt strange touching the actual piece of Sam's Howitzer. Now I like to look at it, as it seems to help connect me directly to Sam's past. But that night it was very disconcerting knowing that it was a piece that both saved Sam and injured him.

On Friday, close to five hundred school kids came out to the festival, visiting different booths to hear the veterans talk about their experiences. I never tire of watching Sammy interact with kids. As groups filed past his table, he allowed each of them to hold his Medal of Honor that was stolen and retrieved from the river in Indianapolis earlier that summer. I got a lump in my throat, and I was so thankful that they were holding Sam's original medal, not a replacement piece. The eyes of some kids grew big, and many of them touched the medal with such awe. Sam patiently answered their questions and made each one feel special. Those young people provided another memorable touch for our wedding weekend.

At noon on Friday, Roxie, the bridesmaids, and I perched on some bleachers on the grounds and tried to figure out the wedding details. The silliest things would send us into fits of laughter, and we weren't making too much headway. Some guy was sitting off to the side, and out of the corner of my eye, I could almost see the wheels turning in his head. He was probably thinking that this wedding going to be some kind of a mess. Or maybe he thought we were soused.

Michael J. Martin was to perform, and right after his last song, the wedding would follow. The ladies asked how they were to arrange themselves on the portable outdoor stage. I had no idea, so I instructed them to line up in a V like a flock of geese. Every now and then somebody throws that line at me, and I will probably never live it down.

As we talked through different plans, I realized we had no music for Sam and me to exit the stage after the ceremony. Because we were at a festival, there were activities going on all over the grounds with various performers on stage at different times. Right then, this guy who played a really hot harmonica walked off stage in the distance, and one of the girls quipped, "Hey, go get that guy to play for you."

We didn't know who he was, but it sounded like a good idea to me. He turned out to be Phil Duncan, a harmonica master known the world over, who had written numerous harmonica instruction books. I'd actually been introduced to him the previous year when Sammy and I got together for the first time, but I guess I was so goofy over Sam that I didn't remember.

After the wedding planning session on Friday afternoon, we spent some time strolling around the grounds, viewing different exhibits and chatting with folks. There were tents with soldiers from Desert Storm and Iraq, and we sure kidded Roxie about a Native American veteran dressed in buckskins who was trying to put the moves on her. Cowboys in chaps manned a covered wagon and kept a coffeepot simmering on the fire. One of the real highlights was a huge bald eagle named Miss Moose with a seven-foot wing span. She had been injured and could no longer fly, and her handler from a rescue organization brought her to the festival every year.

The morning of the wedding, I suddenly remembered I had no flowers to carry. Boy, I was really losing it! I grabbed Rox and Sherry, and we hightailed it to the Super Walmart in nearby Maryville. I kept looking in the flower cooler but couldn't find anything that would match my outfit. Then I looked up and saw a woman standing near the cooler holding a beautiful bouquet of white roses tipped in red.

They were perfect, and I was on a mission; with my biggest smile, I quietly walked up to her and put my hands around the roses she was holding. "This is the color I really need," I told her.

I could see the embarrassment on Roxie's face as she turned to walk away. Sherry rolled her eyes and blurted out, "She's getting married tonight." We didn't know that woman or anything about her, and I think Sherry had visions of a catfight starting right there in the Walmart flower section.

Instead, the woman was very sweet and insisted that I take the roses. We started talking colors and discovered we were both interior decorators. With a sigh of relief, and a lot of laughs, we were on our way with the flowers. And I did invite her to the wedding.

While the girls and I were in town, Sammy had a great reunion with several of the guys who had fought at Firebase Cudgel, many of whom he hadn't seen since that night. Sam said they talked about Vietnam in general, but they didn't linger on the battle. Mostly their conversations centered on kids and grandkids, their lives since Vietnam, and how great it was to be as old as they were. None of them could believe they had lived so long. They wanted to focus on life, not death. Sammy and I both felt such a sense of gratitude that these men had wanted to come celebrate our wedding.

After we returned from town, we visited with several folks on the grounds, including Adrian Cronauer, the air force deejay portrayed by Robin Williams in the movie *Good Morning, Vietnam.*

As the afternoon moved on, I remembered we hadn't put streamers or bows on the flowers I would carry. They were in the fridge in a motor home, and I could just see myself trying to carry an unsecured bouquet, dropping a rose here and a rose there every step of the way.

I motioned to Sherry. "Quick, go to the car, yank some of the ribbons off the wedding packages, and do something with the flowers," I told her. She asked what kind of something she was supposed to do with them; she had flunked bow-making 101 a long time ago. But I knew she was crafty and would come up with an idea, so I could mark that off the list.

Dressing for a wedding in a small motor home with a bunch of women bumping into one another was a trip. We appreciated the use of Lyle and Jane Zoerb's camper, but with minimal lighting and no full-length mirror, it was like getting ready for the prom in a closet.

Finally it was time for the ceremony. My dear friend, Colonel Earl Hopper—or Colonel Dad, to me—escorted me in his motorized wheelchair down the makeshift aisle carrying a shotgun across his lap. How I wished my dad had been there to escort me, but Colonel Dad was a wonderful stand-in. I really loved him. Everybody hooted and hollered as we made our entrance. My nephews, Brett and Brandon, met us at the steps to escort me up on stage.

As a side note, an unusual and unexpected guest showed up to crash the party. A little black and white goat followed a young woman around through the crowd, kind of like "Mary had a little lamb." Mostly he stayed closed to her, but as he got more comfortable, the little fellow roamed freely through the grounds. Whenever he got tired, he'd just plop down to rest next to some-body. It was the cutest thing I've ever seen, and I'm so glad he was a guest at our wedding.

I had finally settled on wearing a straight, white skirt and blouse, covered with a red-fringed lace poncho. For something old, I borrowed blue crystal beads that had belonged to Sherry's mom. I also borrowed my niece Kara Farnsworth's clear acrylic Cinderella heels, the ones that flashed neon colored lights when I walked. Of course, not being used to walking in four-inch heels on dirt, it was actually more of a light and wobble, light and wobble deal. I asked Sam to grab my flip-flops and bring them up on stage because I knew I couldn't stand long in those heels. In true princely fashion, he carefully removed the heels and lovingly slipped the flip flops on my feet. He looked so handsome in his red, white, and blue shirt and jeans.

Kara sang "Love Will Build a Bridge," and our friend Carolyn Zsoltos sang my song for Sammy, "Holding Out for a Hero." The poor thing swallowed a big moth while she was singing, but she never missed a note. Michael J. Martin added his self-penned tune "Do Believe That It's Love."

Then it was time for the traditional vows. When Reverend John Steer, the Vietnam veteran who conducted the ceremony, came to the "obey" part, I kept balking at saying the word. He'd say it again, and I'd balk at it. The crowd burst into gales of laughter. Come to think of it, I'm not sure I ever really did say the "obey" part.

All the lighthearted moments made my heart sing. Then it was time for Sam and me to talk about Peggy and Tim. I could see guests out in the field wiping their eyes with handkerchiefs; many of them had known both Peggy and Tim. Yet, somehow, Sam and I both felt like Tim and Peggy were celebrating with us. Both of them were a natural part of our everyday conversations, so it was important for us to talk about them on our special day as well.

Reverend Steer had known both Peggy and Tim as well. "Do you take Peggy to be your wife?" he asked Sam during the ceremony. When he realized what he'd just said, he was horrified. But it was a slipup anyone could have made, and we moved on with the ceremony. I assured John it wasn't a big deal; in fact, I considered it an honor.

Sam and I had written our own vows to each other, and my heart was bursting as he recited these beautiful words to me:

It is our time, Dixie. Everything we have learned in our lives will make us appreciate each other. Our life together will be so wonderful and full of tremendous joy. I love you more than I ever thought possible. And when people see us walking down the street or dancing in the aisle of Walmart, they will say "aren't they cute." It will be a blessing and it will give people hope—as it has given us.

I remember you saying, "I want a special love between a man and a woman again." You said, "I want that special man to sit on the porch with, rocking and holding hands at eighty kind of love. I want to laugh with him until I can't get my breath, I want to go on adventures together and see things through each other's eyes and I want to be there through thick and thin." I love you, Dixie Marie, and I want to be that man in your life.

Loving you is the easiest thing I have ever done.

People who were at an angle where they could see Sammy as he recited his vows later told me they'd never seen so much love on any man's face. That touched me so much.

In turn I recited my vows to him:

I love you so much Sammy. I want to hold you tight forever. I can't believe we have made it to this point. It just seems like we have been in this process for years. Maybe we have. Anyway it is our time now. I love you with all my heart and soul. You are the joy of my life. Everything that has happened to me has led me to this point and to you. Finally, I hope to put to good use all of the lessons that I have learned in my life and be able to improve with each new day. I want to make you happy. I want to make you laugh. I want to make you cry good tears, tears of joy. More than anything, I want you to be content. I want to be able to hold you when you have nightmares and make you feel safe. I want you to know deep down in your heart that you are not alone. I want to rock with you on the porch when we get old. Sammy Lee, you have made my heart so full it is overflowing.

At that moment, I felt pure joy, and I didn't think I could ever be happier.

Things couldn't stay serious for long, though. For our grand wedding finale, a huge grasshopper jumped on Sam's rear and then leaped up and hit me in the eye. In spite of the jumping bug, the moth that Carolyn swallowed, the preacher's bumbled words, and the less-than-perfect bow on the flowers, it couldn't have been a more beautiful wedding. It was the best celebration of our love that we could have imagined. And Phil Duncan did play harmonica for us as we exited the stage.

To the world, I was now officially Mrs. Sammy Davis. Later that month I was to attend my first Medal of Honor convention as a Medal of Honor wife.

CHAPTER 20

We Are Family

Shortly after our Skidmore wedding, I prepared for the Congressional Medal of Honor Society annual convention in Phoenix, Arizona. Although this was my very first convention, I'd already attended an official Medal of Honor function and met some recipients and their wives a few months earlier in March 2005, when Sammy and I attended the annual Medal of Honor Foundation fund-raiser at the New York Stock Exchange. I reflected on that amazing experience as I looked forward to the convention.

The foundation is the Society's fund-raising arm that supports recipients and society events, educates the public about the meaning of the Medal of Honor, perpetuates the medal's legacy, and generally promotes the values of courage, sacrifice, selfless service, and patriotism.

While Sammy's speaking engagements were often of a serious nature, the fund-raiser was much more of a social event, and I was thrilled to be going to New York and meeting other Medal of Honor recipients and their wives.

That new experience was a defining moment in my life, a new role for me as a Medal of Honor wife. There was no template, and it was something impossible for me to rehearse. When we got married, Sam had told me that as his wife I would become a part of American history, and that scared me to pieces. Women like Martha Washington were part of history, not me.

I hadn't imagined that I would one day travel to support my husband as he carries his message of love and service, or that I would belong to a family of the most valiant American heroes and their wives. Even today, I feel blessed with such a rare privilege and charge, and it still feels surreal at times.

This is a feeling Sammy, himself, knows all too well. Ahead of the trip to New York, I thought of Sam's first Medal of Honor event at President Nixon's inauguration in January 1969. Nobody had told Sam and Peggy what to expect, they weren't given a dress code, and they didn't know a soul; they were really on their own. Attending a presidential inauguration in Washington, DC was heady enough for a couple of country kids, and the Medal of Honor events they were to attend stepped it all up a notch. Sammy had received their airline tickets in the mail, and the hotel room was reserved for them. When they checked in, they were given a schedule of events.

The main Medal of Honor banquet was held at the lower level of their hotel. They took the elevator down, the doors opened, and they could see through large, arched doors into the banquet room. There at the first table sat America's great World War I and World War II heroes, Eddie Rickenbacker, Jimmy Doolittle, Pappy Boyington, and a couple of other recipients. At that time there were 350 Medal of Honor recipients; today there are fewer than eighty. Sam thought at least two hundred recipients were there that night.

Sammy froze in his tracks. He just couldn't make himself walk through those doors; he didn't feel worthy of going into that room. It was a room for heroes, not a young veteran from Flat Rock, Illinois. He smoked five Lucky Strikes right there by the elevator; his feet felt like they were glued to the floor.

That's when he saw Pappy Boyington elbowing Jimmy Doolittle and pointing to him and Peggy. The men talked as long as it took Sam to smoke two more cigarettes, and then all three of them stood up and walked toward the elevator. Sam wanted to make a hasty getaway; he was a basket case. Pappy was a step or two ahead of the rest, and when he approached Sam, he stuck his hand out. In the coarse language he was known for, he said, "You must be the (expletive) new guy."

Jimmy Doolittle and Eddie Rickenbacker took Peggy Jo by the elbows and Pappy took Sam. They marched Sammy and Peggy into the banquet hall and sat them at their table. During the course of the evening, the other recipients came by and introduced themselves. Sammy and Peggy Jo were both totally awestruck.

Sammy will never forget the advice Jimmy Doolittle gave him after everyone welcomed them into their circle. "Son," he said, "You have to always remember, don't let the sound of your own motor drive you crazy."

Sam had just read Jimmy's book about flying the bombers over Japan, and he'd learned that the drone of the motors and the long time it took to get there had mentally affected a couple of the crew. At first, Sam thought that was what he was talking about, but as he gained more life experiences, he realized Jimmy was simply telling him not to get too big for his britches.

Not only was Sam in the company of heroes for the first time; that night he also tucked Jimmy Doolittle's advice into a mental file folder. Because Sam is so often honored at events, and we are blessed to spend time in some elegant places and to be surrounded by impressive people, we realize that Jimmy gave him sound words to live by. Remembering our roots helps to keep us grounded amid the accolades and the grand adventures we are privileged to experience.

Unlike Sammy and Peggy that night in 1969, I fortunately had my husband to prepare me a little bit about what to expect at the foundation event in New York. At the top of my list of questions was what to wear. Some things never change because Sam said Peggy was very concerned about her outfit for that first Medal of Honor banquet. I looked at photos of Peggy at the events to see what she had worn over the years. For the black-tie gala, I chose a floor-length, black skirt with a chiffon overlay and a jacket adorned with black and pearl beadwork. I thought my new strappy pumps with three-inch heels would be the height of fashion, but I had no idea yet how hard it is to stand all night at a cocktail party in skinny heels. My feet were screaming for house slippers. So the one tip I always pass on to the spouses of new recipients is to forget about high heels and wear comfortable shoes.

I was anxious to meet the other Medal of Honor wives, to hear their stories, and to get their advice about what to expect at the upcoming convention in September. I wondered if any of them had a similar story to ours. I was curious about the roles they played as Medal of Honor wives and if they were involved in special projects or interests. I was just in awe of being able to meet this group of special women.

At the same time, I knew that they all had known Peggy Jo when she accompanied Sammy to these events. She was a beautiful woman inside and out, and I didn't know how I would be received. I wanted to fit in, be myself, and hoped to be accepted for who I was. I also wondered about the other recipients. Were they like Sam?

Although I had a lot of trouble remembering names that weekend, the way everyone made me feel welcome warmed my heart.

Kathy Wetzel, who had just married her husband, Gary, invited us to have lunch with them, and Leo Thorsness's wife, Gaylee, invited me to sit next to her on one of the busses. She was very interested in how I met Sammy and made me feel like I belonged. I had already met Joan Kelley in Vermont, so we had common ground. Bob Ingram's wife, Doris, was so sweet and patted a chair next to her, inviting me to sit and talk. Dotti Lu Fox, Wesley Fox's wife, talked about their daughter named Dixie Lee. I told her I hadn't met many Dixies in my life, and we hit it off right away. I took the initiative to bring up Peggy Jo in some of the conversations so it was out in the open, and I think that helped to make us all feel comfortable.

I found out other Medal of Honor recipients came from all walks of life, but to a man, they were very humble. None of them felt they'd done anything extraordinary to earn the Medal of Honor. They were almost embarrassed about the recognition, and each one said he wore the medal for his brothers who lost their lives serving their country.

They all went out of their way to include me, and I was overwhelmed when one gave a speech and made a toast in remembrance of Peggy and to welcome me. It was a great feeling to be so accepted by these men and women and to feel part of the Medal of Honor family.

It was easy to make conversation with everyone. A few couples I met were in a second marriage and, like Sam and me, they had not been together for a great length of time. However, it seemed that Sammy and I were unique in the Medal of Honor Society in that I didn't hear of any other couple traveling together for speaking engagements to the extent that we do.

In New York City, I loved seeing the impressive skyscrapers, the clang and clatter of traffic, and the hustle and bustle on the streets; it was all so out of my realm. I was like a little kid in a candy store, taking in the sights, the people, and everything going on around me. Whoa, Toto, we're not in Texas anymore!

I had been to New York before, but never to an event of the caliber of the Medal of Honor Foundation's fund-raiser. On Thursday evening, we arrived in a special bus with other recipients and guests at the New York Stock Exchange building. After showing our IDs and passing through a metal detector, we were escorted to the boardroom. In the middle of the room sat the biggest wooden table I have ever seen, designed with a lot of high-tech features. I think you could have laid forty people across it. It's strange how certain things stay with you, but when I think of the New York Stock Exchange, that table is one of the first things that come to my mind. Hors d'oeuvres were served, and we each were presented with a gift to commemorate the event. It was a time to meet and greet many of the private donors who support the foundation. Everything was so new and exciting for me, and I was wide-eyed as a school girl making a new discovery.

Several recipients had been asked to ring the closing bell that marked the end of trading for the day, so we were escorted to the main floor of the Exchange where all of the action takes place. With monitor screens everywhere and people rushing here and there, it looked like total chaos. The chatter and din of voices punctuated the air at every turn. To me, it was mind-boggling to realize that much of the world's economy was orchestrated right there. When we entered the floor, the traders stopped what they were doing and started to applaud. The applause continued as we wove our way through the posts and monitors across the creaking wooden floor to the podium. We were told that the trading never comes to a standstill except when Medal of Honor recipients come through; that moved me to tears. I stood with four other wives as the men rang the automated bell. The big gavel that was once used is now just a prop. We were then whisked upstairs for photos, and I was thrilled to hold the gavel for one of the shots.

As a farm girl from Illinois, it was overwhelming to be at the stock market, rubbing elbows with some of the most prominent people in the financial world, and to be in the company of our nation's greatest heroes. Nobody I knew did things like that. How I wished my dad could have been there to experience it all with me. He would have loved it.

It was also a real treat to eat dinner at the famous Tribeca Grill. Richard Grasso, chairman of the board and CEO of the New York Stock Exchange from 1995 to 2003, and his family always host this dinner for the Medal of Honor recipients. We learned that much of the artwork there was done by actor Robert De Niro's father, an abstract expressionist painter and sculptor. Over the years Sammy had bumped into a number of celebrities at the Tribeca Grill, so we were on the lookout to see who might come in.

Amid all the celebrating, however, there were the somber reminders of the tragedy that unfolded in New York City on September 11, 2001. Our room was at the luxurious Millennium Hilton Hotel overlooking Ground Zero. Opening the drapes that evening, I looked down at the black pit where the twin towers had stood. The adjoining buildings were still being repaired, and the location was full of trucks, bulldozers, and construction workers.

I remembered being home alone in Texas when a friend called to tell me to turn on the TV. I just sat there staring at the screen, not believing what I was seeing. When a plane hit the second tower, I thought surely it was the end of the world. Even though my family members weren't in New York, I had to call them to make sure they were all right. Like most Americans, I watched in horror, glued to the continuous coverage, trying to comprehend what had really happened. There I was gazing out at the actual physical place where I had watched such carnage and destruction on TV. It felt surreal.

Thinking about the thousands of families who were affected by that horrific event gave me the shivers, and tears welled up in my eyes. My heart still breaks for the children who will never see their parents again, for the moms and dads who lost their children, for the husbands and wives torn apart in just moments. Such a waste of human life. I was surrounded by luxury and beauty in our hotel, yet four short years before, this same area had been a flaming inferno that had taken innocent lives and shocked our nation to the core.

I thought of the brave firefighters, emergency responders, and others who gave everything they had that awful day. Each one of them deserved a special Medal of Honor. How many of the survivors of that attack and their families suffer horrific PTS symptoms today? How could something so heinous happen in our country? Somehow I think we always believed we were insulated from terrorist attacks, and I pray it never happens again. Watching the attacks unfold on TV had been heart-wrenching enough, but to know that it had all happened outside my window just gripped my heart that evening. For the most part, our time in New York was a joyous occasion, but the impact of seeing Ground Zero for the first time will always stay with me.

On Saturday evening we attended an elegant dinner with one Medal of Honor recipient and his guest seated at each donor table. As I looked at the impressive table settings, I silently thanked Mrs. Otteson, my high school home economics teacher. Stylishly dressed, she always wore spike heels, and she'd made Emily Post, the grand dame of etiquette and manners, required reading for her students. Because of Mrs. Otteson, I knew how to navigate the array of silverware surrounding my plate. But I sure wondered how on earth she'd been able to stand in those spike heels all day.

While we were eating, Sam was talking and not paying attention as he cut his roll with a serrated butter knife. Wearing his white jacket mess dress, he was holding his hand in his lap surrounded by a white dinner napkin. He sliced his finger and palm with the knife and began bleeding profusely. We quietly slipped out of the room to see to his hand, but someone insisted we call the EMTs. By the time they bandaged it, it looked like he'd lost the entire hand. The medics thought he should have had stitches, but Sammy declined. They left me more tape and wrapping, just in case. The dressing was so cumbersome that we rewrapped it, and the bleeding finally stopped.

There is never a dull moment with that boy, and the best part is, he never got a speck of blood on his white uniform! We returned to the dinner, and the dessert made Sam feel much better. During the program, Sam was featured in a video that was shown. Needless to say, I was proud beyond words.

My first Medal of Honor event had exceeded all my expectations. Being in the company of the Medal of Honor recipients and their wives that first time had helped me to better grasp and become a little more comfortable with the concept that, by marrying Sammy, I had by association become a part of history as well. Still, it is something that has always stayed in the back of my mind. I know that if I don't conduct myself with grace and kindness that also becomes part of my history. My mother's words to "act right" are always with me.

As I planned for my first Congressional Medal of Honor Society convention in Phoenix, Arizona, shortly after our Skidmore wedding, once again the protocol for dress was at the top of my list. For the numerous events during the week, I knew attire could run from business casual to formal black-tie galas. I learned that wives rarely ever wear jeans unless they're at a ranch or some outdoor activity where it would be appropriate.

However, it wasn't all about the clothes. Sam and I talked at length about the Medal of Honor Society. He mentioned that the general public and the media often mistakenly referred to the recipients as Medal of Honor "winners." They had not been in a competition; therefore, the correct term is recipients.

I discovered that the Medal of Honor goes back to the Civil War and the only woman to receive it was Dr. Mary Walker for her actions at the Battle of Bull Run on July 21, 1861. Historically, women have not been on the frontlines of battle, which is why all other recipients have been men.

World War II brought a new focus to the Medal of Honor, and the current Medal of Honor Society was chartered by Congress in 1958 to perpetuate the legacy of the Medal of Honor and to create a bond of brotherhood among living recipients. Among the many functions of the group is a commitment to veterans and those currently serving in the military, as well as fostering patriotism among the public. During the conventions, the recipients are also involved in a character development program to educate students about core values of courage, integrity, sacrifice, commitment, citizenship, and patriotism.

The 2005 Phoenix convention—themed "Forever Honoring Valor and Service"—was spectacular from the moment we arrived at the Pointe Hilton Tapatio Cliffs Resort. Nestled in the Phoenix North Mountain Preserve, this luxury retreat would be our home for the next several days. My mind was boggled. I had never stayed in a luxury resort before, so that really had me dancing in circles. I wanted to be sure that I was dressed appropriately, that I was brushed up on formal etiquette, and that I would complement Sam in all that I did. Not all of the recipients and their wives had attended the New

York foundation event, so I knew I would be meeting many more recipients and their spouses. I couldn't wait.

At each convention, the host city provides the recipients and guests the opportunity to visit special attractions in their area. An afternoon at the world-class Heard Museum in Phoenix, which is devoted to Native American culture and the art of the Southwest, was right up my alley. Of course, it reminded me of Tim and his great love for the Native American culture. I could have stayed there for hours. The necklace with turquoise beads and buffalo nickels pounded into heart shapes that we bought in the gift shop is still a treasured memento of that first convention.

Being outdoor people, Sam and I loved the tour of the Desert Botanical Garden with its huge cacti and succulents plus an array of desert critters and birds.

I didn't take advantage of the shopping trip provided for the wives, but when they offered an option of getting our nails done at a spa, it was wonderful. It was my first time ever at a spa, and I felt so pampered.

I chose to accompany Sam on one of the school visits, and once again, I loved watching him interact with the students. Kids were curious and honest, and they asked such interesting and thoughtful questions. When Sam talked about the major flying in to tell them there was a one hundred percent chance they would be attacked that night at Firebase Cudgel, one elementary student asked Sam why the major didn't take Sam with him when he flew away.

We ate lunch at the Arizona State Veterans Home where my heart was touched by the elderly veterans we talked to. At one point, one of them just nodded at Sammy and Sammy nodded back. No words passed between them, but the look in the old gentleman's eyes said it all. They were brothers of combat, and both of them understood. No words were needed. It was one of those encounters that just filled my heart.

At each convention there is a public book signing, and time is set aside for recipients to sign *Medal of Honor: Portraits of Valor Beyond the Call of Duty.* The *New York Times* best seller profiles Medal of Honor recipients from World War II to the war in Afghanistan. People may bring their own books or purchase a copy there. The evening book signing in Phoenix brought an unexpected surprise for Sam. As we were making our way with other recipients through the roped off line to the autograph table, a man on the other side of the rope yelled, "Sammy, Sammy!"

Sammy took one look and rushed to the man; they hugged, laughed, and cried. It was Darrell Ereth, who had been on guard duty with Sammy at his first Vietnam duty station, the 3rd Ordnance Battalion at Long Binh Ammunition Depot. They had not seen each other since 1967. Darrell sat with us at the autograph table, and people took many pictures of him and Sam together that night. Darrell signed autographs as well.

We also enjoyed a sunset concert at the Phoenix Museum of History and dinner at the Arizona Science Center.

A patriotic "Fabulous Forties Night" let us travel back to that memorable decade with the USO Liberty Bells performance troupe. The thing I remember most about the black-tie gala was Wayne Newton. He was so tall, and I was also impressed that he was willing to stick around for photos with everyone. That made me realize that it means a great deal to others when they want a photo with Sammy, and I hoped we could always accommodate them with the same grace.

While much of the convention was fun, inspirational, and uplifting, the annual memorial service for recipients who had passed away the previous year was very touching. I didn't know the names that year, but in succeeding years, many whom I had come to know would be on that list. It is always a time of great tribute, honor, and remembrance of these brave men who are part of our Medal of Honor family.

During our time in Phoenix, a light bulb went on for me about the magnitude of the Congressional Medal of Honor Society. It is one thing to be married to someone who made valiant sacrifices to save others, but I stood in a room full of men who had done the same. Each man had a story just as riveting as Sammy's, and each one had defied the basic human instinct to save himself in order to save others. To the man, they will tell you they were just doing their jobs.

I thought of each person saved by a recipient and wondered how many children, grandchildren, and great-grandchildren are in this world today making their mark on humanity because of one Medal of Honor recipient's bravery. Each recipient in Phoenix had his own Jim Deister, Gwyndell Holloway, or Billy Ray Crawford. Multiply that by nearly thirty-five hundred recipients who have earned the Congressional Medal of Honor since the Civil War, the offspring of each one saved, and their contributions to society; it is easy to see how each recipient, through extraordinary and valiant efforts, championed the cause of freedom and changed the course of history. What a powerful concept to contemplate.

Having attended numerous Medal of Honor conventions now, I have learned that for whatever reason, people look up to the wives of the recipients as well as the recipients themselves. I choose my words carefully so as not to offend anyone and strive to always act appropriately because someone is watching. I've learned to pretend I am not exhausted and dying for some rest while there is still an autograph line. I try to talk to everyone, including the bus drivers and the hotel's housekeeping personnel, and thank them for their services. They, too, are important. Dressing modestly but with style is protocol at the conventions. Courtesy matters, and we look the other way when someone else makes a mistake. Wearing comfortable shoes is paramount, and above all I laugh at myself if I mess up, because it helps everyone else feel comfortable.

Sam and I, along with all the other recipients, now reach out to the newer recipients and their wives and try to help them learn the ropes of what it means to belong to the Medal of Honor Society. In 2010, Sal Guinta of the 173rd Airborne became the first living recipient since Vietnam, and we ran into him and his beautiful wife, Jen, at another function before they had attended any of the Medal of Honor events. Sam talked to Sal about the society, and I told Jen what kind of clothes to bring and what a typical day at the convention might look like. Our inside joke is that first we eat and then we get on a bus, and then we eat and we get on another bus, and then we eat again and get on another bus. We are always overweight when we get home. I assured her she would get to know and love the Medal of Honor wives just as I had.

Someone once asked me if the novelty of being a Medal of Honor wife and attending conventions has worn off. The answer is that it hasn't. Each one is held in a different city, each with special attractions, and the festivities and celebrations are unique to that city. People in each city are special. Every event is a new adventure, and I look forward to them all. The conventions also requires incredible planning, legions of volunteers, and tremendous numbers of people working together to make them happen.

Each event creates special memories. At a recent convention, two women police officers accompanied us on a school visit where they sat with me while Sam addressed the students. He asked the students who had questions to come forward and speak into the microphone because he has "artillery ears" and sometimes doesn't hear everything. As always, Sam had a knack for making each student feel special. Before long, one of the officers whispered to me that it was the best day of her life, and she was so glad she was chosen to escort Sam and me.

I also remember a young police officer who was checking IDs at the door to our hospitality room so that only recipients and guests entered. He had been there all day. "Aren't you getting tired?" I asked him late that night. "No, ma'am," he replied, "It is my day off, and I consider it a privilege to be here."

Over the years, no matter where the convention takes place, we've watched communities come together with wonderful people who make great sacrifices to honor the Medal of Honor recipients. I think it is as edifying for them to work together as it is for us to receive the fruits of their labor, and we are so grateful to each one for his or her time and commitment.

These conventions have also granted me the privilege to see the best of the best in people. Our media peppers us with all the bad and ugly, but we seldom get to see much of the good. I meet wonderful kids with great minds, our future leaders, when media often casts the younger generation in the worst light. I see dedicated people willing to give of themselves while asking for nothing in return. I see people who love their country and honor the ideals that were the foundation of America. It is not only a privilege to be part of the Medal of Honor family, but also a great opportunity to see so much that is positive in a world that is often portrayed in such a negative light. I am grateful for that opportunity.

With each experience, I was learning that life on the road with Sam would be like a college education. I would have the opportunity to meet fascinating people, visit exciting places, and participate in events that I could never have imagined. The veterans, the children, and others along the way would teach me important life lessons. I also had a unique opportunity to contribute. I've always wanted to light my candle in the world and make a difference to others whether in a big or small way. With Sam, I've been given the opportunity to reach out to people in a way I never would have had without him. I hoped that would be my legacy to history as a Medal of Honor wife. The new adventures to come were all part of the privilege and responsibility of being Mrs. Sammy Davis.

CHAPTER 21

Unforgettable

Reflecting on my own life, I see how my experiences, both good and bad, have helped me grow and broadened my scope of understanding in many ways. The people I've met along the way have inspired me and helped me become more compassionate, more understanding, and more grateful for the blessings I have. Others have shown me what great courage and selflessness means. My travels with Sam have opened doors I would have never walked through, and he has been my teacher as well as my husband. We have become an extension of each other, yet maintaining our separate personalities. Working as a team, I find that each experience continually brings us closer together, and our mission has given me a broader purpose in life.

As I sifted through my story, I thought of a little book entitled *My Beautiful Broken Shell* by Carol Hamblet Adams. The author had just discovered that her husband had been diagnosed with multiple sclerosis, and she was feeling frightened and alone. As she picked up a broken shell on her walk along the beach, it seemed to be a symbol of her life at that point. The shell had been pounded and tossed around by the sea. She, too, had been tossed and pounded by life; her heart was broken and crushed. Yet, even in its broken state, the little shell had fought to keep from being totally crushed, and it still survived on the beach. The author, in her pain, fear, and loneliness still survived, and the message of her story was how God can restore us in our brokenness and allow us to still find beauty in life. The broken shell represents those who are hurting, those who are frightened by what life has handed them, those who have lost loved ones, are lonely, or have broken families, those who have gone through traumatic experiences, and those with unfulfilled dreams.

That broken shell reminded me of who I was when Tim was diagnosed with cancer. It symbolized all the pain, fear, and anguish I experienced through his illness and death. Tossed by the storms of life, I didn't think I could go on. When I was crushed by grief, I learned to lean on friends, family, and most of all, my Heavenly Father. When I think of how God began to restore me, He showered me with more strength, courage, and resolve than I could have ever imagined I had. On days when I felt like throwing in the towel, I was given a lifeline of faith. Because of that, I can share the gift of hope with others who are hurting.

When Sam came into my life, there were still times of brokenness. Leaving Texas was one of those times; it was excruciating to give up my life and memories there. In some ways, I felt like I was abandoning Tim. I was also used to being in charge of running my food business, and suddenly I was no longer in charge of anything. That was very hard for me. I wondered if I was doing the right thing. At times I felt very much alone, but I learned more about love and faith through those trials. I learned gratefulness for the many blessings I still had as I left a place I loved for the man I loved. God had a much greater plan for me than I had for myself in Texas. Even through sharing our story in this book, I'm blessed to have been given an opportunity to broaden my reach to those in search of hope.

The seashore is full of broken shells that are often overlooked by people combing the beach. Because the shells are not perfect, they are passed over. How the people miss out on the uniqueness and beauty of those jagged shells. As humans, we want what is painless and comfortable, yet sometimes it's the pain and adversity that teaches us the most and opens new doors in our lives. Both Sammy and I have walked through those doors, and we've been given the privilege of meeting many, especially veterans, whose lives have been tossed and turned in the storms of this life. Then we meet people, some who have also traveled a difficult path, who give of themselves and reach out to help those in need. All of these folks are truly unforgettable to both of us.

In the early 1990s, Sammy received a call from a second lieutenant at the Pentagon. The call was to tell him that a movie company from California had requested all film footage and written material about Sammy L. Davis, Medal of Honor recipient. Medal of Honor history is a matter of public record. In 1994, the critically acclaimed movie *Forrest Gump* was released and went on to win numerous awards. Forrest Gump became a household name. However, few people knew that the scene in which Forrest receives the Medal of Honor was the actual footage of Sammy receiving the Medal of Honor from President Lyndon Johnson. Actor Tom Hanks's head had been superimposed on Sammy's body.

While numerous scenes in the movie had more than a familiar ring to Sammy, the film opened the door for us to meet Lieutenant Dan from the *Forrest Gump* movie. In real life, Lieutenant Dan is award-winning actor, musician, and film director Gary Sinise. In 2006, Sammy was scheduled to speak at Cantigny Park, near Chicago, where Gary and his Lieutenant Dan Band were playing for a veterans function.

Gary was such a gentleman and so humble; we just clicked with him from the very beginning. He had a ready smile and was welcoming to two strangers. He seemed like an ordinary guy helping the band to set up, not some star on an ego trip.

Gary knew the actual film footage from the White House Medal of Honor ceremony in the *Forrest Gump* movie was Sam receiving the medal from President Johnson. The actors were told that Forrest was fictional, but Gary was glad to meet the "body" from the movie. Sam spoke on stage that day before Gary and the Lt. Dan Band played. That meeting with Gary began a friendship that grows stronger with each passing year.

As a well-known entertainer, Gary could easily bask in his celebrity status. Instead, he chose to start a foundation to honor our veterans and first responders and to help them in times of need. Gary has such a heart for America and for those who serve, and donations made to his foundation truly do go to assist veterans and responders in need. Among the many services provided by Gary's foundation is the building of custom smart homes for our most severely wounded heroes. These are houses designed with state-of-the-art technology so that those who have lost limbs can function in their own homes. Gary also takes his Lieutenant Dan Band to military bases around the world to boost morale for the troops, and he performs benefit concerts to promote awareness for defenders and veterans; he's our modern-day Bob Hope. Today, Sammy is honored to be a member of the ambassador's council for the Gary Sinise Foundation, and we consider Gary as one of America's true heroes. Gary gives of his time because he cares about the broken shells of this world. He is an inspiration to all who meet him, and he continues to inspire Sam and me in our mission to reach out to veterans.

There are those veterans and their families whose names I don't know, yet the pictures of their faces are forever etched in my heart. During an event in 2007, a young veteran in a wheelchair sat across the table from us at dinner. He had lost a limb. His mother, who was strikingly beautiful, accompanied him. We learned that her husband was also a soldier and was still serving in the Middle East. I could not imagine coping with her son's injuries as well as worrying if her husband would return safely. Her burden was heavy. Arrangements of tall glass tubes containing stunning, red-orange floral pieces graced the table where we sat. From our vantage point, we could see the face of this brave mother and wife between the tubes. Her lipstick was the color of the flowers, and flickering candlelight bounced off her dark hair and olive complexion. It was one of those unforgettable scenes that an artist or a photographer dreams of capturing with the perfect combination of light, color, and expression. Her strength during the patriotic speeches was even more captivating, the way she closed her eyes, her lips trembling, at times almost hyperventilating as she blew out tiny breaths to keep from breaking down. She couldn't let go; she had to be strong for her son. The beautiful face between the vases was a study of so many layers of humanity and emotions, a poignant reminder that the families of our veterans make incredible sacrifices, too. Her bravery and courage spoke volumes to me that night.

That same evening, former ABC TV news anchor Bob Woodruff and Canadian cameraman Doug Vogt were being honored with awards. On January 29, 2006, both Bob and Doug were seriously injured by an improvised explosive device (IED) near Taji, Iraq, and Bob's traumatic brain injury almost cost him his life. At the time, both were embedded journalists with the United States 4th Infantry Division.

It had been a long day and we were tired, so shortly after the presentations we were leaving to return to the hotel. As we walked toward the vehicle, our driver asked whether we minded if a couple more people rode back with us. Climbing into the van, we were delighted to see Bob and Doug, who were staying at the same hotel. After some light chitchat, we asked them one serious question: What was the most important thing they'd learned from their devastating experience in Iraq? Neither of them missed a beat. "Family," they answered in unison.

I loved their answer. They could have gone into some long diatribe, but when faced with death their thoughts were reduced to the single most important thing in their lives, the love and support of their families. I share their belief that no matter what else happens in life, our families are paramount.

Despite their harrowing experience in Iraq, Bob certainly didn't lose his sense of humor. When it came time to get out of the van, we heard a lot of groaning and moaning. Among us, there were knee problems, back problems, Sammy was recovering from surgery, and some were having an issue stepping down from the van. When the driver placed a small stool at the door, Bob announced, "OK, everybody step off, state your name, and state your injury." Cocking his head to the side with a big grin, he quipped, "Bob Woodruff, head injury." He had us all in stitches, and the laughter carried on in the hotel elevator as we headed up to our rooms. Since that time Bob and his wife have also started a foundation to help wounded veterans.

Sam and I visit many military hospitals to encourage the wounded and try to spread a little hope; sometimes what we encounter is heartbreaking. Exceptional medics and corpsmen in the military and the advances in medicine help severely wounded soldiers survive; that's the good part.

As I see these young people, I think of Tim and his work in Vietnam as a hospital corpsman. I don't know how he handled horrific situations to care for the wounded from his war. Now it is a different war and a different generation, but the harrowing aftermath remains the same. These kids (I use that term endearingly because as a mom—all of these young people are our kids) are blown up and have lost limbs or have traumatic brain injuries.

In a traumatic brain injury unit, we visited a young soldier lying in bed, seemingly not moving or responding to outside stimuli. A TV played just a few inches from the injured man's face. The young man's wife and children, a toddler and a baby, lived in the hospital room with him. A child playing, talking, giggling, occasional high-pitched laughter, the TV blaring, and Sam and I trying to talk to the wife was a little disconcerting to me. There was just too much going on, but we were told that the veteran's brain was registering what was happening in the room. The activity, the TV, and having the family continually interacting in the room were encouraging his brain to heal. How I hoped for a miracle that would someday allow them to be a whole family again.

There is another young man I will never forget. He was missing both his legs, and he looked like he was about twelve years old. When we arrived in his hospital room, he was eating lunch and yelled, "Come on in!"

He was the most positive, upbeat kid I've ever seen. He explained how he'd lost his legs and told us what he remembered about the battle. Then he told us the doctors said he would be ready for his new legs in about six months and out of the hospital and back to his life in another six months. With great confidence, he told us he would just show those doctors, and he would be back with his unit in less than six months. I thought of how important it was for Sammy to be back with his unit after he was injured in Vietnam, and this young soldier needed to be with his brothers as well. I wanted so much to believe he would be back with them on his timetable; his enthusiasm was catching. I cried when I left his room.

A cute young lady with blue hair (her nickname was Blue) was watching TV and folding clothes. As she folded, she sang, just little ditties that had no meaning. She looked so young. A traumatic brain injury had left her with the mentality of a twelve-year-old. She was laughing and appeared to be happy. Blue was the first female combat veteran with a traumatic brain injury that I had ever met, and it really hit me hard. Here was a lovely young woman who enlisted for her country, but now she has to have help doing the simplest things like laundry. I wondered what her dreams of the future might have been before she served her country. I don't know what she could remember, but I grieved for what she had lost.

There were other young veterans in wheelchairs with attendants, and many had either one or both of their parents beside them. Every last one of the parents was positive, telling their kids how good they looked and how well they were doing. Then I looked into their eyes as one parent to another and saw the desperation, the sadness, and the grief. I've lost a spouse, but I cannot imagine losing a child. To have your child living and breathing but half his head blown away is beyond comprehension.

I get goose bumps when I remember visiting a young man who had just returned from surgery in a VA facility in Tampa, Florida. A nurse said we could go in, but he might not be awake enough to know we were there. Sam walked over to the bed where the soldier's arm was in an L-shaped cast attached to a pulley over his head. Sam quietly leaned over to see if he was awake and the young man's eyes popped open.

"Sergeant Davis!" he exclaimed.

I about fell over that this young man recognized Sam. Sam was startled, too, and was really taken aback when the soldier asked Sam if he had his harmonica with him. The young man explained that when he was six years old, he had attended the veterans reunion in Kokomo, Indiana, with his grandpa. Once again I realized just how many soldiers and their families have been touched by Sam and his story. How amazing that two generations later, this young man felt a connection to Sam.

"You played 'Shenandoah' for my grandpa and all of his brothers so they could rest and find peace in their hearts," he told Sam. "Sergeant Davis, I really need to rest. Could you play 'Shenandoah' for me?"

So we stood by his bed and Sam played "Shenandoah" over and over until the young man's eyes closed, and he fell asleep. Try to get through something like that without tears pouring down your face.

That same young soldier reminded me of the story Sam had told me about his hospital stay in Vietnam. At that point, Sam didn't really care if he lived or died. His fever was so high that he was in and out of consciousness. Then a young nurse touched him, feeling his head and arms for fever. Sam could smell her, and she smelled so sweet. It was then that he decided he wanted to live. I wondered if Sam's visit would be the moment that this young man decided to live and continue on.

It also reminded me of a song, "Suitcase Full of Secrets" that Tim used to sing, a tribute to all the nurses in war who tended the wounded and dying. Being part of this encounter was very powerful for me, and once again I hoped that perhaps I could impart a smile or a word of encouragement to someone the way Sammy's song brought peace to this soldier.

I often think of these young people and pray for them, wondering about them and the lives of their families. I think of all the young wives who stand vigil in many hospital rooms as their husbands lie wounded in bed. They are no different than the wives from the Vietnam War, World War I, World War II, or Korea. The generations between them don't matter; they are part of a sisterhood of women who loved their husbands and tended their wounded warriors. Their broken shells are jagged and sharp, and I pray for them to find courage, strength, healing, and peace through their difficult situations.

I have been touched not only by young veterans; those aged veterans in nursing homes tug on our hearts as well. At the Ben Atchley Tennessee State Veterans' Home in Knoxville, several veterans, many in wheelchairs, were assembled in the common room for Sam to speak to them. Some were sleeping, and some were in a world of their own, perhaps remembering happier times in their lives. When Sam started to speak, he asked if there were any veterans in the room. With prompting from staff and family members, several raised their hands. Two elderly gentlemen in wheelchairs, Vietnam veterans, feebly raised their hands and proudly stated where they had served.

Sam always invites questions, and someone asked where he had met his wife. I started telling the shortened version of our story. But like so many couples who have been married for years, we now sometimes finish each other's sentences. As Sam kept adding to the story, I jokingly took the microphone away from him and told him he couldn't talk. That statement was met by a lot of laughter, hoots, and hollers. There were more questions and laughter, and as we were getting ready to leave, the applause started. Then it happened.

The two Vietnam veterans in wheelchairs struggled to stand up for Sammy. They wanted to honor one of their own. The one man managed to make it to his feet as an attendant rushed to assist him; the other gentleman didn't have enough strength to stand. I couldn't hold back the tears. Sam went to the one who was standing, and I knelt by the one still in his chair. We each hugged them and thanked them for their service. I will never forget that day and those two veterans who gave what they had left to try to stand for Sammy and for freedom.

In 2013, the Medal of Honor Convention was held in Gettysburg, Pennsylvania. There are as many impressions of Gettysburg as there are people who visit the battleground, and I had my moment as we visited the historic area. A print of artist Larry Winborg's heartrending painting "To Save a Nation," depicting Abe Lincoln in prayer at the Gettysburg battlefield, hangs in our home. Illuminated by shafts of sunlight, Lincoln has one knee on the ground, his head bowed, with the written words of the Gettysburg Address stuffed in his top hat on the dried grass next to him. The field in the distance smolders in a haze. I am touched by the power of that painting, and as we stood on the ground where that horrible battle was fought, I thought not only of the soldiers who lost their lives, but I imagined Lincoln in prayer overlooking that field of carnage. There really aren't words to describe the depths of feeling and sense of history I felt at that sacred place. I reflected on all the sacrifices that Americans made on both sides of the Civil War, and I wished there never had to be war anywhere.

We were told that never before had a concert been performed on the battlefield, but that night a concert celebrating America's heroes, past, present, and future was held at the Pennsylvania Monument. It was fitting to be entertained by the United States Marine Band and the West Point Cadet Glee Club, culminating with a breathtaking fireworks display to honor those who have served.

The memorial to those killed at Pearl Harbor, Hawaii, in 1941 on the battleship Arizona evoked similar deep emotions for me. At a Medal of Honor reunion in Hawaii in 2012, we dropped wreaths in the water to honor the 1,177 crewmen who lost their lives. I thought of those who never got to see their loved ones again and of the children and grandchildren of these men who never had the chance to be born. How very sad. It's eerie to look below and see bubbles still rising up from beneath the ship. We were told that some of the surviving crewmembers still request to have their ashes buried with their buddies, and a diver will take the ashes into the water and lay them to rest with their brothers.

I have visited some of the hallowed places where American history was made, and I have been privileged to meet ordinary Americans with extraordinary courage who have faced things I hope I never have to face. They have taught me to never take my blessings for granted. Among my many roles with Sam is that of a student; when he shared what it was like to be a wounded soldier in a hospital bed, it helped me understand what that soldier might be thinking and feeling. I always learn so much through Sam's eyes.

While life will always throw challenges our way, I've come a long way from the broken shell I was in Hawkins, Texas. I thank God for the healing of my heart and the incredible opportunities to expand my knowledge of our country, to encounter unforgettable people, and to continue our mission. I thank God for second chances and for the amazing adventures I continue to experience with Sam, some poignant and others exciting and downright glamorous.

CHAPTER 22

Celebrate

While some of our experiences are deeply moving and at times heart-wrenching, on occasion we are also privileged to take part in less solemn but memorable activities. We have also found ourselves in some funny situations that I will never forget. In addition, we are invited to gala celebrations where we sometimes rub elbows with celebrities and other glamorous people. I still have to pinch myself when I realize how much my life has exceeded the dreams I had as a small-town farm girl.

Who gets the chance to shoot with the Navy SEALs? I have such great respect for them, and I sure never thought it would be me. In July 2005, Sammy took me to Camp Atterbury in Indiana where Navy SEALs are trained to be snipers. When they invited me to try my luck with a target, somebody was kind enough to put down a tarp so I wouldn't get dirty as I laid flat on the ground at the shooting range. Somehow I don't think they do that in combat. Other than pumping a little BB gun as a kid and shooting at dirt banks with Tim, I had very little experience with guns and really didn't know what I was doing. The Navy SEALs let me shoot everything in the arsenal, including a .50 caliber machine gun. Sam said I kept the shots within one minute of angle from fifty yards out to one thousand yards. In nonmilitary lingo, I think that means I kept within a few inches of the bull's eye. I was so excited! The bad news is that women do not have the muscle mass that men have in the front of their shoulders to absorb the recoil. I was a canvas of black and blue the next day. Sam almost cried when he saw my shoulder. It reminded me of when Tim took the splinter out of my arm all those years before. It touched me that both of them could go through any amount of pain, but they had tender hearts when it came to me. Shooting with the SEALs was an exhilarating experience, and a Navy SEAL coin and sniper cap are now among my special mementos.

Anybody who knows me well will tell you that I can get myself tangled up in the silliest, sometime embarrassing situations. On one occasion, Sam and I rode in a convertible around the track at the Indianapolis 500, the annual Memorial Day auto race in Indianapolis, Indiana. With a grandstand seating upward of 250,000 people, the event is considered part of the Triple Crown of Motorsport. Sam and I had been given small American flags to wave, and as our Medal of Honor car came into view, the crowd stood, yelled, and cheered. It was like a giant wave at the ballpark and something to behold. I was having the time of my life, wildly waving my flag to the beat of the band. Later, as we were getting out of the convertible, I looked up and realized there was no flag on the stick. It had fallen off along the way, and there I was like a crazy woman waving that stick around. To add insult to injury, when we got home, a friend who had seen us on TV called. "Why were you waving a stick?" he asked. Oh, boy!

When it comes to meeting celebrities, Sammy and I are no different than anyone else. We're often like school kids, awed to be in the same room with famous people, not to mention getting to speak with them. Sometimes we just shake hands with them in passing, and then there are those who leave lasting memories in a very personal way. Many have left their marks on us, often enriching our lives, even though they tell us that we are the ones who have made the impression on them.

I will never forget sitting next to Tony Award-winning actress and comedian Carol Channing one evening. She and her husband were the cutest little couple. That million-dollar smile that we all loved in *Hello, Dolly!* was captivating, and I told her how much I enjoyed her performance in that production. Then we talked about kids and grandkids. I was so surprised when Carol said she was nervous about saying a few words on stage later in the evening. She was so human and so real, and I felt like I was talking with an old friend. What sticks with me the most is that this bigger-than-life Broadway icon was wearing orthopedic shoes. It put everything into perspective and reminded me that we are all fragile human beings. No matter how much fame one achieves in life, in the end we are all alike. Carol was truly a lovely person.

At a fund-raiser for wounded veterans in Los Angeles, Sammy caught his shoe on a step and tripped. None other than actor Clint Eastwood lunged to his aid, insisting that he help Sam up the remaining steps. Later, I thanked Clint for catching Sammy. "I am usually the one that trips," he whispered to me. I loved that he was just a regular guy, too.

At another fund-raiser, Sam and I found out that comedian and actor Tim Allen is as funny off stage as he is on, and he kept us in stitches with his wry comments on everything from politics to kids. The fact that he placed the highest bid for one of Sam's harmonicas was really heartwarming for us as well.

Meeting Willie Nelson was so exciting; I've long been a fan of his. His music speaks to my heart, and Tim used to sing a lot of Willie's songs. Over the years, Sam had played harmonica on stage with Willie several times, so when we attended Willie's 75th birthday party in Texas in 2008, I was thrilled to go backstage to meet him. Before the concert, we were told to stand by the stage door, where we talked with country music legend Merle Haggard and his wife. Soon Willie, wearing his trademark headband, leaped up the steps with a flourish and grabbed Sam, and then me. The band kept playing his entrance music, and he kept talking to us while the crowd screamed wildly for him. Later, he introduced us on stage. For me, that was certainly one for the books!

When we returned to our seats, the people behind us leaned over and said, "We just knew y'all were somebody important." What a hoot; I really got a kick out of them.

On a number of occasions, Sammy and I attended gala fund-raisers at the Ronald Reagan Library in California, and it became one of our favorite annual events. I respected Ronald Reagan not only as a great president, but he also came from Dixon, Illinois, not far from where I grew up. He was a favored son in our area.

Hollywood is always well represented at this event, and celebrities stand behind the roped-off red carpet when Medal of Honor recipients and their guests enter. At one of the Reagan Library events, actor Jon Voight, whom we had previously met at other functions, jumped the rope and came rushing toward me, yelling "Dixie". Then he gave me a big hug. It was a little embarrassing, but what fun.

The imposing Air Force One of the Reagan era stood sentry over the celebration, and I was amazed to find out that Sammy had flown with the Reagans on that very plane, as well as a couple of other times when they were not onboard. More American history that Sammy was part of! I couldn't wait to walk through the plane and see it all through his eyes.

In 2013, our assigned table was near the front, just to the left of the stage. Nancy Reagan was being honored with a Lifetime Achievement Award. Having broken her hip earlier in the year, she didn't attend the dinner but came for the award. Double doors opened to the rear of the room, and Mrs. Reagan slowly made her entrance with a cane, escorted by Medal of Honor recipient Gary Littrell. Partway up the aisle, they stopped at a table where the dashing Tom Selleck stood and took her arm. Nancy Reagan was elegance personified in a red, floor-length gown, and Tom Selleck was the picture of handsome. He guided her up the steps to the stage where she said she was so happy to host the Medal of Honor recipients and that we were invited back the following year. She told the crowd she considered it a high honor to receive the award from the Medal of Honor Society.

When she exited the stage, she walked past our table. We made eye contact, and I smiled. She nodded. I had always admired Nancy Reagan. She supported her husband with such grace but also kept her own identity. I loved how she and President Reagan showed their love for each other; their countenance together said it all and that reminded me of Sam and me. I was more than a little excited and starstruck when I grabbed Sam and said that Mrs. Reagan had smiled at me.

"No," Sammy quipped with a grin, "she was smiling at me." So I snitched his dessert. We still chuckle about that.

In Bentonville, Arkansas, I met former President George W. Bush at a function where he posed for official photos with Medal of Honor recipients and their guests. The former president signed a photo of he and Sam together that had been taken at the White House. I told him I had lived in Texas.

When he asked where, I mentioned Hawkins, saying it was such a small town he had probably never heard of it.

"I know exactly where that is," he replied. "Remember, I was once governor of Texas." Mr. Bush was very personable and gave us hugs. After his speech, he told the crowd that he had to leave to get back to his new grandbaby in Texas.

In both 2009 and 2013, we attended the inaugurations of President Barack Obama, and I was giddy with the anticipation of participating in such historical events. Sammy has not missed a single presidential inauguration since he received his Medal of Honor in 1968. In 2009, on a cold, clear January day, a jubilant atmosphere prevailed in Washington, DC. The Capitol Building was festooned in red, white, and blue, and I was amazed at the sea of people behind us reaching clear back to the National Mall area. It was just the way Sam had described his first presidential inauguration. Under tight security, forty or fifty Medal of Honor recipients and their guests were led to white folding chairs on the lawn in a reserved section close to the front. Both times we were seated next to the Tuskegee Airmen and the Navajo Code Talkers. A jumbo TV screen to our left made it easier to watch the proceedings. Even though we had dressed for the cold, three hours outside was enough to nearly turn us into popsicles. That year Aretha Franklin belted a riveting rendition of "My Country, 'Tis of Thee," and her hat, embellished with a huge, sparkling bow, was talked about for days. Before the oath of office, we listened to the most stirring music by Yo-Yo Ma (cello), Anthony McGill (piano), Gabriela Montero (violin) and Itzhak Perlman (violin). Right after the president was sworn in, security quickly whisked us away from the area. Throughout the inaugural weekend, the Medal of Honor recipients and their guests were never without security.

I particularly enjoyed people-watching at the Salute to Heroes Inaugural Ball, one of several balls held around the city. Men wore tuxedos or military dress and women glittered from head to toe. Before attending, I had visions of people dancing the night away, but in reality it's more of a cocktail party and dinner, unless the president or vice president comes in to dance. President Obama did not attend the Salute to Heroes Ball either year, although all past presidents since Eisenhower have made an appearance. In 2009, a few of us stopped in at another ball to see the new president and his wife. I remember that Michelle Obama's white silk chiffon gown embellished with Swarovski crystals was stunning, and Jill Biden looked radiant in a regal red dress. Being from northwest Illinois, I was especially interested in the live feed to that ball from Afghanistan; it featured members of the Illinois National Guard from Rockford, Illinois, a neighboring city to Freeport.

Our 2013 experience was similar, and I was excited that my sister, Roxie, accompanied us. The tone of that inauguration seemed more subdued than in 2009, however, and there appeared to be fewer people in attendance. I just didn't feel the excitement we'd observed at the previous inauguration. Once again, it was incredibly cold. On the balcony of the Capitol Building, every living former president and first lady was on the platform with the incumbent President Obama. The jumbo screen allowed us to watch the cabinet members and other dignitaries make their entrances. After Vice President Biden was sworn in, James Taylor sang "America the Beautiful." Following the swearing-in of the president, Kelly Clarkson performed an impressive version of "My Country, 'Tis of Thee," and Beyoncé closed the ceremonies with our national anthem.

I thought of my ancestors who had migrated to the United States for a better life, and how amazed they would be to know that their granddaughter had witnessed two presidential inaugurations.

In 2014, I made my first-ever trip abroad to Stuttgart, Germany. We were invited to attend the 239th birthday of the United States Army Ball. Sammy would speak to the American troops at the United States base, and we would visit a German farm, dine in local restaurants, and attend a church service.

I was ecstatic to visit another country, especially the home of my ancestors. I had heard so much about Germany from grandparents on my dad's side, and they would have been thrilled to know that I was going to visit their homeland.

I will never think about this trip without remembering how Sammy made me laugh. On the plane, we were given a little gift bag with toiletry items, socks with nonskid lines, and eye masks for sleeping. I glanced over at Sam;

he had one of the socks with the nubby lines draped over his eyes, thinking it was the eye mask that you somehow tied behind your head. We do have fun when we travel.

Our accommodations in Germany included a two-day stay at the beautiful Schloss Weitenburg castle. I think most little girls dream about Cinderella stories and fairytales, but I'd never imagined that I would one day get to stay in a real castle! I felt like a princess. We had dinner with the baron whose family had owned the castle since the 1700s. Because of my German heritage, many of the dishes that included noodles, sauerkraut, and sausage were not only delicious but very familiar to me.

Sam was especially excited to tour a Lamborghini plant, and he took a ride in a Lamborghini Diablo that zoomed up to 160 kilometers per hour in just a few seconds. I sat that one out. I had hair to worry about.

We toured museums and other castles, but what I loved most about the trip was the friendliness of the people and visiting farms; I was especially impressed with how neat and clean the countryside was. It reminded me so much of my home in Illinois.

Then there are those surprises and humbling moments that I will lock in my heart forever. When we were in Salt Lake City, Utah, for a speaking engagement in 2014, the timing happened to coincide with the semiannual conference of the Church of Jesus Christ of Latter-day Saints. The conference was held in their 21,200 seat conference center, and as church members, Sam and I both were so excited to hear the music of the world renowned Mormon Tabernacle Choir. We were going to be introduced to the choir after the performance, but as they sang their closing number, the church elders escorted us up the center aisle and around to the side of the stage. I was so embarrassed because the service had not yet ended. They told us they had to get us moving because we would not have been able to get through the thousands of people there at the end of the service.

We were met by choir directors and taken up an elevator to the choir level and then led to the conductor's wooden platform, where we were introduced to the choir. I don't do well with heights, and looking over my shoulder, I could see we were about four tiers up from the main floor. I was told to hang on to a bar on the platform; the knuckles on my one hand were clenched white while I clenched Sam with the other.

Sammy spoke a few words, and then he handed the microphone to me. Good grief, I thought I might pass out. What could I say to this world famous choir? I told them how happy we were to be there to hear their wonderful voices, that their songs filled my heart with joy, and how much I felt the spirit of God as they sang. At least, I think that's what I said. How can I remember when the entire Mormon Tabernacle Choir gave us a standing ovation? Sammy cried. He later said he was totally amazed that this group he looked up to and had admired for so many years had honored him. We were so humbled, and it was a stirring moment for both of us.

When I was feeding cows as a kid on the farm, in my wildest dreams, I could never have conceived such dazzling encounters. Yet, of all the grand experiences I've had, what ranks right up at the top for me is visiting with school kids.

CHAPTER 23

Only in America

While we are involved in official school visits at Medal of Honor functions, Sam and I often accept invitations from schools and visit students on our own. We love veterans, but often they immediately fall into military mode with Sam. Kids, on the other hand, especially the little ones, are just so honest. Boys will ask about weapons and trucks and jeeps. They want to know if Sam saw any snakes or tigers, and what he ate. Little girls often ask if Sam missed his mom, or how he felt about the war. Sometimes they wonder why Sam calls all of the servicemen his brothers. Schoolchildren haven't yet put on the veneer that adults wear, and they say whatever is on their minds. I love the openness and looks on their faces; sometimes they appear quizzical, and sometimes I see admiration for Sam in their eyes. If they ask a question, they really want to know the answer. In every school I've been to with Sam, I've been impressed with the respect I've felt from students. I also appreciate the teachers who give so much of themselves to kids.

Each presentation is a little different, but the theme is always the same: "Duty, Honor, Country." Sammy almost always asks the students if they have seen the movie *Forrest Gump*. Even today's young people seem to connect with Forrest Gump, and they are all ears when Sammy says that like Forrest, he was also shot in the buttocks. Personally, I love Forrest's kind heart and the great love he had for his mama and Jenny. Children often ask if I'm Jenny.

"The only similarity between Jenny and Dixie is that I love Dixie as much as Forrest loved Jenny," Sammy always tells them. He doesn't want them to think I did drugs, hung out with the Black Panthers, or protested against the

Vietnam War. Then he explains how the real footage of him receiving the Medal of Honor from President Johnson was used in the film. Discussion of the movie often prompts many questions about the Vietnam War.

Sammy tells students how he got to hold the grandbaby of Jim Deister, one of the men he saved in Vietnam. He also advises that no matter what they face in life, whether in school, in their home lives, or in the military under duress, giving up is the worst option. "You don't lose till you quit trying," he tells them, just like his mom and dad used to tell him. That phrase has become Sammy's anthem, and he points out that Jim didn't give up either. He encourages the students to do all that they can to help their brothers and sisters, their parents, and their schoolmates and friends, no matter what situation they find themselves in.

Because Sammy believes that the group will better grasp the meaning of the Medal of Honor if they get to actually touch it, he takes it off and passes it around for each student to hold so that he or she feels a part of it.

My job in the audience is to keep Sam on track if he forgets what questions were asked. One story leads to another, and it is sometimes hard to reel him in. The audience doesn't care because all his stories are interesting, but sometimes we're on a tight schedule, so I try to make sure we don't get off on too many rabbit trails. Also, if questions get tense, I can insert some humor to lighten things up.

Over the years, Sam has addressed the schools that all fifteen of our grandchildren attend. I was especially thrilled to be able to visit the three schools in West Monroe, Louisiana, where six of our grandchildren are enrolled.

One of our favorite questions was from our grandson's elementary school. Remember how we thought our grandparents were really old, no matter how young they were? Now we are those grandparents. Kids do get off topic sometimes, and one young man asked Sammy just what year the Titanic sank. I'm sure he thought we were alive at that time. It's a good thing Sammy remembered it sank in 1912.

At our grandkids Zac and August's West Monroe High School, Sam addressed four thousand students. August was his escort to the stage. Next we talked to West Ridge Middle School where Hannah is a student. Finally

Benjamin and Reuben got to escort Grandpa into their room at the elementary school. The children on each side of the aisle raised flags to form an arch when Sam and the boys walked in. Of course, the flags hit Sam in the head all the way down the aisle. It was precious. Our little Olivia, who was in preschool, wanted Grandpa to come to her school, too, so he put his uniform back on, and we went to pick her up at school. She showed us her room and playground and that made her a very happy little girl.

We never know what will happen on school visits. After a presentation in an Illinois school, Sammy did not expect the teacher to present him with a chain attached to a peace sign emblem. As the teacher removed the chain from his neck, he explained that he had protested the Vietnam War, and he had worn that symbol all these years. He wanted Sam to have the pendant because he no longer needed it. With tears in his eyes, he apologized, saying that he had been misinformed. He concluded that sometimes it takes years to grow up and really understand. That was a lump-in-the-throat moment for both Sammy and me.

Following a school visit, we will often receive an envelope full of handwritten notes and letters from students we have addressed. Some of the most precious, poignant, and sometimes hilarious letters come from them. We treasure the one that came on a three-by-five card decorated in red, white, and blue. Referring to Jim Deister, this young person put it very succinctly: Sammy held Jim's grandbaby, he saved three of his brothers, and his bravery caused a grandbaby!

"Sergeant Davis, you changed my life today," some of the notes read. We get those often, and they always tug at both our hearts. Then there are those like the carefully written two-page letter from an older student who expressed her thoughts most eloquently. She was upfront about not supporting war, but she supported loyalty and bravery and protecting others. She told Sam she cared about those for whom he'd risked his life and that he had a big heart. She also revealed that she didn't have a very positive outlook on humanity because of all the hate, greed, and pain she saw around her, but Sammy's story had given her hope and helped her believe there are genuine people left in the world. Her letter suggested that she struggles in life and that Sammy's words made a difference. That is why we do what we do.

Touching someone like that young lady in a positive way and providing a glimmer of hope is why we stay out on the road when we are tired and worn-out, sometimes driving hundreds of miles. It is why we leave home three hours before a flight and deal with delayed planes and cancellations. It is why we've traded the comforts of privacy for a public life. The little mantra that runs through my head each day is "Make a difference, make a difference." Perhaps it's through the young people that we can make the biggest difference of all, inspiring them to look for clarity and truth, letting them know others care, and encouraging them to never give up, no matter how difficult the situation.

Conversely, the enthusiasm and positive spirits of these young people encourage and carry us when we are tired, weary, and facing our own challenges. And like everyone else, life throws a fair share of curveballs our way.

CHAPTER 24

I Made It through the Rain

More than once someone has told me that Sam and I live a charmed life. To that, I would answer that we have certainly been blessed beyond measure, but life has also thrown in a bucket load of challenges along the way. We don't dwell on them, but they have been as much a part of our lives as all the exciting adventures we've experienced in our marriage.

The onset of my mom's illness in 2005 until she passed away in 2009 was an especially trying time for my family, as well as for Sam and me. As a child I was probably closer to my dad than to my mom, but as I got older and after Dad passed away, my mom, Doris Busch, and I developed a special relationship. I came to a better understanding of what it meant for her to be a farmwife and a stay-at-home mom who worked as hard as my dad. She busied herself with gardening, putting up food, housework, and feeding three square meals a day to a family of five, plus a hired hand. In addition, she took care of her children and sometimes extra kids to boot. One of my favorite memories of Mom is her constantly singing, "You are My Sunshine" as she did her chores.

Mom taught us to respect our elders and proper table manners. That meant clean hands, no hats at the table, shirts on, holding your utensils properly, and keeping your left hand in your lap and elbows off the table. Using our napkins and not a sleeve to wipe our hands on was a must, too. We were to act right at all times, obey the teachers, and if we got in trouble at school, we'd get it ten times worse when we got home. I wasn't sure what that meant, exactly, but I didn't want to find out, so I made sure to toe the mark. We were to listen in school, make good grades, and read everything available. Talking back to parents or teachers was not even thinkable at that time, and we didn't interrupt adults but waited our turns to speak. Extreme fashions were not allowed; for church I wore a hat, a dress, white gloves, and my shoes had to be polished.

While there were strict rules about some things, Mom saw to it that we were still free to be kids, to play, daydream, and just have fun without every minute being structured. She made it possible for us to have piano lessons, took us to Bible school in the summer, and she was the chauffer who drove us to school activities. She also made sure that we learned all about spring cleaning, and when she and Dad hosted card club, Roxie and I had the privilege of cleaning the entire house, including washing every dish in the china cupboard. My sister and I didn't think too much of her plan then, but now I see how much of what she taught me prepared me for my life today.

As an adult, I realized the sacrifices Mom had made for our family, and I appreciated her in many ways that a child doesn't understand. In her later years, we had so many laughs together, and I cherish those moments.

When Mom started falling and could no longer stay in her home, I was frustrated that doctors never did pinpoint a cause for her weakness. We had her in several facilities trying to find a place where she would be comfortable. Sadly, she was never able to go back home again, and that took its toll on her. I struggled with the guilt of being away from her during her illness and not being there to help my sister with Mom's needs. I needed to be with my husband, and I needed to be with my mom. The conflict tugged at my heart.

Anyone who has dealt with an elderly parent probably has stories that are terribly sad yet funny at the same time. As Mom's condition deteriorated, she lost her volume control and would blurt out statements meant just for our ears. That was so unlike her. She had always been very shy around our friends and at school functions. Once Sam and I were with her during a rehab session where several other residents were doing their exercises in the same room. Mom glanced toward one lady. "That woman over there sure is homely," she suddenly boomed in a loud voice. The whole room heard her, and there was no place for us to hide.

She became feistier in the nursing home; she was not happy and just wanted to go home. It was hard to visit and see her that way, but equally hard to leave her. We moved her to a nursing home near us for about a year in order to take the burden off of my sister and brother. After a year she was homesick and wanted to return to the nursing home where her own mom and dad had spent their last days. We took her back, but she wasn't happy there either and was often cantankerous with the staff.

One of the sweet moments occurred when Mom encountered her old school chum in the same nursing home. Mom and Izzy had been friends forever, and I remember Izzy coming to our house when I was growing up. My brother, Roger, was in Mom's room the day Izzy wheeled herself in and rolled over to the bed where Mom was propped up. Both were in their last days. They looked at each other, and Mom finally recognized her. "Izzy," she whispered. "Doris," Izzy whispered back. Then they just sat there together, not talking, but holding hands for a very long time. I cry each time I think of them; both were lonely and miserable, but they found each other and some moments of peace together.

Mom had told a friend that she wanted Sam to play the old Stephen Foster song, "Beautiful Dreamer" on the harmonica at her funeral. I do remember that Dad's barbershop quartet sang that song years ago, so Mom would have played the piano for them. Or perhaps it had to do with her secret. A faded photo of a soldier in uniform leaning on an old sedan with his arms crossed over his chest had been in our family photo album for as long as I can remember. He had once been Mom's beau. Mom told me that Grandma had hidden letters from him that were addressed to her so she couldn't read them. Mom was in high school, and Grandma must have thought that she was too young for this soldier. We always assumed he had been killed in the war, but Mom was pretty tight-lipped about details. I wished I knew the answer and what that song really meant to her.

Sam didn't know "Beautiful Dreamer," but he immediately got a recording and learned it. On our last visit with Mom, she was unable to speak to us. Sam pulled out his harmonica and played her request; she never took her eyes off of him. Sam gave her a special gift, and she passed away peacefully in her sleep that night. Sam was my rock through it all. He stayed by my side as we made funeral arrangements, and when we had to clean out Mom's apartment, he was right there, willing to do anything. I don't know how I would have survived without him.

Unfortunately, tragedy was to strike my family again. It had taken my sister, Roxie, four and a half years to move forward after her husband, Phil, died in the racquetball accident. Everyone was so happy for her when she started to date Donnie, an old friend from high school. She didn't expect to fall in love again, but she did. One day at a horse sale, a man driving the auctioneer's truck lost control and plowed into the crowd. Donnie saved others when he pushed people out of the way, but the truck hit him, and he died instantly. My heart broke for my sister as she faced another crushing loss from a freak accident. Why should anyone have to cope with so much grief? It just wasn't fair.

While Sam was my strength through my family situations, he had to deal with multiple physical challenges himself. He had long been plagued with knee problems, intense pain resulting from shrapnel in Vietnam, other injuries, and from a lifetime of playing hard: four-wheelers, football, jeeping, and jumping out of airplanes. In 2006, he consulted an orthopedic surgeon about his knees. Tests revealed that Sammy suffered from severely pinched nerves as the result of his back injuries in Vietnam. In addition, he suffered greatly with back pain and numbness in his legs. Some of his organs weren't functioning properly, and it was urgent for him to have back surgery or the organs would shut down, and he would lose feeling in his legs. Knee surgery would have to wait.

Sam's daughter, Nikki, sat with me through the surgery, and we were told it would probably take two hours. When the two hours turned into three, and then five, I grew frantic. Any surgery is risky, especially for a diabetic. Even though a surgical nurse assured us hourly that all was going well, I convinced myself that something had gone wrong and that the doctors and nurses didn't want to tell me. In reality, everything really had gone well and there were no additional problems. The nurse later told me it took so long because the doctor was a particularly detailed and meticulous surgeon. I wished the medical staff could have been a little more forthcoming with information. It was a long, draining day.

I stayed in the hospital with Sam and tried to sleep in the chair, but memories of Tim's illness wouldn't go away. I felt like I was back in the hospital with Tim. I never left him alone in all of his hospital stays, and that night, I relived the trauma and fears of losing Tim each time he had been hospitalized. I was so thankful that this time, the news was good, and that my Sammy would recover and be better than before. This time, there was hope. However, in that darkened room after the mental exhaustion of the day, painful memories of Tim, as well as fears of losing Sam kept taunting me.

Living on a gravel road, grains of grit and sand sometimes settle on our deck. When we got home, Sam walked out on the deck barefoot and said, "Wow, I can feel sand under my feet." It had been a long time since he'd felt grass on his feet, too, and he was elated. Although one critical problem was fixed with that surgery, Sam still suffers from back problems from his Vietnam injuries.

Scar tissue in his back continues to cause nerve pain, and he also has severe muscle spasms. When Sam says, "I have to look for nickels" I know he has to bend over and try to relieve the pain. I have also learned how to apply pressure by squeezing his back. It looks like a giant hug and sometimes helps. Lying flat for a little bit often helps, as well, but that is not possible when we are on the road.

Sammy gave me another major scare in September 2008. Our hotel room was quite a distance from the front desk, and as he carried our luggage, he started getting short of breath. He didn't have any pain, but he said it felt like the bone in his arm got cold.

"If I didn't know better, I'd think I was having a heart attack," he told me. The symptoms soon subsided, and Sam blamed it all on low blood sugar. I was very concerned, however, and when we got home three or four days later, I urged him to go to the doctor. He balked at going, so I finally called the doctor and made him an appointment.

Sam failed the stress test, and the doctor told him he'd had a silent heart attack. Three of his arteries were blocked, and open-heart surgery was scheduled three weeks later. Heart disease is another health issue related to Agent

Orange, and Sammy was told years ago that he would someday have to have heart surgery. To reassure us, Sam's doctor told us he had performed six thousand heart surgeries, and his confidence helped us have faith in him. Also, the doctor's assistant had been a hospital corpsman like Tim, so I knew Sam would be in good hands. Sam's attitude was positive, which helped me as well. He was cracking jokes even as he went into surgery. Still, thinking about him undergoing such a serious procedure was not easy. Before Sam went into surgery, I was on my knees in the chapel, praying for him and the doctors and nurses—just as I had before his back surgery.

I was grateful for Sam's family while we passed the long hours in the waiting room. Our relationship was getting better, and we were united for a common cause. Once again, the hourly updates from an OR nurse were encouraging, and I wasn't as fearful as I had been during his previous surgery. As it turned out, the surgeon did a quadruple bypass. There was evidence that Sam had previously suffered another heart attack: one artery had formed its own bypass. But the procedure went well, and I was so thankful that my prayers had been answered.

One of my most treasured mementos is a white paper plate from the snack Sam ate shortly after his heart surgery. On it, he wrote "Sammy Loves Dixie Marie 2008." The plate is yellowed from spilled Betadine but worth a million dollars to me.

We were told that as soon as Sammy could walk around the nurse's station, he could go home. When he was recovering from his wounds in Vietnam, Sam's colonel told him if he could walk down the stairs to the weapons room, clean a weapon, and come to his office three days in a row he would be allowed to return to his unit. Both times Sam was determined to get out of the hospital in record time, and after heart surgery, he was able to leave on the third day. His recovery time has always amazed me; Sam always says the good Lord has a hand in it, and I suspect a tiny bit of stubbornness helps, too.

In 2011 and 2012, Sam finally underwent the much-delayed knee replacements as well.

Health scares weren't the only challenges along the way. We knew we needed to find a home of our own where we were free to merge our personalities.

In 2007, after much thought and discussion, we decided to build. However, that meant we first had to sell both my home in Texas and Sam's home in Flat Rock. We were fortunate that Sam's son bought his house, but being on the road and unable to oversee things in Texas, I had to deal with difficult tenants at my house. It took time and much frustration to get them out and to find a suitable buyer for the eleven acres of heaven in the Piney Wood Hills. I tried not to let Sam know just how hard it was for me to put my home on the market, but I grieved all over again. It felt like I was turning my back on Tim and the life we had there. I was ready for my life with Sam, but I knew a piece of my heart would always remain in the Piney Wood Hills of Texas.

Between speaking engagements, the search was on for the right building site. Because we travel so much, proximity to the Indianapolis airport was a top priority. We finally found a beautiful spot surrounded by woods in the rolling hills of southern Indiana near Bloomington, an hour-and-a-half drive from the airport. The land plot was located in Freedom, a very small town with a wonderful name. Given Sam's story and our mission together, it seemed more than coincidence, and we couldn't have found a more perfect place. Wild turkeys, deer, squirrels, and birds would be our neighbors, and we would have a sanctuary when returning home from long days of travel.

As a decorator, I was in heaven. I pored over house plans for hours and tried to remember every house design snafu I'd ever heard about. I wanted to be sure to avoid those. Sam and I had both lived in the Southwest and were interested in Native American culture. We loved the Southwestern colors, we chose a traditional design covered in stucco, and we both had many items that would make wonderful accessories. Sam has very good taste, and we conferred on everything. There were not many things that we disagreed on. Whenever we did, he would say, "Well, Dix, you are the decorator."

Because we have so much Medal of Honor memorabilia and so many beloved gifts and mementos, storage was a high priority. I covered every detail I could imagine, and I was so excited; it was our dream house, and everything was going to be perfect. We started building in 2008, but quickly found out how tricky it is to try to direct building plans when you can't be there to make certain things are done correctly. One day we went to check on the house and the garage was up, but they'd omitted the side door in the plans. Much to our surprise, changes had been made to the front of the house, as well, and it was too late to change it back. The contractor was rarely around when we were home. We were thankful for our wonderful neighbors Bill and Sandy McCowan. At least Sandy was able to document progress at the construction site almost daily with photos and updates.

Finally, we moved in at Thanksgiving time in 2009. However, as time moved on, we had to replace the furnace twice, and I was horrified to come home one day and find that the cupboards upstairs had literally fallen off the wall. They had not been installed properly, and my grandmother's crystal stemware and other heirlooms were smashed to pieces, not to mention gouges in the hardwood floor and walls. I was just sick. Traveling and building do not make good bedfellows.

Then it was my turn to upset the apple cart. In 2012, Sam and I were at Fort Benning, Georgia, to speak to the troops and to a group from Morgan Stanley Smith Barney. We stayed in a restored bed-and-breakfast cottage and had to be ready at 4:30 a.m. to catch an early morning flight. In the dim light, I left the room first with both hands full of luggage, and I was attempting to navigate the few cement steps that led to a brick walkway. Sam was locking the door, and I turned to him and said, "Be careful on the ste…"

The next thing I remember, I was flying through the air. Then I landed on my head at the bottom of the steps. Putting my hands on my face, I felt blood. Initially, I didn't feel much pain, but my first thought was that I wouldn't be able to fly home that day. I had no idea how bad it was, but Sam told me not to move, and he ran for towels. Meanwhile, our friend Bob Jerome, who was going to the airport with us, came around the hedge from the cottage next door. Seeing me lying across the steps, he yelled, "Dixie, are you all right?" I wasn't. He later said he feared I was dead.

Sam returned and wrapped my face in towels, and they somehow got me into the car and to the hospital. In hindsight, with a head injury, they probably should have called an ambulance, but I'm thankful for the help that was at hand. The emergency room doctor said he had been a hospital corpsman before becoming a doctor, and that made me feel safe. The medical staff took care of me, but as I was lying on the gurney inside a curtain, sticking my arm out and pointing to my head, they were in the outer room asking Sam for his autograph. Sam's appearances had made the morning paper, so everyone in the hospital knew who he was. Now I find it funny, but in that moment, I was aggravated with both Sam and the staff.

I had a hole at the base of my nose, a tear over my lip, and a hematoma the size of a baseball over my left eye. They stitched me up and did a CT scan. I had also broken my mandible from ear to ear above my lip line, and there was an orbital fracture below my left eye. The doctor said I couldn't fly home because the pressure would affect my injuries.

An angel in the form of Derek Scrivner, branch manager for Morgan Stanley in Columbus, Georgia, said he'd be happy to drive us all the way back to Indiana. Before I could leave the hospital, I had to see the ophthalmologist in the same medical complex to determine whether or not I had a detached retina. By then, I was a black and blue mess. When I later saw pictures that Sam had taken to send my sister, they about scared me to death. It looked like I'd emerged from the depths of some horror movie.

So an entourage of Bob, Derek, Sam, a couple of men from Morgan Stanley Smith Barney, and one bruised, beat-up woman entered the eye-clinic waiting room. I'm sure the other patients thought I was either a convict or a battered woman. One very loud individual walked right up to me and asked, "What happened to you?"

Sammy explained the situation.

"Well, OK then," she continued, "because if you had surgery here, I am not coming back!"

Fortunately my vision was OK, and the retina was not detached. However, a nerve was caught in the orbital fracture in my face, which later required surgery. Sam had to mince and liquefy all my food for a couple of weeks, and then it was soft foods for a while. I couldn't chew, but I sure was hungry for a bag of chips or a handful of nuts. Nerve damage also necessitated additional surgery the following year to lift the left side of my face to match the right. Yet, considering what could have happened, I was really thankful to be alive.

In 2014, it was Sammy's turn again, with carotid artery surgery. Because of plaque, his arteries were one hundred percent blocked on one side and eighty percent on the other. The surgery went well, and Nikki and I sat in the waiting room once again. I am thankful that our family feels like a real family now and relationships are good. I am also grateful that Sam bounced back so quickly. In just a short time, he was back on the speaking circuit doing what he feels called to do.

When we married, it was for better or worse. Like all couples, we've had our share of "worse," but the "better" has far outweighed the challenging times. Our faith in God and in each other has made the difference. When times get tough, I'm glad we can return to a comfortable home, family, and friends to help renew our bodies and spirits.

CHAPTER 25

Back Home Again in Indiana

While we love traveling and meeting people, Sam and I relish relaxing at home. The house we built truly is a sanctuary where we can spend time together and enjoy family and friends. We can actually start a conversation and are able to finish it. Interruptions are just part of being in the public eye, whether it's at an event, on an elevator, walking to our room, or eating in a restaurant. People want to chat, or they ask for a photo or autograph. But when we are at home, it is just about us. We can laugh, act as goofy as we want to, work together on a project, or just help each other with chores that are always waiting for us when we get home. We also have the option of companionable silence if we choose. It's wonderful not to have a schedule and not to set an alarm clock. When we are away, I long for the peace and quiet of our woods and grass instead of cement walks. I guess it's really true that you can take the girl out of the country, but you can't take the country out of the girl. It also means a lot to me to have some time when I don't have to share Sammy with the world.

Then there is the pleasure of sleeping in our own bed. We are put up in the nicest hotels, and I truly appreciate that, but I've yet to find a pillow as comfortable as my own. Sam has to have a light on in the room, so a drapery is always open to the blazing neon lights in big cities; I think they damage my brain. Garbage trucks in the wee hours of the morning and sirens wailing are not very conducive to sleep. The lull of crickets and tranquil night sounds at home help us to recharge for the next event.

Both of us are early risers; we don't want to miss anything. I enjoy the morning sunshine streaming through the windows and the music of chirping birds at daybreak. A long bank of windows off the kitchen allows us to see what is going on at the edge of the woods in the early morning. Birds and squirrels show up at the feeders for breakfast, and Sam puts out corn for the deer, turkeys, and whatever else might be wandering through.

After a while, I started to recognize the deer that came, and of course, I had to name them all. We had Gordy and Jane for a short while, then Gordy left, but baby Jeff still accompanied his mama for a meal. We also had two youngsters named Caroline and Ron. Wild turkeys enjoyed the corn last winter, and Steve and Bob, two handsome gobblers with long beards, showed up, accompanied by Mary Margaret. All went well until another female crashed the party. She pecked at everyone, especially Mary Margaret. I called her Jezebel, the troublemaker. The simplicity of connecting with nature is a balm for the hectic pace we keep on the road.

When a friend mentioned house sounds that gave him comfort as a child, I realized that early morning kitchen sounds also give me a feeling of well-being. I hear the water running, the sound of the cupboards opening, and the gurgle of the little coffee pot as Sam heats water for his morning tea. The refrigerator door opens as he gathers all the ingredients to cook his breakfast. Then I might hear his feet padding across the floor to look out the windows. As Sam's breakfast sizzles in the skillet, inviting smells drift from the kitchen to the office where I'm checking e-mails. Losing Tim and having lived with deafening silence in the house, I've come to treasure simple things like the sound of my husband puttering in the kitchen.

Yogurt, toasted homemade bread or ciabatta, and fruit usually start my day. We take our breakfast to the reclining love seat in the great room, where we settle in to check the morning news on TV. On chilly mornings we build a crackling fire in the fireplace; sharing breakfast together in this room gives us both a feeling of peace and contentment.

Sam likes to cook, I enjoy baking, and we both like to can and freeze food. We live in an Amish community, so we have a country store and an

Amish greenhouse nearby where we buy our spring plants. Our name is on a list for summer fruits and vegetables, and we get a call when they are ripe.

Because the abundant wildlife roaming the woods behind our house likes nothing better than tender garden plants, we don't try to grow much ourselves except for what flourishes in pots on the deck. Last year, it was jalapeno peppers, Brussel sprouts, tomatoes, and butternut squash. A gate at the top of the steps has deterred the larger furry friends. So far.

We both love the outdoors and spending summer hours on the deck. Sam is my chief watering expert, and he keeps the flowering rose trees, hibiscus, and bougainvillea happy. Hardwood trees are full of singing birds, and the darting little hummingbirds are regular visitors to the blossoms. There is nothing better than relaxing on the overstuffed wicker sofa, gazing up at the blue sky as a gentle breeze rocks the nearby pine trees. We are blessed with our own little piece of heaven on the edge of the woods.

Sam is also the chief lawn care expert who rides the Dixie Chopper lawn mower at breakneck speed. He really scares me sometimes. With five acres to tend, there is always something to prune, pinch back, deadhead, or trim. In addition, Sam is Mr. Chainsaw. I won't touch that thing. However, I'm the queen of wood splitting. We have a big log splitter, and as I work, I think of the cold days to come and know we'll love sitting in front of that warm fire while the snow flies.

Sam and I are not good couch sitters. Sometimes we will hop on the brand-new side-by-side ATV, a gift from Sammy's kids, and take a ride on our country roads to enjoy the beauty. We go fishing, or if we have company, we take the 1946 Willys jeep out for a spin. The windshield folds down and there are no seat belts, but it travels at a wild thirty-five miles per hour.

Decorating the house is always a work in progress, whether I'm designing a new floral creation or figuring out how to incorporate family pieces into our Southwest theme. Because Sammy's family moved a lot, we only have a few heirlooms on his side, but my family stayed on the farm much of their lives, so I'm fortunate to have a number of their treasures, which are very precious to me. My grandmother's china closet is filled with old dishes and crystal from both sides of the family. Mom's cedar chest is full of handmade items from my grandmothers, and it also contains Mom's wedding dress and her gym suit from the early 1940s. My hope chest from the 1960s is filled with Tony's baby things.

The oak table and chairs that belonged first to my grandparents, then to my parents, is where we ate all our meals during my childhood. When I run my hands over that furniture and remember the many hands that prepared the food, the family members that congregated there together, and all the card games played at that table, it gives me a tangible connection to all of those I loved. Since Sam and I live a largely nomadic life, we are grounded in family when we return. These heirlooms help provide comfort and stability.

Sam spent much of his childhood fishing, hunting, and trapping. That put food on the table and was also something his family did together. Baiting a pole at his favorite fishing hole is still Sam's passion. He doesn't care if he catches anything; it's all about being outside and enjoying the natural beauty around him.

Wanting to do something special and unique for Sam, I designed a fishing bathroom for him. The idea came from an old cane fishing pole that belonged to his grandpa. It was fun to utilize old lures, mounted fish, the cane pole, and photos of us with our favorite catches to create a bathroom to showcase one of his hobbies. A plaque above the door reads, "What happens in the outhouse stays in the outhouse."

Sam's bathroom turned out to be so much fun to design that I decided to decorate the guest bathroom in a cowgirl motif. When I was a little girl, I wanted to be Dale Evans or Annie Oakley. Even though Dad had tractors, he loved his horses, and we still had a team when I was small. He kept Tom and Maud around to pull a rack with fencing equipment. Dad would swing us up on their backs when he came in for lunch or at the end of the day, and to a little girl, the ground looked like it was two miles down. We would ride Tom and Maud over to the water tank, perched high on their backs while they drank their fill. How I loved those times.

So using a gate from an old barn, I mounted my childhood Hopalong Cassidy cowgirl suit and the little red straw hat that I used to wear, riding my pony, Snowball, in the Pearl City homecoming parades. I was a cowgirl from the Old West. My dad would get my pony all cleaned up, and I remember using saddle soap on my little saddle. We hauled Snowball into town in the back of Dad's truck and unloaded her at my grandparents' house, which was about two blocks from where the parade started. Dad fluffed her mane and tail, and ribbons were added to the bridle and tied into her mane. When I was really small, Dad would walk the entire parade route behind the spectators just to make sure I was all right. I especially remember the year that I won the blue ribbon. My pony did really well until she got to the railroad tracks going through the middle of the town. She came to a dead stop and wouldn't budge. She had never encountered a railroad track before. I tried everything I knew, and then all of a sudden there were two giant palominos behind me. One was ridden by my dad's friend Joe Raders. Those two big horses pushed my pony across the tracks. Boy, was I scared. I thought I was a goner. But it all turned out well; on the way back Snowball marched right across those tracks like she did it every day. She probably was afraid that those giants would come up behind her to push so she pretended bravery. Everything from a horse halter bit to a shelf with cowboy cats helped to create my whimsical bathroom. More than that, it's a room full of fond memories.

As a Christmas present for Sam a few years ago, I had some of Peggy Jo's drawings framed for the office. They had been rolled up and tucked away for years. I believe all of these special mementos—Sam's cane pole, my cowgirl suit, and Peggy Jo's drawings—should be out where we can enjoy them.

In 2013, we built a new wooden barn where we have the best barn porch parties with the family and grandkids. I'm grateful that we've now grown into one big family, and it is a joy to have Sammy's grandchildren as well as mine for extended visits. Both our families have come at the same time, and the little ones love playing together. When we built the barn, I wanted to recreate some of my wonderful childhood memories for them. There just had to be a hayloft with a ladder where they could build hay houses

As kids, my brother, sister, and I spent so much time in the hayloft of Dad's barn. We built hay houses and played with the never-ending batches of kittens. We were the ones who threw the hay down for the cows to eat. Sometimes I went up to the loft just to be alone, to read a book, or daydream. Sam's childhood was similar to mine in that we used our imaginations and had the best of times out in the country.

There are no stairs to the loft, so if the kids want to take anything large up there, they use a rope and pulley attached to the outside of the barn. It makes my heart sing to see them having such a good time, playing and using their imaginations like we used to do.

The large barn porch faces north, and we installed ceiling fans, so it's always cool and comfortable. I sometimes wonder what I was thinking when I decided to paint all the porch furniture red, white, and blue. It seemed like such a good idea at the time! Thank goodness Sam pitched in, and a month of Sundays later, two colorful tables, ten chairs, one chaise lounge, a bench, and two rockers gave the appearance that Uncle Sam himself resided there. I hung all my dad's farm tools on the porch wall, making it is so homey and welcoming. In the fall, a firebox that doubles as a grill keeps us warm, and nothing tastes better than hot dogs and s'mores over a wood fire. We love to have company, and the informal porch is a magnet for fun.

Being gone as much as we are, it seems when we come home there are always errands to run, so we do them together. I'm glad Sam likes to shop when we go to the grocery store, because I don't. However, even a shopping trip can turn into something very special as it did one day while we were picking up groceries in nearby Spencer, Indiana.

Upon returning to the car, we found an envelope tucked under the windshield wipers. It was evident the person who left it had seen the Medal of Honor plates on our vehicle. A twenty-dollar bill was inside, and the donor had written these words on the outside of the white envelope.

Hello,
I just want to take a moment to appreciate you for your service and sacrifice to our country. I wish I could have the honor of shaking your hand and knowing your name. I pray that God blesses you for what you have done. I also pray that you bless and honor Him with your life.
I want to give you a small monetary gift out of the abundance He has given me.
God bless you.

There was no signature. This person wasn't looking for recognition but just gave from the heart. Sammy and I both were so touched by this generous gesture and the beautiful spirit and character of this anonymous individual.

Antique shops seem to call our name when we're out, and we always find something that reminds us of our childhood. How many times have we exclaimed to each other, "Oh, I remember this!" Usually that sparks a nostalgic conversation that involves our separate families, how we used the item, and the memories it brings back. For us, old kitchen utensils are the best. Many people don't know about old, wooden potato mashers or the handheld mashers with the green wooden handle, egg baskets, milk strainers, and cherry pitters. I think the fact that we both grew up during a simpler time helped shape our values and experiences, and being able to share these stories just brings us closer. Our rule is that if we buy something new, something old has to go. So far, that has not worked out very well. How can we throw out memories?

We're constantly busy, so on quiet evenings at home, especially in the winter, it's wonderful to curl up in the great room with a crackling fire to watch TV. Sam also likes to sit back and catch up on his e-mail or peruse his Facebook account. I love knowing he is there by my side, and he says he likes knowing he can reach over and touch me.

For many years, Hobbie, one of the two cats that Tim brought home from the shelter, would sit on my lap as I did needlework. She was over nineteen years old when we lost her in 2015, and I still miss her sitting with me when I am stitching. Annie, Hobbie's sister, passed when she was fourteen. They were my babies, a part of Tim and a part of Texas, and it's still hard to know they aren't there to curl up with me before the fire.

I need to keep my hands busy whether traveling or relaxing at home, so I always have a stitchery piece in the works. It's been great fun to enter my projects at the Indiana State Fair, and Grandma Busch would be proud that I won a Best in Show in the needlepoint category.

People often say they don't think they could be together twenty-four seven like we are, but Sam and I are as glad to be together at home as we are out on the road. We couldn't imagine it any other way. I think it's because we are best friends before anything else and because we have known loss and know that we are never promised tomorrow. We want to make the best of today and make every minute count. We've learned that you can't take each other for granted.

In the serene surroundings of home, I can also reflect on the great blessings I've been given, and I am reminded that when I put God first in my life, even through adversities and pain, He will somehow work everything out. I've learned that when I reach out to others and look for people who need a helping hand, the blessings come back tenfold. Perhaps it's only a smile to share or helping a mom who is trying to hang on to a little one while lugging a big bag of groceries; there are opportunities all around us to share a kindness and lighten someone else's load. I've learned that a positive attitude begets a positive attitude, and that we all have the privilege and responsibility of caring about our fellow men and women. I know that strong families are the backbone of our great country, and much can be accomplished with perseverance. I applaud the bright, young people I've met along the way who will be tomorrow's leaders, and I am thankful for the selflessness of our young soldiers who put themselves in harm's way to serve our nation. Looking back on my life with Tim and the mission of the Last Patrol to reach out to veterans, I am amazed to see how much that experience prepared me for my role with Sam now. More than anything, I reflect on how grateful I am that I was given a second chance to find great love in a man with whom I can sit on the porch for the rest of my days, and that I can be a helpmate in his mission to serve veterans and others who seek hope.

Epilogue

When I started writing our love story, in my mind, the title applied just to Sammy and me. As the book unfolded, however, it became increasingly clear to me that the love story in this journey was much broader than just between two people. Love really is a circle that has no ending, and it gathers momentum and continues to grow. As each of us share our love and our lives with others, many become inspired to reach out to another, and another, and yet another.

Writing the early chapters, I often consulted Tim's former singing partner, Michael J. Martin, about a Tim story or one of their songs. Michael was a good friend. We could have never imagined that before this book was complete, on December 2, 2014, cancer would take him, as well. Veterans and former members of Tim and Michael's veterans awareness group, the Last Patrol, once again gathered and poured out their love via e-mails and Facebook messages. Their appreciation for Michael's life, and for his and Tim's influence, has been heartwarming. Tim and Michael made a difference to others. They will always live on in many hearts.

Tim and Peggy continue to leave their mark on Sammy and me, as well as our families, friends, and others we encounter. Those who cared for us through our spouses' illnesses will never be forgotten, and they taught us to reach out to others who are going through a tough time. The many people who put so much effort into finding Sammy's Medal of Honor in the White River did it out of respect for Sammy and love for their country. Each time Sammy or another veteran tells the story of his fallen comrades, the spirits of those soldiers live on, and the brotherly love they had for one another touches someone else. Those who reach out to veterans and their families do it out of compassion. Each act of love, passed on through generations of our families, builds on another. It is our wish that the love Sam and I have, not only for each other, but for the many people who cross our paths, will also offer hope and inspiration to others.

When I think of Peggy Jo closing Tim and Michael's concerts singing "Will the Circle Be Unbroken," I realize that, because of love, the circle will always remain intact. Miracles still happen, and second chances come along when we least expect them.

Michael J. Martin and Tim "Holiday" Taylor

Sammy Davis and Tim "Holiday" Taylor at Daley Plaza, Chicago, Illinois

Dixie Busch Davis, age five

Grandma Flory and Grandpa John Busch
Back row: my dad, Howard Busch, and his sister Irene

Grandma Bess and Grandpa Lester Fehr

My mom, Doris Fehr Busch

The old home place near Kent, Illinois. Photo by Gary Sinise

The Busch kids: Roger, Dixie, and Roxie. We all had
whooping cough the day the photographer arrived.

Peggy Jo and Sammy Davis

Dixie and Tim in Colorado

Annie and Hobbie

Our engagement in Vermont

Happy New Year

Cutting our wedding cake in Skidmore, Missouri

Sam's favorite hobby

Sam's note to me after his heart surgery

Aunt Mary Fry's chicken hat.

That really is Sammy Davis riding a motorcycle in a chicken suit

At the New York Stock Exchange. Sammy really should have moved his hand.

In the woods. Photo by Katie Kunzelman

Our fireplace at home

Snow fun with Sam in Freedom

Smooching in front of the Christmas tree

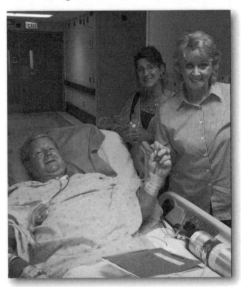

Sam coming out of surgery with Dixie and daughter, Nikki

Our barn porch.

Log splitter queen

Dixie, sister Roxie, and my forever friend Sherry

Sam playing his harmonica

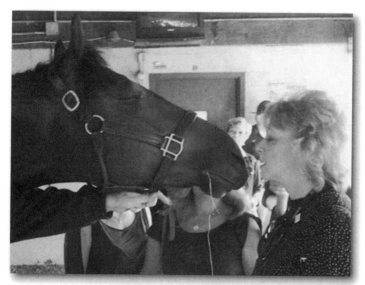

We both closed our eyes

Sam and Dix with the Oscar Mayer Wienermobile

Our fairytale castle in Germany

We fired the cannon at the Brigham Young University football game

Sam and Dixie with Gary Sinise

Surfin' on the East Coast

Front row: Son, Tony, and grandchildren: Reuben, Benjamin, Zach
Back row: Daughter-in-law, Christie, and grandchildren: Hannah, Olivia, and August

Daughter, Nikki, her husband, Donnie Johnson, and
their family in our 1946 Willys jeep

Johnson grandchildren: Draegan, Savannah, Dylan,
Samantha and Stevie Raye

Grandson Johnny, daughter-in-law Jerri, granddaughter
Katelynn, and son, Beau

Grandson Hudson, son Blue, granddaughter Harper, daughter-in-law Carrie

My hero

Recipes: Food, Glorious Food

Home, comfort, and cooking go hand in hand at our house, and we hope you will enjoy some of the special recipes we like. In addition, I've included the recipe for juicing that helped Tim and Peggy Jo during their cancer.

Our church is big on being prepared, so we try to have enough basic ingredients on hand to be able to sustain ourselves during an emergency. This bread from scratch is very nutritious and freezes well. The recipe makes three loaves, one to eat, one to freeze, and one to give away. Bread making is good for what ails you. Kneading the dough is therapeutic. Watching it rise gives you hope. Eating the finished product and giving one away is pure joy. This bread toasted is heavenly.

MITCH MITCHELL'S WHOLE WHEAT BREAD

In one bowl cream together:

1 stick of melted butter. Cool

Add 2 eggs

In another bowl mix together:

1 can (12 oz) evaporated milk

1 can (12 oz) hot water

¼ teaspoon salt

½ cup brown or white sugar

1 level tablespoon rapid rise dry yeast

Let stand for 15 minutes

Add butter mixture to yeast mixture. (You can do this by hand, but a KitchenAid mixer with bread kneading attachment is great!)

Add nuts and seeds: 1 cup walnuts, 2 tablespoons caraway seeds, 1 teaspoon poppy seeds, 1 teaspoon flax seeds and 1 teaspoon sesame seeds. I go heavy on caraway, but adjust all measurements to taste.

Add: 8 cups of flour (Use 6 cups of wheat and 2 cups of white)

Dump the mixture onto a floured counter top. Knead for ten minutes unless you have used the mixer. Keep adding additional flour until the dough no longer sticks to your fingers or the counter top. Divide into three loaves. Sprinkle more seeds on the counter and roll the shaped loaves across them for a pretty loaf. Put into greased bread pans and let rise until doubled.

Bake at 375° F for twenty-five minutes.

LORETTA MOON'S BUTTERMILK PIE

1 premade or homemade pie shell

Mix together:

3 tablespoons of flour

1 ½ cups of sugar (You may substitute Splenda. Another twist is using brown sugar. It adds a bit of a butterscotch taste.)

Pinch of salt

Beat together:

3 eggs

1 ½ cups buttermilk (Powdered buttermilk can be found in the refrigerator section at the grocery store. Just add water to it.)

3 tablespoons melted butter

1 teaspoon vanilla

Pour into an unbaked pie shell, sprinkle with cinnamon or apple pie spice, and swirl with a knife.

Bake at 350° F for forty-five minutes.

DIXIE'S PEACH PIE

2 premade or homemade pie crusts

Mix together:

1 ¼ cups sugar

1/3 cup flour

½ teaspoon cinnamon

Add: 4 cups fresh peaches, and mix together until peaches are covered with the sugar mixture.

Dot with 1 tablespoon butter

Pour into pie crust, and cover with vented top crust (If not vented, poke holes in crust with fork.)

Bake at 375° F degrees for forty to forty-five minutes.

Tip: To make a pretty top crust, take tiny cookie cutters and make designs out of the left over pie dough. Place these around the edge of the crust.

Dixie's Blonde Brownies (the ultimate comfort food)

1 cup flour

½ teaspoon baking powder

1/8 teaspoon baking soda

½ teaspoon salt

½ cup nuts

1/3 cup butter

1 cup brown sugar

1 egg

1 teaspoon vanilla

2/3 cup chocolate, white chocolate, or butterscotch chips (my favorite is peanut butter chips.)

In a large bowl, melt the butter, cool, then add brown sugar, eggs, and vanilla. Mix well. Add remaining ingredients and mix well. Pour into a nine-inch greased pan.

Bake at 350°F for twenty to twenty-five minutes. (You may frost if you like.)

Mom's Card Club Barbeque

Brown together in a frying pan:

3 pounds of hamburger until no longer pink

3 chopped onions

1 cup chopped celery

Drain fat

Add:

3 tablespoons sugar

1 cup tomato soup

4 tablespoons Worcestershire sauce

1 tablespoon mustard horseradish

1 cup chili sauce

½ teaspoon salt (adjust to taste)

½ cup water

Simmer for thirty minutes, or cook ingredients in a crockpot one hour on high. Turn down to low setting until ready to serve.

GRANDMA BUSCH'S CHOCOLATE CAKE

Cream together:

2 cups sugar

1 cup butter-flavored Crisco

½ teaspoon salt

2 eggs

Add:

1 cup sour milk (Add 1 teaspoon vinegar to regular milk to make it sour.)

2 teaspoons baking soda (add to the milk mixture)

½ cup cocoa

2½ cups flour

Mix well and add 1 cup of boiling water. Mix all ingredients together.

Bake in nine x thirteen pan at 350° F for twenty-five minutes. Check with toothpick. Frost with chocolate powdered sugar frosting or other chocolate frosting, and add one perfect hickory nut half on each piece.

Grandma Fehr's Golden Angel Food Cake

1½ cups granulated sugar (scant)

½ cup water

6 egg whites

½ teaspoon salt

½ teaspoon cream of tartar

6 egg yolks

1 cup cake flour

1 teaspoon vanilla

In a medium saucepan, cook sugar and water to thread stage (240° F). In a large bowl, beat egg whites and salt until foamy, add cream of tartar, and continue to beat until stiff but not dry. Gradually pour syrup over the egg whites, beating constantly. Cool.

In a separate bowl, beat egg yolks until thick and lemon colored, and fold into cooled mixture. Sift flour over top, a little at a time, folding in lightly. Add vanilla with the last addition of flour. Bake in a nine-inch ungreased angel food cake pan at 325° F for one hour. Invert pan and cool.

Sammy's Ebony and Ivory Dish

I use venison tenderloin that I have harvested and cleaned myself and a half section of pork tenderloin purchased from the local meat market.

Cut a tubelike hole the long way through the center of the loin. I use a long filet knife. Make the hole large enough to stuff the trimmed venison tenderloin inside of the pork loin. You want it to fit snug into the hole.

Put roasts into an appropriate-sized baking dish. I like to put cornbread dressing around all the meat because it helps retain the moisture in the meat and adds even more flavor to the dish. You can place potatoes, onions, and carrots around the meat instead if you prefer.

Tightly cover the dish and bake it at 350° F for two hours or until done. As you slice off the portions, you will see a distinct ebony and ivory color of the meat, hence the name I gave it.

Enjoy the wonderful meal!

JUICING FOR ONE PERSON

Wash everything with mild dish soap or a fruit and veggie wash. Juice ¾ orange or yellow veggies to ¼ green veggies. (Note: the cabbage family tends to have a bitter taste.) Use organic veggies when possible. Add all ingredients to the juicer. Veggies are pushed one at a time into the juicer. The apples make great cleaners so I use them after a few veggies and then it is easier to add more food. Carrots make great pushers for the greens or smaller pieces. Do not juice vegetables and fruits together. Apples are the only exception. Something in the enzymes of each cancel out the other.

1 pound of carrots (remove tops)

2 stalks of celery

1-inch slice of fresh ginger

1 clove of garlic

1 bell pepper

1 handful of greens (I like spinach best because it has the most nutritional value. Iceberg lettuce is the last choice unless it is from your garden.)

2 or 3 apples (Don't peel but remove seeds and core)

1 tablespoon of ground flaxseed (add after everything else is juiced).

Nutrients are lost if the juice sits out, so drink it right away.

About the Authors

Dixie Davis, the wife of Medal of Honor recipient Sammy Davis, is the only Medal of Honor wife in recent history to write a memoir. She and Sammy travel the country approximately two hundred days a year as Sammy shares his Vietnam experience and message of "Duty, Honor, Country" with veterans, schoolchildren, and a wide variety of audiences. Dixie has long been involved with veteran organizations and was a member of the Last Patrol veterans awareness group. Together, she and Sammy share a mission to inspire hope and encouragement to veterans and people from all walks of life. Her greatest hope is to make a difference to others.

Off the road, Dixie loves the outdoors and country life, decorating their home, spending time with Sam, and enjoying family and friends. She and Sam make their home in Freedom, Indiana.

Sherry Maves has been a freelance writer for more than three decades. Her published work includes multiple features for newspapers and magazines and a long-standing music column for the *Journal Standard* in Freeport, Illinois. Sherry was also involved with a veterans organization and the Last Patrol. She and Dixie are sisters-of-the-heart and have shared many of the experiences in this book together. Sherry currently lives in northwestern Illinois.

Contact the author at dixiedavis1946@gmail.com.